THE PRINCETON REVIEW

Cracking the AP:
Chemistry Exam

1998-99 Edition

THE PRINCETON REVIEW

Cracking the AP:
Chemistry Exam

By Paul Foglino

1998-99 EDITION
RANDOM HOUSE, INC.
NEW YORK 1997

Princeton Review Publishing, L.L.C.
2315 Broadway
New York, NY 10024
E-mail: info@review.com

ISSN: 1076-5395
ISBN: 0-375-75109-2

AP is a registered trademark of The Educational Services.

Editor: Rachel Warren
Designer: Illeny Maaza
Production Editor: Amy Bryant

Manufactured in the United States of America on partially recycled paper.

9 8 7 6 5 4 3 2 1

ACKNOWLEDGMENTS

I'd like to thank John Katzman for entrusting me with this project, and my editor, Rachel Warren, whose guidance and tireless effort helped me in converting chemistry into English. I'd also like to thank Eric Payne, whose rigorous attention to detail helped me in separating chemistry from fantasy. I'd like to thank Tom Meltzer for his advice and Libby O'Connor for her patience.

I'd also like to thank The Princeton Review's editorial and production crew; Amy Bryant, Greta Englert, Effie Hadjiioannou, Evelin O'Hara, John Pak, and Matthew Reilly.

CONTENTS

INTRODUCTION

WHAT IS THE PRINCETON REVIEW?

The Princeton Review is a test-coaching service. Since 1981, it has provided the single best way for high school students to prepare for the SAT. In the following years, The Princeton Review also began to provide the best way for college students to prepare for the GRE, GMAT, LSAT, and MCAT.

The success of The Princeton Review can be traced to the simple, but previously untried, approach to test preparation taken by its founders, John Katzman and Adam Robinson. That approach is to *study the test, as well as the subject*. Every test has idiosyncrasies that you can use to your advantage. Another way of saying this is that you should *think like the test makers and test graders*. Obviously, you need to be well versed in chemistry to do well on this test, but you should remember that *any standardized test is partly a measure of your ability to think like the people who write standardized tests*.

In this book, we'll review chemistry, but we'll also examine the structure and idiosyncrasies of the AP Chemistry test and practice the best approaches to both multiple-choice and free-response questions.

1
ORIENTATION

WHAT IS THE AP PROGRAM?

The Advanced Placement (AP) Program joins high schools and colleges by allowing high school students to do college-level work for college credit. The AP Chemistry test is one of 29 college-level examinations offered every year.

AP courses are offered by more than 10,000 high schools in the United States, Canada, and more than sixty other countries. About 2,900 colleges around the world offer college credit to students who have performed well on AP tests. The specific score required for credit varies from school to school and from subject to subject.

The AP Program is coordinated by The College Board. The College Board is a national nonprofit organization composed of representatives from various schools and colleges. They see it as their mission to set educational standards.

The College Board appoints a Development Committee for each of the 29 subjects. The Development Committee decides what should be covered in an AP course and how it should be covered on the AP test. The AP Chemistry Development Committee is composed of three high school chemistry teachers, three college professors who teach general chemistry, and an additional college professor who chairs the group. Each member of the Development Committee serves a three year term.

The test is administered by the Educational Testing Service (ETS), the same folks who bring you the SAT. ETS also plays a role in developing the test.

WHAT IS THE AP CHEMISTRY TEST?

The AP Chemistry test is a three-hour long, two-section test that attempts to cover the material you would learn in a college first-year chemistry course. The test has two parts. The first part, which counts for 45 percent of your grade, consists of multiple-choice questions. The second part, which counts for 55 percent of your grade, is composed of free-response questions, such as short essays and problems involving calculation.

The test is offered once every year, in May. It's scored in June. The multiple-choice section is scored by computer and the problems and essays are scored by a committee of high school and college teachers. The problems and essays are graded according to a standard set at the beginning of the grading period by the chief faculty consultants. Inevitably, the grading of Section II is never as consistent or accurate as the grading of Section I.

When the grading is done, the results are curved and each student receives a grade based on a five-point scale. For the AP Chemistry test, the results break down as follows.

Grade	What it means	Approximate % of test takers who get this score
5	Exremely well qualified	13%
4	Well qualified	18%
3	Qualified	30%
2	Possibly qualified	25%
1	No recommendation	14%

Although standards vary from school to school, it's safe to say that most colleges will give credit for a 4 or 5, some will give credit for a 3, and very few will give credit for a 2.

CRACKING THE MULTIPLE-CHOICE SECTION

THE BASICS

Section I of the test is composed of 75 multiple-choice questions, for which you are allotted 90 minutes. This part is worth 45 percent of your total score.

For this section, you will be given a periodic table of the elements and you may NOT use a calculator.

The first fifteen multiple-choice questions, give or take a few, will be formatted with five answer choices followed by a series of questions, as shown.

Questions 1-4

(A) O_2
(B) H_2O
(C) Ni
(D) Fe
(E) NaCl

1. This species contains ionic bonds. (E)

2. This species is a gas at standard temperature and pressure. (A)

3. This species is more dense as a liquid than as a solid. (B)

4. This species contains a double bond. (A)

These are mostly straightforward, "you know it or you don't," questions. Notice that an answer can be used once, more than once, or not at all.

The rest of the multiple-choice questions are in the standard question-and-answers format shown below.

16. Which of the following species is a gas at standard temperature and pressure?

(A) O_2
(B) H_2O
(C) Ni
(D) Fe
(E) NaCl

On the multiple-choice section, you receive 1 point for a correct answer, and $\frac{1}{4}$ point is subtracted for an incorrect answer. There is no penalty for leaving a question blank.

Your raw score on this section will just be the number of questions you answered correctly minus one-fourth of the number of questions that you answered incorrectly. You can make a rough prediction about your overall score from your raw score on the multiple-choice section, assuming that you do about as well on the free-response section.

Roughly speaking:

If you get a raw score of at least 50, you probably will get a 5.

If you get a raw score of at least 35, you probably will get at least a 4.

If you get a raw score of at least 25, you probably will get at least a 3.

PACING

So you can get a 5 with a raw score of 50, a 4 with a raw score of 35, and a 3 with a raw score of 25. That's a pretty generous curve. According to The College Board, the multiple-choice section of the AP Chemistry test covers more material than any individual student is expected to know. Nobody is expected to get a perfect or near-perfect score.

What does that mean to you?

Don't answer all the questions!

You can skip every third question and still get a 5. You can skip half the questions and still get a 4. You can skip two out of every three questions and still get a 3. Obviously, you should answer any question that you have a chance of getting right, but you should be aware that the grading curve gives you plenty of slack.

Okay, so you know that you can skip questions. So how do you know which questions to skip?

Use the Two-Pass System

Go through the multiple-choice section twice. The first time, do all the questions that you can get answers to immediately. That is, the questions with little or no math and questions in chemistry topics in which you are well versed.

The first time through, skip the questions in the topics that make you uncomfortable. Also, you might want to skip the ones that look like number crunchers (even without a calculator, you might still be expected to crunch a few numbers). Circle the questions that you skip in your test booklet so you can find them easily during the second pass.

Once you've done all the questions that come easily to you, go back and pick out the tough ones that you have the best shot at.

In general, the questions near the end of the section are tougher than the questions near the beginning. You should keep that in mind, but be aware that each person's experience will be different. If you can do acid-base questions in your sleep, but you'd rather shoot yourself in the eye than draw a Lewis diagram, you might find questions near the end of the section easier than questions near the beginning.

That's why the two-pass system is so handy. By using it, you make sure that you get to see all the questions that you can get right, instead of running out of time because you got bogged down on questions you couldn't do earlier in the test.

Which brings us to another important point.

Don't turn a question into a crusade!

Most people don't run out of time on standardized tests because they work too slowly. Instead, they run out of time because they spent half the test wrestling with two or three particular questions.

You should never spend more than a minute or two on any question. If a question doesn't involve calculation, then either you know the answer, you can take an educated guess at the answer, or you don't know the answer. Figure out where you stand on a question, make a decision, and move on.

Any question that requires more than two minutes worth of calculations probably isn't worth doing. Remember, skipping a question early in the section is a good thing if it means that you'll have time to get two right later on.

GUESSING

You get one point for every correct answer on the multiple-choice section. You lose $\frac{1}{4}$ point for every wrong answer. Each question has five answer choices, so if you were to guess randomly on every single question you would get one out of five right. That's 15 right and 60 wrong.

$$(15 \text{ right} \times 1 \text{ point}) - (60 \text{ wrong} \times \frac{1}{4} \text{ point}) = (15) - (15) = 0$$

So guessing randomly neither helps you nor hurts you. Educated guessing, however, will help you.

Use Process of Elimination (POE) to find wrong answers

There is a fundamental weakness to a multiple-choice test. That is, the test makers must show you the right answer, along with four wrong answers. Sometimes, seeing the right answer is all you need. Other times, you might not know the right answer, but you might recognize one or two of the answers as clearly wrong. Then you should use POE to take an educated guess.

Look at this hypothetical question:

1. Which of the following compounds will produce a purple solution when added to water?

   (A) Brobogdium rabelide
   (B) Diblythium perjuvenide
   (C) Sodium chloride
   (D) Hynynium gargantuide
   (E) Carbon dioxide

You should have no idea what the correct answer is here because I made up three of these compounds, but you do know something about the wrong answers. You know that sodium chloride (C) and carbon dioxide (E) do not turn water purple. So, using POE, you have a one-out-of-three chance at the correct answer. Now the odds are in your favor. Now you should guess.

If you can eliminate even one wrong answer, you should guess

In the example above, we eliminated two wrong answers, but even eliminating one wrong answer puts the odds in your favor. The guessing penalty ($\frac{1}{4}$ point) assumes that you're taking a one-out-of-five guess, so even a one-out-of-four guess will gain points. Of course, the more wrong answers you can eliminate, the better.

Once you've done POE and decided to guess, guess and move on

Remember, you're guessing. Pondering the possible differences between brobogdium rabelide and diblythium perjuvenide is a waste of time. Once you've taken POE as far as it will go, pick your favorite letter and move on.

Remember, the multiple-choice section is the exact opposite of the free-response section. It's scored by a machine. There's no partial credit. The computer doesn't know, or care if you know, why an answer is correct. All the computer cares about is whether you blackened in the right oval on your score sheet. You get the same number of points for picking (B) because you know (A) and (E) are wrong and B is a nicer letter than C or D as you would for picking (B) because you fully understood the subtleties of an electrochemical process.

ABOUT CALCULATORS

You will NOT be allowed to use a calculator on this section. That shouldn't worry you. All it means is that there won't be any questions in the section that you'll need a calculator to solve.

Most of the calculation problems will have fairly user-friendly numbers. That is, numbers with only a couple of significant digits, or things like "11.2 liters of gas at STP" or "160. grams of oxygen" or "a temperature increase from 27 °C to 127 °C". Sometimes these user-friendly numbers will actually point you toward the proper steps to take in your calculation.

Don't be afraid to make rough estimates as you do your calculations. Sometimes knowing that an answer is closer to 50 than to 500 will enable you to pick the correct answer on a multiple-choice test (if the answer choices are far enough apart). Once again, the rule against calculators works in your favor here because The College Board will not expect you to do very precise calculations by hand.

There might be a couple of real number-crunching problems on the test. If you can recognize them quickly, these are good ones to skip. There's no point in spending five minutes crunching numbers to get one problem right if that time could be better used in getting three others right later in the test.

CRACKING THE FREE-RESPONSE SECTION

Part II is composed of a series of free-response questions, some of which you may choose from and some of which are required. You will be allotted 95 minutes to complete this section, which is worth 55 percent of your total score. You get exactly 10 minutes for Part A, then 85 minutes to divide as you see fit among the other parts.

PART A—WRITING CHEMICAL EQUATIONS

For this section, you will be given a table of standard reduction potentials and a periodic table and you may NOT use a calculator.

For Part A, you will be given 8 sets of chemical reactants. You'll be asked to choose 5 sets and write the appropriate equation for the reaction that will occur for each. You are allotted exactly 10 minutes for this section.

Each reaction is worth 3 points; 1 point for reactants and 2 points for products, so you can earn a total of 15 points for this section. Based on information released by The College Board, the average score for this section is usually about 5 out of the available 15 points.

We'll talk about how to approach this section in Chapter 17.

PARTS B AND C—PROBLEMS

For Parts B and C, you will be given a table of commonly used chemical equations, a table of standard reduction potentials, and a periodic table. You may use a calculator, which you will need.

About Part B—The Required Equilibrium Problem

All students must do this problem, which is a multipart question involving calculation to determine some aspect of equilibrium.

This question will be divided into four or five parts, with partial credit available for correct answers on each part. The question is worth a total of 9 points. The average score for this section is usually between 3 and 4 points.

About Part C—Choice of One Additional Problem

Here you must choose one out of two additional multipart questions that will involve calculation. These questions, like the equilibrium question, will be divided into four or five parts, with partial credit available for correct answers on each part. Each question is worth a total of 9 points. The average score for this section is usually between 4 and 5 points.

CRACKING THE PROBLEMS

On Parts B and C, you want to show the graders that you can do chemistry math. Here's the best way to do that.

Read both of the optional problems all the way through before deciding which one to do

Each question will have at least three or four parts, so you won't be able to tell how easy or tough it is unless you've read it all the way through. Sometimes questions that look like cake at first turn out to be pretty tough when you get to parts (b), (c), and (d). Alternatively, sometimes a problem will have an intimidating facade that disguises the fact that the questions are simple.

Show every step of your calculations on paper

This section is the opposite of multiple-choice. You don't just get full credit for writing the correct answer. You get most of your points on this section for showing the process that got you to the answer. The graders give you partial credit when you show them that you know what you're doing. So even if you can do a calculation in your head, you should set it up and show it on the page.

By showing every step, or explaining what you're doing in words, you ensure that you'll get all the partial credit possible, even if you screw up a calculation. You also ensure that you won't lose points on a correct answer for not showing where it came from.

Include units in all of your calculations

Scientists like units in calculations. Units make scientists feel secure. You'll get points for including them and you might lose points for leaving them out.

Remember significant figures

You can lose one point per question for having the incorrect number of significant figures. Without getting too bent out of shape about it, try to remember that a calculation is only as accurate as the least accurate number in it.

The graders will follow your reasoning, even if you've made a mistake

Often, you are asked to use the result of a previous part of a problem in a later part. If you got the wrong answer in part (a) and used it in part (c), you can still get full credit for part (c), as long as your work is correct based on the number that you used. That's important, because it means that botching the first part of a question doesn't necessarily sink the whole question.

Remember the mean!

So, you could only do parts (a) and (b) on the required equilibrium problem. That's 4 or 5 points out of 9, tops. Are you doomed? Of course not. You're above average. If this test is hard on you, it's just as hard on everybody else. Remember, you don't need anywhere near a perfect score to get a 5, and you can leave half the test blank and still get a 4!

PARTS D AND E—ESSAYS

For Parts D and E, you will be given a table of commonly used chemical equations, a table of standard reduction potentials, and a periodic table. You may use a calculator for this section, although you probably won't need it.

About Part D—The Required Essay Problem

All students must do this question, which will involve written responses to a multipart conceptual question about some aspect of chemistry. This required question was added to the test to deter students and teachers from ignoring parts of the curriculum, since any topic in General Chemistry may turn up here.

This is another multipart question, with partial credit given for correct answers on each part, for a total of 8 points. The average score for this section is usually between 2 and 3 points.

About Part E—Choice of Two Additional Essays

For the final part, you must choose two out of four additional multipart essay questions.

Each question is worth a total of 8 points, with partial credit given for each question. The section is worth a total of 16 points. The average score for the two questions on this section is usually about 7 out of the available 16 points.

CRACKING THE ESSAYS

This section is here to test whether you can translate chemistry into English. The term "essay" is a little misleading because all of these questions can be answered in two or three simple sentences, or with a simple diagram or two. Here are some tips for answering the three essay questions on Part II.

Read all of the optional essay questions all the way through before deciding which ones to do

Just like in the problem section, each question will have at least three or four parts, so you won't be able to tell how easy or tough it is unless you've read it all the way through. Sometimes questions that look like cake at first turn out to be pretty tough when you get to parts (b), (c), and (d). Alternatively, sometimes a problem will have an intimidating facade that diguises the fact that the questions are simple.

Show that you understand the terms used in the question

If they ask you why sodium and potassium have differing first ionization energies, the first thing you should do is tell them what ionization energy is. That's probably worth the first point of partial credit. Then you should tell them how the differing structures of the atoms make for differing ionization energies. That leads to the next tip.

Take a step-by-step approach

Grading these tests is hard work. Breaking a question into parts in this way makes it easier on the grader, who must match your response to a set of guidelines he or she has been given that describe how to assign partial and full credit.

Each grader scores each test based on these rough guidelines that are established at the beginning of the grading period. For instance, if a grader has 3 points for the question about ionization energies, they might be distributed this way:

- One point for understanding ionization energy.

- One point for explaining the structural difference between sodium and potassium.

- One point for showing how this difference affects the ionization energy.

You can get all three points for this question if the grader thinks that all three concepts are addressed *implicitly* in your answer, but by taking a step-by-step approach, you better your chances of *explicitly* addressing the things that a grader has been instructed to look for. Once again, grading these tests is hard work; graders won't know for sure if you understand something unless you tell them.

Which leads us to an obvious point.

Write neatly

Even if writing neatly means you have to work at half-speed. You can't get points for answers if the graders can't understand them. Of course, this applies to the rest of the free-response section as well.

The graders will follow your reasoning, even if you've made a mistake

Just like in the problem section, you might be asked to use the result of a previous part of a problem in a later part. If you decide (incorrectly) that an endothermic reaction in part (a) is exothermic, you can still get full credit in part (c) for your wrong answer about the reaction's spontaneity, as long as your answer in (c) is correct based on an exothermic reaction.

Do the easiest optional essay first

You should make sure that you've accumulated all the easy points before time runs out. Also, the level of difficulty will vary among the four optional essays. You should be aware that you get exactly the same score when you do well on an easy essay as on a hard one. That is, there is no distinction in the grading curve based on the essays you choose.

Don't do more than is required

There is no extra credit for doing extra problems, essays, or descriptive reaction questions.

ABOUT THE TOPICS COVERED ON THE TEST

These are the topics covered on the AP Chemistry test, as described by The College Board.

  I. Structure of Matter
      A. Atomic theory and atomic structure
          1. Evidence for atomic theory
          2. Atomic masses and how to determine them experimentally
          3. Atomic number and mass number; isotopes
          4. Electron energy levels: atomic spectra, quantum numbers, atomic orbitals
          5. Periodic trends (atomic radii, ionization energies, electron affinities, oxidation states)
      B. Bonding
          1. Forces
              a. Types: ionic, covalent, metallic, hydrogen bonding, van der Waals (including London dispersion forces)
              b. Relationships to states, structure, and properties of matter
              c. Polarity, electronegativity
          2. Molecular models
              a. Lewis structures
              b. Valence electrons, hybridization of orbitals, resonance, sigma and pi bonds
              c. VSEPR
          3. Geometry of molecules and ions; structural isomerism of simple organic molecules and coordination complexes; dipole moments; relation of properties to structure
      C. Nuclear chemistry: nuclear equations, half-lives, and radioactivity; chemical applications
  II. States of Matter
      A. Gases
          1. Ideal gas laws
              a. Equation of state for an ideal gas
              b. Partial pressures, Dalton's law

      2. Kinetic-molecular theory
         a. Interpretation of ideal gas laws on the basis of this theory
         b. Avogadro's hypothesis and the mole concept
         c. Dependence of kinetic energy of molecules on temperature, Graham's law
         d. Deviations from ideal gas laws

  B. Liquids and solids
      1. Liquids and solids and kinetic-molecular theory
      2. Phase diagrams
      3. Changes of state, including critical points and triple points
      4. Structure of solids; lattice energies

  C. Solutions
      1. Types of solutions and factors affecting solubility
      2. Molarity, molality, mole fraction, density
      3. Raoult's law, colligative properties, osmosis
      4. Non-ideal behavior

III. Reactions
  A. Reaction types
      1. Acid-base reactions; Arrhenius, Brønsted-Lowry, and Lewis theories; coordination complexes; amphoterism
      2. Precipitation reactions
      3. Oxidation-reduction reactions
         a. Oxidation state
         b. The role of the electron in oxidation-reduction
         c. Electrochemistry: electrolytic and galvanic cells; Faraday's laws; standard half-cell potentials; Nernst equation; spontaneity of redox reactions

  B. Stoichiometry
      1. Ionic and molecular species present in chemical systems: net ionic equations
      2. Balancing of equations, including redox reactions
      3. Mass and volume relations, using the mole concept in finding empirical formulas and limiting reactants

  C. Equilibrium
      1. Dynamic equilibrium, physical and chemical; Le Chatelier's principle; equilibrium constants
      2. Quantitative treatment
         a. Equilibrium constants for gaseous reactions: K_p, K_c
         b. Equilibrium constants for reactions in solution
            (1) Constants for acids and bases; pK; pH
            (2) Solubility product constants and their application to precipitation and the dissolution of slightly soluble compounds
            (3) Common ion effect; buffers; hydrolysis

D. Kinetics
   1. Reaction rate
   2. Use of rate laws to determine order of reaction and rate constant from experimental data
   3. Effect of temperature change on rates
   4. Activation energy, catalysts
   5. Reaction mechanisms and rate determining step
E. Thermodynamics
   1. State functions
   2. First law: enthalpy change; heat of formation; heat of reaction; Hess's law; heats of vaporization and fusion; calorimetry
   3. Second law: entropy; free energy of formation; free energy of reaction; dependence of change in free energy on enthalpy and entropy changes
   4. Relationship of change in free energy to equilibrium constants and electrode potentials

IV. Descriptive Chemistry
   A. Chemical reactivity and products of chemical reactions
   B. Relationships in the periodic table: horizontal, vertical, and diagonal with examples from alkali metals, alkaline earth metals, halogens, and the first series of transition elements
   C. Introduction to organic chemistry: hydrocarbons and functional groups (structure, nomenclature, chemical properties)

V. Laboratory
   Questions based on experiences and skills students acquire in the laboratory: making observations of chemical reactions and substances; recording data; calculating and interpreting results based on the quantitative data obtained; lab safety; experimental errors

The following list summarizes types of specific chemical calculations problems that may appear on the test.

1. Percentage composition

2. Empirical and molecular formulas from experimental data

3. Molar masses from gas density, freezing-point, and boiling-point measurements

4. Gas laws, including the ideal gas law, Dalton's law, and Graham's law

5. Stoichiometric relations using the concept of the mole; titration calculations

6. Mole fractions; molar and molal solutions

7. Faraday's law of electrolysis

8. Equilibrium constants and their applications, including their use for simultaneous equilibria

9. Standard electrode potentials and their use; Nernst equation

10. Thermodynamic and thermochemical calculations

11. Kinetics calculations

PREPARING FOR THE AP CHEMISTRY EXAM

IN THE MONTHS BEFORE THE TEST

Start your review early

Try to spend a half-hour to an hour reviewing Chemistry three or four times a week. Leave your chem books around so you can leaf through them when there's a really bad sitcom on TV between two shows that you like. If you study consistently, even for very short sessions over a few months, you'll find that by the time test week arrives, you'll know the material and you won't have to study for six hours a day for the last six days, which doesn't work very well anyway.

Read this book and do all of the questions in it

This book covers all of the important information required for the AP Chemistry test and the questions in the book test AP Chem material in AP Chem style. If you do well on the questions at the end of each chapter and on the diagnostic test at the end of the book, you will do well on the AP Chemistry test.

Get some real AP Chemistry tests

The College Board releases some test material after the test has been given. It releases a multiple-choice section every five years or so and the free-response section every year, along with the guidelines that were used in grading it. This is the most valuable study resource you have. Remember, you're not just studying chemistry, you're studying the AP Chemistry test.

Ask your teacher or guidance counselor if they have copies of released exams. Many teachers keep them on file and use them every year for in-class tests and practice material. The free-response sections with grading guidelines are especially useful; if you know what the graders are looking for, it's a lot easier to give it to them.

If real AP material is not available at your school, you can buy it directly from The College Board and ETS. Call them at **609-771-7300** or **609-771-7243** and ask them to send you a catalogue of what's available this year.

Use the Internet

If you have access to a computer or you know someone who does, get on the Internet and try typing "Advanced Placement Chemistry" (or some variation) into a couple of different search engines. Here's what you should find:

The College Board home page: This site gives general information about the test and some test-taking tips. This is one place to go to find out if there have been any last-minute changes to the test.

Old AP tests: Sometimes people post old tests on Websites. Sometimes you can download the material for free and sometimes it's available for sale (probably at a lower price than The College Board charges). This stuff won't be as accurate as the official material, but it's almost as good. Also, The College Board only offers selected tests for sale each year, while the material on the Internet tends to be more complete.

AP Students and Teachers: Some AP Chemistry classes have home pages. It might be worth a look to see what other AP classes around the world are up to.

Get a second textbook

Don't get a new one. New science textbooks are way too expensive and you've probably had to buy one already, not to mention what you've had to shell out for this book.

Go to one of those slightly stale smelling used book stores that has books piled randomly from floor to ceiling. Somewhere in there, they should have a first-year chemistry textbook that was printed within the last twenty years. It will probably cost less than ten bucks. You should buy it. Don't worry if it's old; first-year chemistry hasn't changed all that much since you were born.

The reason that it's good to have a second book is that all textbook writers have strengths and weaknesses. An author who can make you understand thermodynamics may leave you totally confused when it comes to kinetics. You don't have to read everything in both books, just use the index to see what the second author has to say about any topic that the first author can't make you understand. Sometimes a second point of view is all you need.

Teach somebody else

The best way to really learn something is to explain it to someone else. Work with the other people in your class whenever you can. When someone else explains something to you, you're learning. When you explain something to someone else, you're learning even more.

IN THE WEEK BEFORE THE TEST

Maintain your usual routine

Go to sleep at your usual time. Don't start a strange new diet. You can step up your studying a bit, but if you've been studying with any consistency in the last few months, you probably won't have to. Don't try to cram the night before the test; it's a waste of time and effort.

Review this book

In assembling the information presented in this book, I pared away everything that was not absolutely necessary to do well on the AP Chemistry test. So if it's in this book, then you need to know it. If it's not in this book, you can get a 5 without it.

Review old AP Chemistry tests

By now you should know the science pretty well. Practice the test. Read the directions on the test carefully, so you will already know them on the day of the test. You should know exactly what you're supposed to do on each section long before you sit for the test. Look for the themes and topics that come up on every test; the more familiar the AP test seems to you when you take it, the easier it will be.

ON THE DAY OF THE TEST

Eat breakfast

Food gives you energy and you'll need it for the test.

Bring everything you need

You need number 2 pencils for the multiple-choice section because that's what the grading machines like to read. You can use either pen or pencil for the free-response section. You will need an eraser.

You will need a watch. Without getting obsessive, you should keep track of the time as you do both sections. Never trust a proctor to do this for you.

Wear comfortable clothing

You don't want anything to distract you from the business at hand.

Bring a snack

A piece of fruit or a candy bar during the break provides a handy energy boost.

Relax

If you're well prepared, the test is simply an opportunity to show it.

3

ATOMIC STRUCTURE AND THE PERIODIC TABLE

How often does this topic appear on the test?
In the multiple-choice section, this topic appears in about 7 out of 75 questions.
In the free-response section, you'll see this topic almost every year.

THE PERIODIC TABLE

Your most important tool for use on this test is the Periodic Table of the Elements.

Periodic Table of the Elements

1 H 1.0																	2 He 4.0
3 Li 6.9	4 Be 9.0											5 B 10.8	6 C 12.0	7 N 14.0	8 O 16.0	9 F 19.0	10 Ne 20.2
11 Na 23.0	12 Mg 24.3											13 Al 27.0	14 Si 28.1	15 P 31.0	16 S 32.1	17 Cl 35.5	18 Ar 39.9
19 K 39.1	20 Ca 40.1	21 Sc 45.0	22 Ti 47.9	23 V 50.9	24 Cr 52.0	25 Mn 54.9	26 Fe 55.8	27 Co 58.9	28 Ni 58.7	29 Cu 63.5	30 Zn 65.4	31 Ga 69.7	32 Ge 72.6	33 As 74.9	34 Se 79.0	35 Br 79.9	36 Kr 83.8
37 Rb 85.5	38 Sr 87.6	39 Y 88.9	40 Zr 91.2	41 Nb 92.9	42 Mo 95.9	43 Te (98)	44 Ru 101.1	45 Rh 102.9	46 Pd 106.4	47 Ag 107.9	48 Cd 112.4	49 In 114.8	50 Sn 118.7	51 Sb 121.8	52 Te 127.6	53 I 126.9	54 Xe 131.3
55 Cs 132.9	56 Ba 137.3	57 *La 138.9	72 Hf 178.5	73 Ta 180.9	74 W 183.9	75 Re 186.2	76 Os 190.2	77 Ir 192.2	78 Pt 195.1	79 Au 197.0	80 Hg 200.6	81 Tl 204.4	82 Pb 207.2	83 Bi 209.0	84 Po (209)	85 At (210)	86 Rn (222)
87 Fr (223)	88 Ra 226.0	89 †Ac 227.0	104 Unq (261)	105 Unp (262)	106 Unh (263)	107 Uns (262)	108 Uno (265)	109 Une (267)									

*Lanthanide Series:	58 Ce 140.1	59 Pr 140.9	60 Nd 144.2	61 Pm (145)	62 Sm 150.4	63 Eu 152.0	64 Gd 157.3	65 Tb 158.9	66 Dy 162.5	67 Ho 164.9	68 Er 167.3	69 Tm 168.9	70 Yb 173.0	71 Lu 175.0
†Actinide Series:	90 Th 232.0	91 Pa (231)	92 U 238.0	93 Np (237)	94 Pu (244)	95 Am (243)	96 Cm (247)	97 Bk (247)	98 Cr (251)	99 Es (252)	100 Fm (257)	101 Md (258)	102 No (259)	103 Lr (260)

The periodic table gives you very basic, but very important, information about each element.

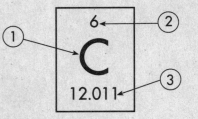

1. This is the **symbol** for the element, carbon in this case.

On the test, the symbol for an element is used interchangeably with the name of the element.

2. This is the **atomic number** of the element.

The atomic number is the same as the number of protons in the nucleus of an element; it is also the same as the number of electrons surrounding the nucleus of an element in its neutral state.

3. This is the **atomic weight** of the element.

The identity of an atom is determined by the number of protons contained in its nucleus. The nucleus of an atom also contains neutrons. The mass number of an atom is the sum of its neutrons and protons. Atoms of an element with different numbers of neutrons are called isotopes; for instance, carbon-12, which contains 6 protons and 6 protons, and carbon-14, which contains 6 protons and 8 neutrons, are isotopes of carbon. The atomic weight given on the periodic table is the average of the mass numbers of a large sample of isotopes of an element.

The atomic weight of an element will give you a pretty good idea of the most common isotope of that element. For instance, the atomic weight of carbon is 12.011 and about 99% of the carbon in existence is carbon-12.

The horizontal rows of the periodic table are called **periods**.

The vertical columns of the periodic table are called **groups**.

ELECTRONS

QUANTUM NUMBERS

The positions of the electrons in relation to the nucleus are described by their **quantum numbers**. Each electron has four quantum numbers, which apply to its **shell**, **subshell**, **orbital**, and **spin**.

Shells: $n = 1, 2, 3...$

In a hydrogen atom, the principal quantum number, or shell, of an electron determines its average distance from the nucleus as well as its energy. So electrons in shells with higher values are farther away on average from the nucleus and will have more energy and less stability than electrons in shells with lower values.

Subshells: $l = 0, 1, 2...$

The angular momentum quantum number, or subshell, describes the shape of an electron's orbital.

- The first shell ($n = 1$) has one subshell: s, or $l = 0$.
- The second shell ($n = 2$) has two subshells: s ($l = 0$), and p ($l = 1$).
- The third shell ($n = 3$) has three subshells: s ($l = 0$), p ($l = 1$), and d ($l = 2$).

The orbitals of s subshells are spherical, while the orbitals of p subshells are dumbbell-shaped.

Orbitals: $m_l = ...-1, 0, +1...$

The magnetic quantum number, or orbital, describes the orientation of the orbital in space. Roughly, that means it describes whether the path of the electron lies mostly on the x, y, or z axis of a three-dimensional grid.

- The s subshell ($l = 0$) has one orbital: $m_l = 0$.
- The p subshell ($l = 1$) has three orbitals: $m_l = -1$, $m_l = 0$, and $m_l = +1$.
- The d subshell ($l = 2$) has five orbitals: $m_l = -2, -1, 0, 1$, and 2.

Spin: $m_s = +\dfrac{1}{2}, -\dfrac{1}{2}$

Each orbital can contain two electrons, one with a positive spin and one with a negative spin.

Here are a couple of graphical ways of looking at quantum numbers.

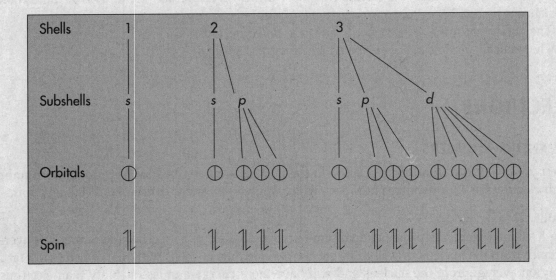

n	l	m_l	m_s
1	0	0	$\pm\frac{1}{2}$

n	l	m_l	m_s
2	0	0	$\pm\frac{1}{2}$
	1	−1	$\pm\frac{1}{2}$
		0	$\pm\frac{1}{2}$
		1	$\pm\frac{1}{2}$

n	l	m_l	m_s
3	0	0	$\pm\frac{1}{2}$
	1	−1	$\pm\frac{1}{2}$
		0	$\pm\frac{1}{2}$
		1	$\pm\frac{1}{2}$
	2	−2	$\pm\frac{1}{2}$
		−1	$\pm\frac{1}{2}$
		0	$\pm\frac{1}{2}$
		1	$\pm\frac{1}{2}$
		2	$\pm\frac{1}{2}$

THE PAULI EXCLUSION PRINCIPLE

The **Pauli Exclusion Principle** states that within an atom, no two electrons can have the same set of quantum numbers. So each electron in any atom has its own distinct set of four quantum numbers.

QUANTUM NUMBERS AND THE PERIODIC TABLE

You can use the periodic table to tell the first two quantum numbers of the valence electrons of any element.

You can also tell the order in which shells and subshells are filled by following the table from left to right across each period.

You should note that after the third period, the filling of subshells becomes more complicated. Notice, for instance, that the 4s subshell fills before the 3d subshell.

Here's a simple tool that many people use to keep track of the order in which orbitals are filled.

1s 2s 2p 3s 3p 4s 3d 4p 5s 4d 5p 6s 4f 5d 6p 7s 5f

HUND'S RULE

Hund's rule says that when an electron is added to a subshell, it will always occupy an empty orbital if one is available. Electrons always occupy orbitals singly if possible, and only pair up if no empty orbitals are available.

Watch how the 2p subshell fills as we go from boron to neon.

	1s	2s	2p
Boron	⇅	⇅	↑
Carbon	⇅	⇅	↑ ↑
Nitrogen	⇅	⇅	↑ ↑ ↑
Oxygen	⇅	⇅	⇅ ↑ ↑
Fluorine	⇅	⇅	⇅ ⇅ ↑
Neon	⇅	⇅	⇅ ⇅ ⇅

DIAMAGNETISM AND PARAMAGNETISM

Diamagnetic elements have all of their electrons spin paired. So diamagnetic elements are elements with all of their subshells completed.

Some diamagnetic elements are:

Helium	$1s^2$
Beryllium	$1s^2\,2s^2$
Neon	$1s^2\,2s^22p^6$

Most of the elements do not have all of their electrons spin paired, and are called **paramagnetic** elements.

Paramagnetic elements are strongly affected by magnetic fields, whereas diamagnetic elements are not very strongly affected.

Molecules can also be diamagnetic or paramagnetic, depending on the pairing of electrons in their molecular orbitals, but the same basic rule holds: Paramagnetic molecules are affected by magnetic fields, and diamagnetic molecules are not.

ELECTRONS AND ENERGY

The positively charged nucleus is always pulling at the negatively charged electrons around it, and the electrons have potential energy that increases with their distance from the nucleus. It works the same way that the gravitational potential energy of a brick on the third floor of a building is greater than the gravitational potential energy of a brick nearer to ground level.

The energy of electrons, however, is **quantized**. That's important. It means that electrons can only exist at specific energy levels, separated by specific intervals. It's kind of like if the brick in the building could only be placed on the first, second, or third floor of the building, but not in-between.

The quantized energy of an electron can be found if you know its principal quantum number, or shell.

Energy of an Electron

$$E_n = \frac{-2.178 \times 10^{-18}}{n^2} \text{ joules}$$

E_n = the energy of the electron
n = the principal quantum number of the electron

When atoms absorb energy in the form of electromagnetic radiation, electrons jump to higher energy levels. When electrons drop from higher to lower energy levels, atoms give off energy in the form of electromagnetic radiation.

The relationship between the change in energy level of an electron and the electromagnetic radiation absorbed or emitted is given below.

Energy and Electromagnetic Radiation

$$\Delta E = hf = \frac{hc}{\lambda}$$

ΔE = energy change
h = Planck's constant, 6.63×10^{-34} joule-sec
f = frequency of the radiation
λ = wavelength of the radiation
c = the speed of light, 3.00×10^8 m/sec ($c = \lambda f$)

The energy level changes for the electrons of a particular atom are always the same, so atoms can be identified by their emission and absorption spectra.

NAMES AND THEORIES

Quantum Theory
Max Planck figured out that electromagnetic energy is quantized. That is, for a given frequency of radiation (or light), all possible energies are multiples of a certain unit of energy, called a quantum (mathematically, that's $E = hf$). So energy changes do not occur smoothly, but in small but specific steps.

The Bohr Model
Neils Bohr took the quantum theory and used it to predict that electrons orbit the nucleus at specific, fixed radii, like planets orbiting the Sun. The Bohr model worked for atoms and ions with one electron, but not for more complex atoms.

The Heisenberg Uncertainty principle
Werner Heisenberg said that it is impossible to know both the position and momentum of an electron at a particular instant. In terms of atomic structure, this means that electron orbitals do not represent specific orbits like those of planets. Instead, an electron orbital is a probability function describing the possibility that an electron will be found in a region of space.

The de Broglie Hypothesis

Louis de Broglie said that all matter has wave characteristics. This is important because sometimes the behavior of electrons is better described in terms of waves than particles.

There is a simple relationship between an electron's wave and particle characteristics.

The de Broglie equation

$$\lambda = \frac{h}{mv}$$

λ = wavelength associated with a particle

m = mass of the particle

v = speed of the particle

$mv = p$ = momentum of the particle

h = Planck's constant, 6.63×10^{-34} joule-sec

De Broglie's hypothesis is useful for very small particles, such as electrons. For larger particles, the wavelength becomes too small to be of interest.

PERIODIC TRENDS

You can make predictions about certain behavior patterns of an atom and its electrons based on the position of the atom in the periodic table. All the periodic trends can be understood in terms of three basic rules.

1. Electrons are attracted to the protons in the nucleus of an atom.
   a. The closer an electron is to the nucleus, the more strongly it is attracted.
   b. The more protons in a nucleus, the more strongly an electron is attracted.

2. Electrons are repelled by other electrons in an atom. So if other electrons are between a valence electron and the nucleus, the valence electron will be less attracted to the nucleus. That's called shielding.

3. Completed shells (and to a lesser extent, completed subshells) are very stable. Atoms prefer to add or subtract valence electrons to create complete shells if possible.

ATOMIC RADIUS

The atomic radius is the approximate distance from the nucleus of an atom to its valence electrons.

Moving from left to right across a period (Li to Ne, for instance), atomic radius decreases

Moving from left to right across a period, protons are added to the nucleus, so the valence electrons are more strongly attracted to the nucleus, decreasing the atomic radius. Electrons are also being added, but they are all in the same shell at about the same distance from the nucleus, so there is not much of a shielding effect.

Moving down a group (Li to Cs, for instance), atomic radius increases

Moving down a group, shells of electrons are added to the nucleus. Each shell shields the more distant shells from the nucleus and the valence electrons get farther and farther away from the nucleus. Protons are also being added, but the shielding effect of the negatively charged electron shells cancels out the added positive charge.

Cations (positively charged ions) are smaller than atoms

When an electron is removed from an atom, forming a cation, the electron-electron repulsions are reduced and all of the valence electrons move closer to the nucleus.

Anions (negatively charged ions) are larger than atoms

When an electron is added to an atom, forming an anion, electron-electron repulsions increase, causing the valence electrons to move farther apart and increasing the radius.

IONIZATION ENERGY

Electrons are attracted to the nucleus of an atom, so it takes energy to remove an electron. The energy required to remove an electron from an atom is called the first ionization energy. Once an electron has been removed, the atom becomes a positively charged ion. The energy required to remove the next electron from the ion is called the second ionization energy, and so on.

Moving from left to right across a period, ionization energy increases

Moving from left to right across a period, protons are added to the nucleus, which increases its positive charge. For this reason, the negatively charged valence electrons are more strongly attracted to the nucleus, which increases the energy required to remove them. Electrons are also being added, and the shielding effect provided by the filling of the s subshell causes a slight deviation in the trend in moving from Group 2A to Group 3A.

Moving down a group, ionization energy decreases

Moving down a group, shells of electrons are added to the nucleus. Each inner shell shields the more distant shells from the nucleus, reducing the pull of the nucleus on the valence electrons and making them easier to remove. Protons are also being added, but the shielding effect of the negatively charged electron shells cancels out the added positive charge.

The second ionization energy is greater than the first ionization energy, and so on

When an electron has been removed from an atom, electron-electron repulsion decreases and the remaining valence electrons move closer to the nucleus. This increases the attractive force between the electrons and the nucleus, increasing the ionization energy.

As electrons are removed, ionization energy increases gradually until a shell is empty, then it makes a big jump

- For Na, the second ionization energy is much larger than the first.

- For Mg, the first and second ionization energies are comparable, but the third is much larger than the second.

- For Al, the first three ionization energies are comparable, but the fourth is much larger than the third.

- For each element, when the valence shell is empty, the next electron must come from a shell that is much closer to the nucleus, making the ionization energy for that electron much larger than for the previous ones.

ELECTRON AFFINITY

Electron affinity is a measure of the change in energy of an atom when an electron is added to it. When the addition of an electron makes the atom more stable, energy is given off. This is true for most of the elements. When the addition of an electron makes the atom less stable, energy must be put in; that's because the added electron must be placed in a higher energy level, making the element less stable. This is the case for elements with full subshells, like the alkaline earths and the noble gases.

Moving from left to right across a period, the energy given off when an electron is added increases. Electron affinities don't change very much moving down a group.

ELECTRONEGATIVITY

Electronegativity refers to how strongly the nucleus of an atom attracts the electrons of other atoms in a bond. Electronegativities of elements are estimated based on ionization energies and electron affinities, and follow basically the same trends.

- Moving from left to right across a period, electronegativity increases.

- Moving down a group, electronegativity decreases.

The various periodic trends are summarized in the diagram below.

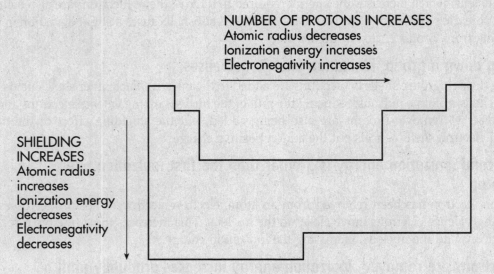

NUMBER OF PROTONS INCREASES
Atomic radius decreases
Ionization energy increases
Electronegativity increases

SHIELDING INCREASES
Atomic radius increases
Ionization energy decreases
Electronegativity decreases

ATOMIC STRUCTURE AND THE PERIODIC TABLE

Questions

Multiple choice

Questions 1–4

    (A) C
    (B) N
    (C) O
    (D) F
    (E) Ne

1. This is the most electronegative element.

2. The nuclear decay of an isotope of this element is used to measure the age of archeological artifacts.

3. All of the electrons in this element are spin-paired.

4. This element, present as a diatomic gas, makes up most of the Earth's atmosphere.

Questions 5–7

    (A) Hg
    (B) Si
    (C) Cu
    (D) Zn
    (E) Ag

5. This element is commonly used in the manufacture of semiconductors.

6. This element is a liquid at room temperature.

7. After oxygen, this is by far the most common element in the Earth's crust.

8. What is the most likely electron configuration for a sodium ion in its ground state?

    (A) $1s^2\ 2s^22p^5$
    (B) $1s^2\ 2s^22p^6$
    (C) $1s^2\ 2s^22p^6\ 3s^1$
    (D) $1s^2\ 2s^22p^5\ 3s^2$
    (E) $1s^2\ 2s^22p^6\ 3s^2$

9. Which of the following statements is true regarding sodium and chlorine?

    (A) Sodium has greater electronegativity and a larger first ionization energy.
    (B) Sodium has a larger first ionization energy and a larger atomic radius.
    (C) Chlorine has a larger atomic radius and a greater electronegativity.
    (D) Chlorine has greater electronegativity and a larger first ionization energy.
    (E) Chlorine has a larger atomic radius and a larger first ionization energy.

10. Which of the following could be the quantum numbers (n, l, m_l, m_s) for the valence electron in a potassium atom in its ground state?

    (A) $3, 0, 0, \dfrac{1}{2}$

    (B) $3, 1, 1, \dfrac{1}{2}$

    (C) $4, 0, 0, \dfrac{1}{2}$

    (D) $4, 1, 1, \dfrac{1}{2}$

    (E) $4, 2, 1, \dfrac{1}{2}$

11. Which of the following elements is diamagnetic?

    (A) H
    (B) Li
    (C) Be
    (D) B
    (E) C

12. Which of the following rules states that no two electrons in an atom can have the same set of quantum numbers?

    (A) Hund's rule
    (B) The Heisenberg Uncertainty principle
    (C) The Pauli Exclusion principle
    (D) The deBroglie hypothesis
    (E) The Bohr model

13. Which of the following is true of the alkali metal elements?

    (A) They usually take the +2 oxidation state.
    (B) They have oxides that act as acid anhydrides.
    (C) They form covalent bonds with oxygen.
    (D) They are generally found in nature in compounds.
    (E) They have relatively large first ionization energies.

14. Which of the following could be the quantum numbers (n, l, m_l, m_s) for the valence electron with the greatest energy in a phosphorous atom in ground state?

    (A) $2, 0, 0, \dfrac{1}{2}$

    (B) $2, 0, 1, \dfrac{1}{2}$

    (C) $2, 1, 0, \dfrac{1}{2}$

    (D) $3, 1, 1, \dfrac{1}{2}$

    (E) $3, 2, 1, \dfrac{1}{2}$

15. Which of the following ions has the smallest ionic radius?

    (A) O^{2-}
    (B) F^-
    (C) Na^+
    (D) Mg^{2+}
    (E) Al^{3+}

Essays

1. Explain each of the following in terms of atomic and molecular structures and/or forces.

    (a) The first ionization energy for magnesium is greater than the first ionization energy for calcium.

    (b) The first and second ionization energies for calcium are comparable, but the third ionization energy is much greater.

    (c) Solid sodium conducts electricity, but solid sodium chloride does not.

    (d) The second ionization energy for sodium is much greater than the first ionization energy, but the second ionization energy for magnesium is comparable to its first ionization energy.

2. Silicon is a nonmetal with four valence electrons.

    (a) Write the ground state electron configuration for silicon.

    (b) Which fundamental atomic theory is violated by the following list of quantum numbers representing silicon's valence electrons?

n	l	m_l	m_s
3	0	0	$-\frac{1}{2}$
3	0	0	$-\frac{1}{2}$
3	1	1	$-\frac{1}{2}$
3	1	1	$-\frac{1}{2}$

    (c) Which fundamental atomic theory is violated by the following list of quantum numbers representing silicon's valence electrons?

n	l	m_l	m_s
3	0	0	$-\frac{1}{2}$
3	0	0	$+\frac{1}{2}$
3	1	-1	$-\frac{1}{2}$
3	1	-1	$+\frac{1}{2}$

    (d) Will a lone silicon atom be diamagnetic or paramagnetic?

3. Use your knowledge of the periodic table of the elements to answer the following questions.

   (a) Explain the trend in electronegativity from P to S to Cl.

   (b) Explain the trend in electronegativity from Cl to Br to I.

   (c) Explain the trend in atomic radius from Li to Na to K.

   (d) Explain the trend in atomic radius from Al to Mg to Na.

4. Use your knowledge of atomic theory to answer the following questions.

   (a) State the Heisenberg Uncertainty principle.

   (b) The absorption spectrum of a hydrogen atom contains dark bands at specific wavelengths. The emission spectrum of a hydrogen atom contains bright bands at the same wavelengths. Explain what causes these bright and dark bands at specific wavelengths.

   (c) Explain why the addition of an electron to a chlorine atom is an exothermic process and the addition of an electron to a magnesium atom is an endothermic process.

   (d) Explain how the valence electron configuration of sulfur is consistent with the existence of Na_2S and SF_6.

ANSWERS

Multiple choice

1. **(D)** is correct. Fluorine, which needs one electron to complete its outer shell, is the most electronegative element, with an electronegativity of 4.0.

2. **(A)** is correct. In carbon dating, the ratio of carbon-14 to carbon-12 in an organic artifact is used to determine the age of the artifact.

3. **(E)** is correct. Neon's second shell is complete, so all of its electrons are spin-paired.

4. **(B)** is correct. Nitrogen gas (N_2) makes up 78% of the Earth's atmosphere. Oxygen is next at 21%.

5. **(B)** is correct. Silicon (Si) is used in semiconductor technology because it has properties that lie in-between metals and nonmetals.

6. **(A)** is correct. Mercury (Hg) is unusual among metals in that it is a liquid at room temperature. Its melting point is –39 °C.

7. **(B)** is correct. Silicon makes up 26% of the Earth's crust by weight (oxygen makes up 50%). In fact, compounds including silicon and oxygen make up nearly all rocks and soils.

8. **(B)** is correct. Neutral sodium in its ground state has the electron configuration shown in choice (C). Sodium forms a bond by giving up its one valence electron and becoming a positively charged ion with the same electron configuration as neon.

9. **(D)** is correct. As we move from left to right across the periodic table within a single period (from sodium to chlorine), we add protons to the nuclei, which progressively increases the pull of each nucleus on its electrons. So chlorine will have a higher first ionization energy, greater electronegativity, and a smaller atomic radius.

10. **(C)** is correct. Potassium's valence electron is in the 4s subshell. That means that $n = 4$, $l = 0$, $m_l = 0$, and $m_s = \dfrac{1}{2}$ or $-\dfrac{1}{2}$.

11. **(C)** is correct. Beryllium's electrons are paired up in the completed orbitals of the 1s and 2s subshells. Choice (E) is wrong because, according to Hund's Rule, carbon's two 2p electrons must be placed in different orbitals.

12. **(C)** is correct. The Pauli Exclusion principle states that no two electrons in an atom can have the same set of quantum numbers.

    About the other answers:

    (A) Hund's rule states that within a subshell, electrons will be placed in empty orbitals while they are available, and will only start to pair up in orbitals when no more empty orbitals are available.

    (B) The Heisenberg Uncertainty principle states that it is impossible to know both the position and momentum of a particle at the same moment with certainty.

(D) The de Broglie hypothesis relates the wave and particle properties of matter, using the following equation.

$$\text{Wavelength} = \frac{h}{\text{momentum}}$$

h is Planck's constant, 6.63×10^{-34} J-sec

(E) The Bohr model of the hydrogen atom (which was disproved by the Heisenberg Uncertainty principle) states that electrons orbit the nucleus in fixed, quantized circular orbits.

13. **(D) is correct.** The alkali metals (Li, Na, K...) are extremely reactive and are found in nature almost exclusively in compounds.

As for the other answers:

Choice (A) is wrong because the alkali metals take the +1 oxidation state. Choice (B) is wrong because alkali metal oxides are basic anhydrides; that is, they form basic solutions in water. Choice (C) is wrong because they form ionic bonds with oxygen. Choice (E) is wrong because they have only one valence electron, so they have relatively small first ionization energies.

14. **(D) is correct.** Phosphorous's valence electrons are in the $3p$ subshell. That means that $n = 3$, $l = 1$, $m_l = -1, 0,$ or 1 and $m_s = \frac{1}{2}$ or $-\frac{1}{2}$.

15. **(E) is correct.** All of the ions listed have the same electron configuration as neutral neon. Al^{3+} has the most protons, so its electrons will experience greater attractive force from the nucleus, resulting in the smallest ions.

Essays

1. (a) Ionization energy is the energy required to remove an electron from an atom. The outermost electron in Ca is at the $4s$ energy level. The outermost electron in Mg is at the $3s$ level. The outermost electron in Ca is at a higher energy level and is more shielded from the nucleus, making it easier to remove.

(b) Calcium has two electrons in its outer shell. The second ionization energy will be larger than the first, but still comparable because both electrons are being removed from the same energy level. The third electron is much more difficult to remove because it is being removed from a lower energy level, so it will have a much higher ionization energy than the other two.

(c) Solid sodium exhibits metallic bonding, in which the positively charged sodium ions are held together by a sea of mobile, delocalized electrons. These electrons move freely from nucleus to nucleus, making solid sodium a good conductor.

Sodium chloride exhibits ionic bonding, in which positively charged sodium ions and negatively charged chlorine ions hold fixed places in a crystal lattice. The electrons are localized around particular nuclei and are not free to move about the lattice. This makes solid sodium chloride a bad conductor of electricity.

(d) Sodium has 1 electron in its outer shell, while magnesium has two. After sodium's one valence electron has been removed, the second electron must be removed from a much lower energy level, requiring a much larger ionization energy.

Magnesium's two electrons are removed from the same energy level, so while the second ionization energy will be larger than the first, it will not be very much larger.

2. (a) $1s^2 2s^2 2p^6 3s^2 3p^2$

(b) The Pauli Exclusion principle is violated. The Pauli Exclusion principle states that no two electrons can have the same set of quantum numbers.

(c) Hund's rule is violated. Hund's rule states that within an energy level, electrons will be placed in empty orbitals while they are available, and will only start to pair up in orbitals when no more empty orbitals are available.

(d) A lone silicon atom will be paramagnetic and will be affected by a magnetic field. If all the electrons in an atom are spin-paired, the atom is diamagnetic. If any of the electrons are not spin-paired, the atom is paramagnetic. Silicon has two electrons in the $3p$ subshell. They will be placed in different orbitals, so they will not be spin-paired.

3. (a) Electronegativity is the pull of the nucleus of one atom on the electrons of other atoms; it increases from P to S to Cl because nuclear charge increases; this is because as you move left to right across the periodic table, atomic radii decrease in size. Increasing nuclear charge means that Cl has the most positively charged nucleus of the three and will exert the greatest pull on the electrons of other atoms.

(b) Electronegativity is the pull of the nucleus of one atom on the electrons of other atoms; it decreases from Cl to Br to I because electron shells are added. The added electron shells shield the nucleus, causing it to have less effect on the electrons of other atoms. So iodine will exert the least pull on the electrons of other atoms.

(c) Atomic radius increases from Li to Na to K because electrons are being added in higher energy levels which are farther away from the nucleus, therefore the K atom is the largest of the three.

(d) Atomic radius increases from Al to Mg to Na because protons are being removed from the nucleus while the energy level of the valence electrons remains unchanged. If there are fewer positive charges in the nucleus, the electrons of Na will be less attracted to the nucleus and will remain farther away.

4. (a) A straightforward statement of the Heisenberg Uncertainty principle is as follows: It is impossible to know both the position and momentum of a particle at one moment with certainty.

(b) When a hydrogen atom absorbs energy, its electrons jump to higher energy levels. The absorbed energy shows up as a dark area on the absorption spectrum.

A hydrogen atom gives off energy when its electrons jump back down to lower energy levels. Electromagnetic waves, which are emitted at these jumps, show up as bright areas on the emission spectrum.

In an atom, energy is quantized, which means that electrons can only exist at specific energy levels. When an electron jumps from one energy level to another, it will always emit or absorb exactly the same amount of energy, and because $\Delta E = hf$, for a particular energy change, radiation of the same frequency will always be emitted or absorbed.

(c) When an electron is added to chlorine, the chlorine ion created has a complete valence shell, which is an extremely stable, low energy configuration. When something becomes more stable, energy is given off, making the process exothermic.

When an electron is added to a magnesium atom, it must be placed by itself in the $3p$ energy level. Adding an electron in a higher energy level makes the magnesium ion created more energetic and less stable, which means that the process is endothermic.

(d) Sulfur has 6 valence electrons in its outer shell. In Na_2S, sulfur gains two electrons to give its outer shell a complete octet. In SF_6, sulfur uses sp^3d^2 hybridization to share all six of its valence electrons with fluorine atoms.

4

BONDING

How often does this topic appear on the test?
In the multiple-choice section, this topic appears in about 8 out of 75 questions.
In the free-response section, you'll see this topic every year.

COULOMB'S LAW

All bonds occur because of electrostatic attractions. Atoms stick together to form molecules, and atoms and molecules stick together to form liquids or solids because the negatively charged electrons of one atom are attracted to the positively charged nucleus of another atom.

Electrostatic forces are governed by Coulomb's law, and the entire study of bonding comes down to understanding how Coulomb's law applies to different chemical situations.

Let's take a look at Coulomb's law.

Coulomb's Law

Attractive Force is proportional to $\dfrac{(+q)(-q)}{r^2}$

$+q$ = magnitude of the positive charge
$-q$ = magnitude of the negative charge
r = distance between the charges

You should be able to tell two things from the math above:

- Bigger charges mean stronger bonds; smaller charges mean weaker bonds
- Charges close together mean stronger bonds; charges far apart mean weaker bonds.

BONDS WITHIN MOLECULES

Atoms join to form molecules because atoms like to have a full outer shell of electrons. This usually means having eight electrons in the outer shell. So atoms with too many or too few electrons in their valence shells will find each other and pass the electrons around until all the atoms in the molecule have stable outer shells. Sometimes an atom will give up electrons completely to another atom, forming an ionic bond. Sometimes atoms share electrons, forming covalent bonds.

IONIC BONDS

Ionic bonds occur between atoms of very different electronegativities. In an ionic bond, electrons are not shared. Instead, one atom gives up electrons and becomes a positively charged ion while the other atom accepts electrons and becomes a negatively charged ion.

The two ions in an ionic bond are held together by electrostatic attraction. In the picture below, a sodium atom has given up its single valence electron to a chlorine atom, which uses the electron to complete its outer shell. The two atoms are then held together by the attraction of the positive and negative charges on the ions.

$$\left[Na\right]^+ \left[:\ddot{\underset{\cdot\cdot}{Cl}}:\right]^-$$

From Coulomb's law we know that more highly charged ions will form stronger bonds than less highly charged ions and smaller ions will form stronger bonds than larger ions.

We'll talk more about ionic bonds when we talk about solids and liquids.

COVALENT BONDS

In a covalent bond, two atoms share electrons. Each atom counts the shared electrons as part of its valence shell, and in this way, both atoms can consider themselves to have complete outer shells.

In the picture below, two fluorine atoms, each of which needs one electron to complete its valence shell, form a covalent bond. Each atom donates an electron to the bond, which is considered to be part of the valence shell of both atoms.

$$:\ddot{F}\cdot \; + \; \cdot\ddot{F}: \; \Rightarrow \; :\ddot{F}:\ddot{F}:$$

The number of covalent bonds an atom can form is the same as the number of electrons in its valence shell.

The first covalent bond formed between two atoms is called a sigma (σ) bond. All single bonds are sigma bonds. If additional bonds between the two atoms are formed, they are called pi (π) bonds. The second bond in a double bond is a pi bond and the second and third bonds in a triple bond are pi bonds.

Polarity

In the F_2 molecule shown above, the two fluorine atoms share the electrons equally, but that's not usually the case in molecules. Usually, one of the atoms (the more electronegative one) will exert a stronger pull on the electrons in the bond, not enough to make the bond ionic, but enough to keep the electrons on one side of the molecule more than on the other side. This makes the molecule a dipole. That is, the side of the molecule where the electrons spend more time will be negative and the side of the molecule where the electrons spend less time will be positive.

Dipole moment

The polarity of a molecule is measured by the dipole moment. The larger the dipole moment, the more polar the molecule. The greater the charge at the ends of the dipole and the greater the distance between the charges, the greater the value of the dipole moment.

LEWIS DOT STRUCTURES

Drawing Lewis dot structures

At some point on the test, you'll be asked to draw the Lewis structure for a molecule or polyatomic ion. Here's how to do it.

1. Count the valence electrons in the molecule or polyatomic ion.

2. If a polyatomic ion has a negative charge, add electrons to the total in (1). If a polyatomic ion has a positive charge, subtract electrons from the total in (1).

3. Draw the skeletal structure of the molecule and place two electrons (or a single bond) between each pair of bonded atoms. If the molecule contains three or more atoms, the least electronegative atom will usually occupy the central position.

4. Add electrons to the surrounding atoms until each has a complete outer shell.

5. Add the remaining electrons to the central atom.

6. Look at the central atom:

    (a) If the central atom has too few electrons, remove an electron pair from an outer atom and add another bond between that outer atom and the central atom. Do this until the central atom has a complete octet.

    (b) If the central atom has a complete octet, you are finished.

    (c) If the central atom has more than eight electrons, that's okay too.

Let's find the Lewis structure for the CO_3^{2-} ion.

1. Carbon has 4 valence electrons; oxygen has 6.
   $4 + 6 + 6 + 6 = 22$

2. The ion has a charge of –2.
   $22 + 2 = 24$

3. Carbon is the central atom.

4. Add electrons to the oxygen atoms.

5. We've added all 24 electrons, so there's nothing left to put on the carbon atom.

6. (a) We need to give carbon a complete octet, so we take an electron pair away from one of the oxygens and make a double bond instead.

Resonance forms

When we put a double bond into the CO_3^{2-} ion, we could have placed it on any one of the oxygen atoms. In fact, the ion can be drawn with the double bond on any of the oxygen atoms as shown below.

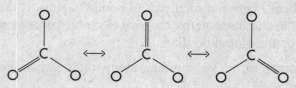

All three resonance forms are considered to exist simultaneously and the strength of all three bonds is the same, somewhere between the strength of a single bond and a double bond.

Incomplete octets

Some atoms can have a complete outer shell with less than eight electrons; for example, hydrogen can have a maximum of two electrons, and beryllium can be stable with only four valence electrons, as in BeH_2.

$$H - Be - H$$

Boron can be stable with only six valence electrons, as in BF_3.

Expanded octets

In molecules that have d subshells available, the central atom can have more than eight valence electrons.

Here are some examples:

PCl₅

SF₄

SF₆

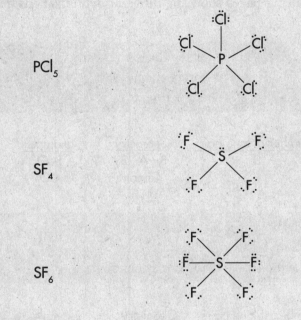

Odd numbers of electrons

Molecules almost always have an even number of electrons, allowing electrons to be paired, but there are exceptions, usually involving nitrogen.

NO

NO₂

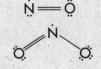

Note that NO_2 could be shown with either of two resonance forms.

MOLECULAR GEOMETRY

Electrons repel one another, so when atoms come together to form a molecule, the molecule will assume the shape that keeps its different electron pairs as far apart as possible. When we predict the geometries of molecules using this idea, we are using the **valence-shell electron-pair repulsion (VSEPR) model**.

In a molecule with more than two atoms, the shape of the molecule is determined by the number of electron pairs on the central atom. The central atom forms **hybrid orbitals**, each of which has a standard shape. Variations on the standard shape occur depending on the number of bonding pairs and lone pairs of electrons on the central atom.

Here are some things you should remember when dealing with the VSEPR model:

- Double and triple bonds are treated in the same way as single bonds in predicting overall geometry for a molecule, but multiple bonds have slightly more repulsive strength and therefore will occupy a little more space than single bonds.

- Lone electron pairs have a little more repulsive strength than bonding pairs, so lone pairs will occupy a little more space than bonding pairs.

The tables on the following pages show the different hybridizations and geometries that you might see on the test.

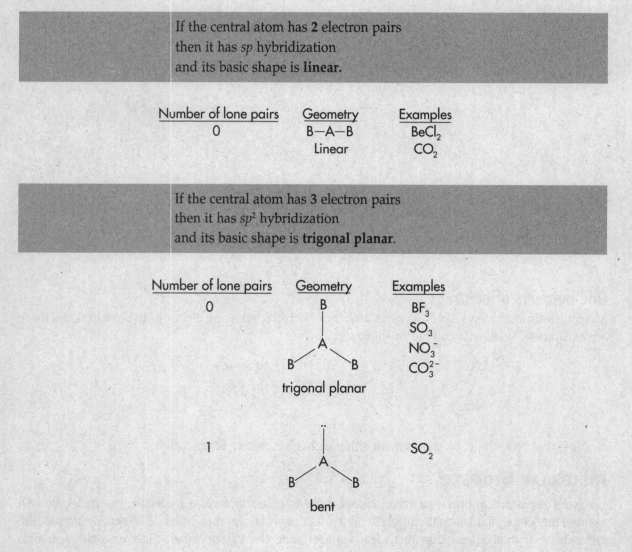

If the central atom has **2 electron pairs**
then it has *sp* hybridization
and its basic shape is **linear**.

Number of lone pairs	Geometry	Examples
0	B—A—B Linear	$BeCl_2$ CO_2

If the central atom has **3 electron pairs**
then it has *sp²* hybridization
and its basic shape is **trigonal planar**.

Number of lone pairs	Geometry	Examples
0	trigonal planar	BF_3 SO_3 NO_3^- CO_3^{2-}
1	bent	SO_2

If the central atom has **4** electron pairs
then it has *sp*³ hybridization
and its basic shape is **tetrahedral**.

Number of lone pairs	Geometry	Examples

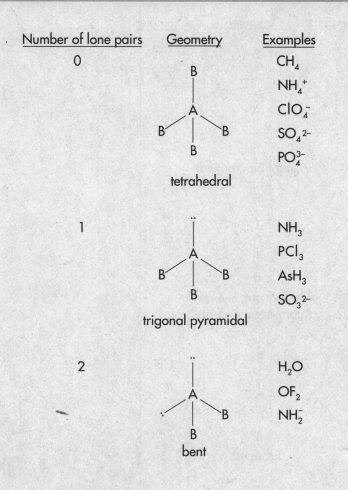

0	tetrahedral	CH_4 NH_4^+ ClO_4^- SO_4^{2-} PO_4^{3-}
1	trigonal pyramidal	NH_3 PCl_3 AsH_3 SO_3^{2-}
2	bent	H_2O OF_2 NH_2^-

If the central atom has **5 electron pairs**
then it has *dsp³* hybridization
and its basic shape is **trigonal bipyramidal**.

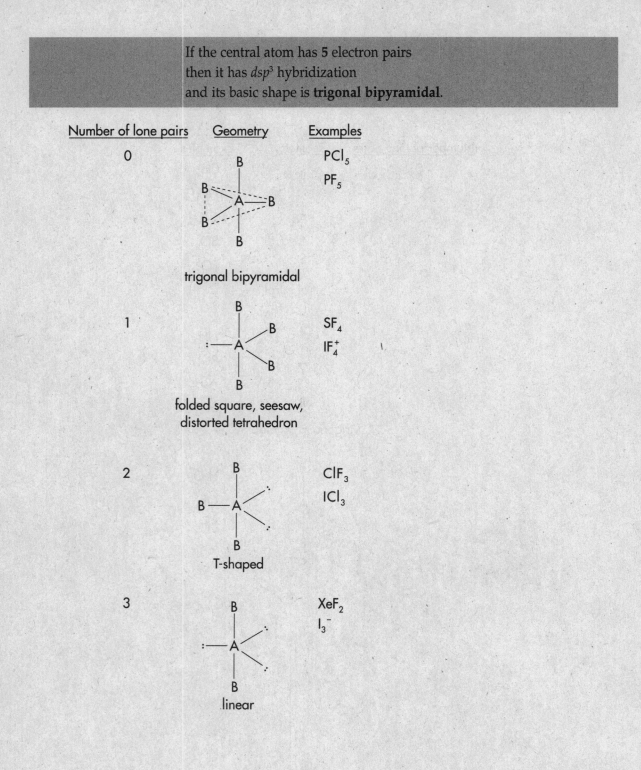

Number of lone pairs	Geometry	Examples
0	trigonal bipyramidal	PCl_5 PF_5
1	folded square, seesaw, distorted tetrahedron	SF_4 IF_4^+
2	T-shaped	ClF_3 ICl_3
3	linear	XeF_2 I_3^-

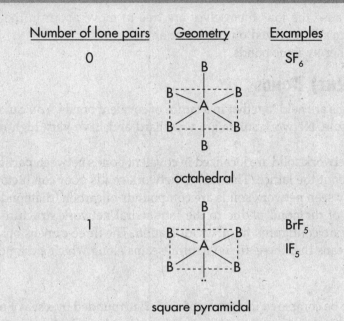

Number of lone pairs	Geometry	Examples
0	octahedral	SF_6
1	square pyramidal	BrF_5 IF_5
2	square planar	XeF_4 ICl_4^-

BONDS BETWEEN MOLECULES—ATTRACTIVE FORCES IN SOLIDS AND LIQUIDS

Sometimes the bonds that hold the atoms or ions in liquids and solids together are the same strong bonds that hold the atoms or ions together in molecules.

IONIC BONDS

An ionic solid is held together by the electrostatic attractions between ions that are next to each other in a lattice structure. The same electrostatic attractions that hold the ions in a molecule of NaCl together hold a block of NaCl together, so there is no real distinction between the molecules and the solid. Ionic bonds are strong and substances held together by ionic bonds have high melting and boiling points.

We know from Coulomb's law that the more highly charged the ions in an ionic bond, the stronger the bond. So an ionic bond composed of ions with +2 and –2 charges will be stronger than a bond composed of ions with +1 and −1 charges. Also from Coulomb's law, we know that the smaller the ions in an ionic bond, the stronger the bond. This is because a small ionic radius allows the charges to get closer together, and increases the force between them.

In an ionic solid, each electron is localized around a particular atom, so electrons do not move around the lattice; this makes ionic solids poor conductors of electricity. Ionic liquids, however, do conduct electricity because the ions themselves are free to move about in the liquid phase, even though the electrons are still localized on particular atoms.

Salts are held together by ionic bonds.

NETWORK (COVALENT) BONDS

In a network solid, atoms are held together in a lattice of covalent bonds. You can visualize a network solid as one big molecule. Network solids are very hard and have very high melting and boiling points.

The electrons in a network solid are localized in covalent bonds between particular atoms, so they are not free to move about the lattice. This makes network solids poor conductors of electricity.

The most commonly seen network solids are compounds of carbon (diamond) and silicon (SiO_2–quartz). The hardness of diamond is due to the tetrahedral network structure formed by carbon atoms whose electrons are configured in sp^3 hybridization. The three-dimensional complexity of the tetrahedral network means that there are no natural seams along which a diamond can be broken.

METALLIC BONDS

Metallic substances can be compared to a group of nuclei surrounded by a sea of mobile electrons. As with ionic and network substances, a metallic substance can be visualized as one large molecule. Most metals are very hard, although the freedom of movement of electrons in metals makes them malleable and ductile. All metals except mercury are solids at room temperature and most metals have high boiling and melting points.

Metals composed of atoms with smaller nuclei tend to form stronger bonds than metals made up of atoms with larger nuclei. This is because smaller sized nuclei allow the positively charged nuclei to be closer to the negatively charged electrons, increasing the attractive force from Coulomb's law.

The electrons in a metallic substance are delocalized and can move freely throughout the substance. The freedom of the electrons in a metal makes it a very good conductor of heat and electricity.

Sometimes the forces that hold liquids and solids together are the weak interactions that occur between distinct, neutral molecules.

VAN DER WAALS FORCES

Dipole-dipole forces

Dipole-dipole forces occur between neutral, polar molecules: the positive end of one polar molecule is attracted to the negative end of another polar molecule.

Molecules with greater polarity will have greater dipole-dipole attraction, so molecules with larger dipole moments tend to have higher melting and boiling points. Dipole-dipole attractions are relatively weak, however, and these substances melt and boil at very low temperatures. Most substances held together by dipole-dipole attraction are gases or liquids at room temperature.

London dispersion forces

London dispersion forces occur between neutral, nonpolar molecules. These very weak attractions occur because of the random motions of electrons on atoms within molecules. At a given moment, a nonpolar molecule might have more electrons on one side than the other, giving it an instantaneous polarity. For that fleeting instant, the molecule will act as a very weak dipole.

Since London dispersion forces depend on the random motions of electrons, molecules with more electrons will experience greater London dispersion forces. So for substances that experience only London dispersion forces, the one with more electrons will generally have higher melting and boiling points. London dispersion forces are even weaker than dipole-dipole forces, so substances that experience only London dispersion forces melt and boil at extremely low temperatures and tend to be gases at room temperature.

HYDROGEN BONDING

Hydrogen bonds are similar to dipole-dipole attractions. In a hydrogen bond, the positively charged hydrogen end of a molecule is attracted to the negatively charged end of another molecule containing an extremely electronegative element (fluorine, oxygen, or nitrogen–FON).

Hydrogen bonds are much stronger than dipole-dipole forces because when a hydrogen atom gives up its lone electron to a bond, its positively charged nucleus is left virtually unshielded. Substances that have hydrogen bonds, like water and ammonia, have higher melting and boiling points than substances that are held together by dipole-dipole forces.

Water is less dense as a solid than as a liquid because its hydrogen bonds force the molecules in ice to form a crystal structure, which keeps them farther apart than they are in liquid form.

BONDING

QUESTIONS

Multiple choice

Questions 1–4

    (A) Metallic bonding
    (B) Network covalent bonding
    (C) Hydrogen bonding
    (D) Ionic bonding
    (E) London dispersion forces

1. Solids exhibiting this kind of bonding are excellent conductors of heat.

2. This kind of bonding is the reason that water is more dense than ice.

3. This kind of bonding exists between atoms with very different electronegativities.

4. The stability exhibited by diamonds is due to this kind of bonding.

Questions 5–7

    (A) CH_4
    (B) NH_3
    (C) NaCl
    (D) N_2
    (E) H_2

5. This substance undergoes ionic bonding.

6. This molecule contains two pi (π) bonds.

7. This substance undergoes hydrogen bonding.

Questions 8–10

    (A) BF_3
    (B) CO_2
    (C) H_2O
    (D) CF_4
    (E) PH_3

8. The central atom in this molecule forms sp^2 hybrid orbitals.

9. This molecule has a tetrahedral structure.

10. This molecule has a linear structure.

11. A liquid whose molecules are held together by which of the following forces would be expected to have the lowest boiling point?

    (A) ionic bonds
    (B) London dispersion forces
    (C) hydrogen bonds
    (D) metallic bonds
    (E) network bonds

12. Hydrogen bonding would be seen in a sample of which of the following substances?

    (A) CH_4
    (B) H_2
    (C) H_2O
    (D) HI
    (E) All of the above

13. Which of the following species does NOT have a tetrahedral structure?

    (A) CH_4
    (B) NH_4^+
    (C) SF_4
    (D) $AlCl_4^-$
    (E) CBr_4

14. Which form of orbital hybridization can form molecules with shapes that are either trigonal pyramidal or tetrahedral?

    (A) sp
    (B) sp^2
    (C) sp^3
    (D) dsp^2
    (E) dsp^3

15. The six carbon atoms in a benzene molecule are shown in different resonance forms as three single bonds and three double bonds. If the length of a single carbon-carbon bond is 154 pm and the length of a double carbon-carbon bond is 133 pm, what length would be expected for the carbon-carbon bonds in benzene?

    (A) 126 pm
    (B) 133 pm
    (C) 140 pm
    (D) 154 pm
    (E) 169 pm

16. Which of the following could be the Lewis structure for carbonate ion, CO_3^{2-}?

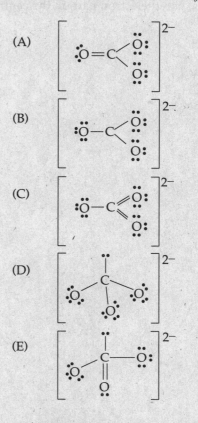

17. In which of the following species does the central atom NOT form sp^2 hybrid orbitals?

    (A) SO_2
    (B) BF_3
    (C) NO_3^-
    (D) SO_3
    (E) PCl_3

18. A molecule whose central atom has d^2sp^3 hybridization can have which of the following shapes?

    I. tetrahedral
    II. square pyramidal
    III. square planar

    (A) I only
    (B) III only
    (C) I and II only
    (D) II, and III only
    (E) I, II, and III

19. Which of the following molecules will have a Lewis dot structure with exactly one unshared electron pair on the central atom?

    (A) H_2O
    (B) PH_3
    (C) PCl_5
    (D) CH_2Cl_2
    (E) $BeCl_2$

20. Which of the following lists of species is in order of increasing boiling point?

    (A) H_2, N_2, NH_3
    (B) N_2, NH_3, H_2
    (C) NH_3, H_2, N_2
    (D) NH_3, N_2, H_2
    (E) H_2, NH_3, N_2

Essays

1. Use the principles of bonding and molecular structure to explain the following statements.

   (a) The boiling point of argon is –186 °C, whereas the boiling point of neon is –246 °C.

   (b) Solid sodium melts at 98 °C, but solid potassium melts at 64 °C.

   (c) More energy is required to break up a $CaO(s)$ crystal into ions than to break up a $KF(s)$ crystal into ions.

   (d) Molten KF conducts electricity, but solid KF does not.

2. The carbonate ion, CO_3^{2-}, is formed when carbon dioxide, CO_2, reacts with slightly basic cold water.

   (a) Draw the Lewis electron dot structure for the carbonate ion. Include resonance forms if they are appropriate.

   (b) Describe the hybridization of carbon in the carbonate ion.

   (c) Describe the relative lengths of the three C–O bonds in the carbonate ion.

   (d) Compare the average length of the C–O bonds in the carbonate ion to the average length of the C–O bonds in carbon dioxide.

3.

Substance	Boiling Point (°C)	Bond length (Å)	Bond strength (kcal/mol)
H_2	–253	0.75	104.2
N_2	–196	1.10	226.8
O_2	–182	1.21	118.9
Cl_2	–34	1.99	58.0

   (a) Explain the differences in the properties given in the table above for each of the following pairs.

   (i) The bond strengths of N_2 and O_2.

   (ii) The bond lengths of H_2 and Cl_2.

   (iii) The boiling points of O_2 and Cl_2.

   (b) Use the principles of molecular bonding to explain why H_2 and O_2 are gases at room temperature, while H_2O is a liquid at room temperature.

4. H_2S SO_4^{2-} XeF_2 ICl_4^-

   (a) Draw a Lewis electron dot diagram for each of the molecules listed above.

   (b) Use the valence shell electron-pair repulsion (VSEPR) model to predict the geometry of each of the molecules.

5. Use the principles of bonding and molecular structure to explain the following statements.

(a)   The angle between the N–F bonds in NF$_3$ is smaller than the angle between the B–F bonds in BF$_3$.

(b)   I$_2$(s) is insoluble in water, but it is soluble in carbon tetrachloride.

(c)   Diamond is one of the hardest substances on Earth.

(d)   HCl has a lower boiling point than either HF or HBr.

Answers

Multiple choice

1.   **(A)** is correct. In metallic bonding, nuclei are surrounded by a sea of mobile electrons. The electrons' freedom to move allows them to conduct heat and electricity.

2.   **(C)** is correct. When ice forms, the hydrogen bonds join the molecules in a lattice structure, which forces them to remain farther apart than they had been in the liquid form. Because the molecules are farther apart in the solid than in the liquid, the solid (ice) is less dense than the liquid.

3.   **(D)** is correct. Electronegativity is a measure of how much pull an atom exerts on another atoms' electrons. If the difference in electronegativities is large enough (greater than 1.7) then the more electronegative atom will simply take an electron away from the other atom. The two atoms will then be held together by electrostatic attraction (the atom that has gained an electron becomes negative and the atom that has lost an electron becomes positive). That's an ionic bond.

4.   **(B)** is correct. The carbon atoms in diamond are held together by a network of covalent bonds. The carbon atoms form sp^3 hybrid orbitals, resulting in a tetrahedral structure which is very stable and has no simple breaking points.

5.   **(C)** is correct. NaCl is composed of two elements of very different electronegativities, so Na gives up an electron to Cl and the two are held together by electrostatic attraction in an ionic bond.

6.   **(D)** is correct. N$_2$ contains a triple bond, so it has one sigma (σ) bond and two pi (π) bonds.

7.   **(B)** is correct. Hydrogen bonding occurs between hydrogen atoms of one molecule and electronegative elements (F, O, N) of another molecule. So in ammonia, hydrogens from one ammonia molecule will form bonds with nitrogens from another ammonia molecule.

8.   **(A)** is correct. In BF$_3$, boron forms three bonds with fluorine atoms and has no unbonded valence electrons, so it must form sp^2 hybrid orbitals.

9. **(D) is correct.** CF_4 forms a tetrahedral structure as shown in the diagram below. The central carbon atom is hybridized sp^3.

10. **(B) is correct.** CO_2 forms a linear structure as shown in the diagram below. The central carbon atom is sp hybridized.

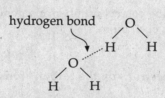

11. **(B) is correct.** A liquid with a low boiling point must be held together by weak bonds. London dispersion forces are the weakest kind of intermolecular force.

12. **(C) is correct.** Hydrogen bonding specifically describes the attraction experienced by a hydrogen atom in one molecule to an extremely electronegative element (F, O, or N) in another molecule. So, in water, a hydrogen atom in one water molecule will be attracted to an oxygen atom in another molecule.

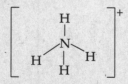

13. **(C) is correct.** SF_4 has 34 valence electrons distributed in the Lewis structure and shape shown below:

In this molecule, sulfur forms dsp^3 hybrid orbitals, which have a trigonal bipyramid structure. Because SF_4 has one unshared electron pair, the molecule takes the "seesaw" or "folded square" shape.

Choices (A) and (B), CH_4 and NH_4^+, each have 8 valence electrons distributed in the same Lewis structure and shape, shown below for NH_4^+:

In these molecules, the central atom forms sp^3 hybrid orbitals, which have a tetrahedral structure. There are no unshared electron pairs on the central atom, so the molecules are tetrahedral.

Choices (D) and (E), $AlCl_4^-$ and CBr_4, each have 32 valence electrons distributed in the same Lewis structure and shape, shown below for $AlCl_4^-$:

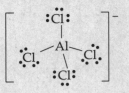

In these molecules, the central atom forms sp^3 hybrid orbitals, which have a tetrahedral structure. There are no unshared electron pairs on the central atom, so the molecules are tetrahedral.

14. **(C)** is correct. sp^3 hybrid orbitals take a tetrahedral shape if the central atom has no unshared electron pairs (CH_4, for instance). If the central atom has one unshared electron pair, the molecule takes the trigonal pyramid shape (NH_3, for instance).

15. **(C)** is correct. Resonance is used to describe a situation that lies between single and double bonds, so the bond length would also be expected to be in-between that of single and double bonds.

16. **(A)** is correct. Choice (A) has the correct number of valence electrons ($6 + 6 + 6 + 4 + 2 = 24$), and eight valence electrons on each atom.

The other choices:

(B) There are only 6 valence electrons on the carbon atom.

(C) There are too many (10) valence electrons on the carbon atom.

(D) There are too many (26) valence electrons.

(E) There are too many (10) valence electrons on the carbon atom and not enough (6) on one of the oxygen atoms.

17. **(E)** is correct. PCl_3 is the only one that doesn't form sp^2 hybrid orbitals, forming sp^3 orbitals instead.

The Lewis structures for all of the choices are shown below (note that boron does not need an octet)

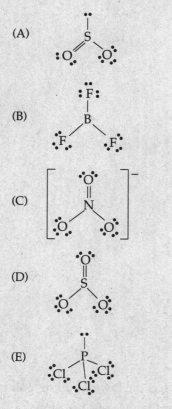

(A)

(B)

(C)

(D)

(E)

18. **(D)** is correct. A molecule with d^2sp^3 hybridization has octahedral structure if the central atom has no unbonded electrons (SF_6, for instance).

If the central atom has one unbonded electron pair, the molecule is square pyramidal (IF_5, for instance).

If the central atom has two unbonded electron pairs, the molecule is square planar (XeF_4, for instance).

A molecule with d^2sp^3 hybridization can never be tetrahedral.

19. **(B)** is correct. The Lewis dot structures for the answer choices are shown below. Only PH₃ has a single unshared electron pair on its central atom.

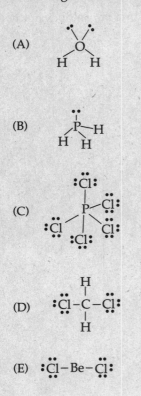

(A)

(B)

(C)

(D)

(E)

20. **(A)** is correct. H_2 experiences only van der Waals forces and has the lowest boiling point.

N_2 also experiences only van der Waals forces, but it is larger than H_2 and has more electrons, so it has stronger van der Waals interactions with other molecules.

NH_3 is polar and undergoes hydrogen bonding, so it has the strongest intermolecular interactions and the highest boiling point.

Essays

1. (a) Molecules of noble gases in the liquid phase are held together by London dispersion forces, which are weak interactions brought about by instantaneous polarities in nonpolar atoms and molecules.

Atoms with more electrons experience stronger London dispersion forces. Argon has more electrons than neon, so it experiences stronger London dispersion forces and boils at a higher temperature.

(b) Sodium and potassium are held together by metallic bonds, positively charged ions in a delocalized sea of electrons.

Potassium is larger than sodium, so the electrostatic attractions that hold the atoms together act at a greater distance, reducing the attractive force and resulting in its lower melting point.

(c) Both CaO(s) and KF(s) are held together by ionic bonds in crystal lattices.

Ionic bonds are held together by an electrostatic force which can be determined by using Coulomb's law.

$$F = k\frac{Q_1 Q_2}{r^2}$$

CaO is more highly charged, with Ca^{2+} bonded to O^{2-}. So for CaO, Q_1 and Q_2 are +2 and –2.

KF is not as highly charged, with K^+ bonded to F^-. So for KF, Q_1 and Q_2 are +1 and –1.

CaO is held together by stronger forces and is more difficult to break apart.

(d) KF is composed of K^+ and F^- ions. In the liquid (molten) state, these ions are free to move and can thus conduct electricity.

In the solid state, the K^+ and F^- ions are fixed in a crystal lattice and their electrons are localized around them, so there is no charge that is free to move and thus no conduction of electricity.

2. (a)

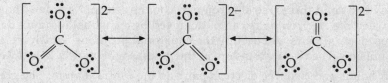

(b) The central carbon atom forms three bonds with oxygen atoms and has no free electron pairs, so its hybridization must be sp^2.

(c) All three bonds will be the same length because no particular resonance form is preferred over the others.

(d) The C–O bonds in the carbonate ion have resonance forms between single and double bonds while the C–O bonds in carbon dioxide are both double bonds.

The bonds in the carbonate ion will be shorter than single bonds and longer than double bonds, so the carbonate bonds will be longer than the carbon dioxide bonds.

3. (a) (i) The bond strength of N_2 is larger than the bond strength of O_2 because N_2 molecules have triple bonds and O_2 molecules have double bonds. Triple bonds are stronger and shorter than double bonds.

(ii) The bond length of H_2 is smaller than the bond length of Cl_2 because hydrogen is a smaller atom than chlorine.

(iii) Liquid oxygen and liquid chlorine are both nonpolar substances that experience only London dispersion forces of attraction. These forces are greater for Cl_2 because it has more electrons, so Cl_2 has a higher boiling point than O_2.

(b) H_2 and O_2 are both nonpolar molecules that experience only London dispersion forces, which are too weak to form the bonds required in order for a substance to be liquid at room temperature.

H_2O is a polar substance whose molecules form hydrogen bonds with each other. Hydrogen bonds are strong enough to form the bonds required in a liquid at room temperature.

4. (a)

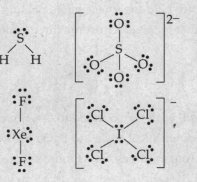

(b) H₂S has two bonds and two free electron pairs on the central S atom. The greatest distance between the electron pairs is achieved by tetrahedral arrangement. The electron pairs at two of the four corners will cause the molecule to have a bent shape, like water.

SO_4^{2-} has four bonds around the central S atom and no free electron pairs. The four bonded pairs will be farthest apart when they are arranged in a tetrahedral shape, so the molecule is tetrahedral.

XeF_2 has two bonds and three free electron pairs on the central Xe atom. The greatest distance between the electron pairs can be achieved by a trigonal bipyramidal arrangement. The three free electron pairs will occupy the equatorial positions, which are 120° apart, to minimize repulsion. The two F atoms are at the poles, so the molecule is linear.

ICl_4^- has four bonds and two free electron pairs on the central I atom. The greatest distance between the electron pairs can be achieved by an octahedral arrangement. The two free electron pairs will be opposite each other to minimize repulsion. The four Cl atoms are in the equatorial positions, so the molecule is square planar.

5. (a) BF_3 has three bonds on the central B atom and no free electron pairs, so the structure of BF_3 is trigonal planar, with each of the bonds 120° apart.

NF_3 has three bonds and one free electron pair on the central N atom. The four electron pairs are pointed towards the corners of a tetrahedron, 109.5° apart. The added repulsion from the free electron pair causes the N–F bonds to be even closer together, and the angle between them is more like 107°.

(b) Polar solvents are best at dissolving polar solutes. Nonpolar solvents are best at dissolving nonpolar solutes.

I_2 is nonpolar, so it dissolves better in carbon tetrachloride, CCl_4, which is nonpolar, than in water, H_2O, which is polar.

(c) The carbon atoms in diamond are bonded together in a tetrahedral network, with each carbon atom bonded to three other carbon atoms. The tetrahedral structure of the network bonds does not leave any planes along which the diamond can be broken, so a diamond behaves as one big molecule with no weaknesses.

(d) HBr and HCl are polar molecules. In liquid form, both substances are held together by dipole-dipole interactions. These interactions are stronger for molecules with more electrons, so HBr has stronger intermolecular bonds and a higher boiling point.

HF has a higher boiling point than HCl because HF undergoes hydrogen bonding, while HCl does not; this causes HF to remain a liquid at higher temperatures than HCl, even though HF is a polar molecule with fewer electrons than HCl.

STOICHIOMETRY AND CHEMICAL EQUATIONS

How often does this topic appear on the test?

In the multiple-choice section, this topic appears in about 10 out of 75 questions.
In the free-response section, you'll see this topic almost every year.

SOME MATH

SIGNIFICANT FIGURES

When you do calculations on the AP Chemistry test, you'll be expected to present your answers with the proper number of significant figures, so let's review the rules.

- Nonzero digits and zeros between nonzero digits are significant.

245	3 significant figures
7.907	4 significant figures
907.08	5 significant figures

- Zeros to the left of the first nonzero digit in a number are not significant.

0.005	1 significant figure
0.0709	3 significant figures

- Zeros at the end of a number to the right of the decimal point are significant.

12.000	5 significant figures
0.080	2 significant figures
1.0	2 significant figures

- Zeros at the end of a number greater than 1 are not significant, unless their significance is indicated by the presence of a decimal point.

1,200	2 significant figures
1,200.	4 significant figures
10	1 significant figure
10.	2 significant figures

- The coefficients of a balanced equation and numbers obtained by counting objects are infinitely significant. So if a balanced equation calls for 3 moles of carbon, we can think of it as $3.\overline{00}$ moles of carbon.

When multiplying and dividing, the result should have the same number of significant figures as the number in the calculation with the smallest number of significant figures.

$$0.352 \times 0.90876 = 0.320$$
$$864 \times 12 = 1.0 \times 10^4$$
$$7 \div 0.567 = 10$$

When adding and subtracting, the result should have the same number of decimal places as the number in the calculation with the smallest number of decimal places.

$$26 + 45.88 + 0.09534 = 72$$
$$780 + 35 + 4 = 820$$

The whole point is that the result of a calculation cannot be more accurate than the least accurate number in the calculation.

LOGARITHMS

Let's review some basic facts about logarithms.

If $10^x = y$ then $\log y = x$

If $e^x = y$ then $\ln y = x$

$e = 2.7183$

$\ln y = 2.303 \log y$

$$\log(ab) = \log a + \log b$$

$$\log\left(\frac{a}{b}\right) = \log a - \log b$$

MOLES

The mole (Avogadro's number) is the most important number in chemistry, serving as a bridge connecting all the different quantities that you'll come across in chemical calculations. The coefficients in chemical reactions tell you about the reactants and products in terms of moles, so most of the stoichiometry questions you'll see on the test will be exercises in converting between grams, liters, molarities, etc. and moles.

MOLES AND MOLECULES

The definition of Avogadro's number gives you the information you need to convert between moles and individual molecules and atoms:

$$1 \text{ mole} = 6.022 \times 10^{23} \text{ molecules}$$

$$\text{Moles} = \frac{\text{molecules}}{\left(6.022 \times 10^{23}\right)}$$

MOLES AND GRAMS

Moles and grams can be related by using the atomic weights given in the periodic table. Atomic weights on the periodic table are given in terms of atomic mass units (amu), but an amu is the same as a gram per mole, so if 1 carbon atom weighs 12 amu, then 1 mole of carbon atoms weighs 12 grams.

You can use the relationship between amu and g/mol to convert between grams and moles by using the following equation:

$$\text{Moles} = \frac{\text{grams}}{\text{molecular weight}}$$

MOLES AND GASES

We'll talk more about the ideal gas equation in the chapter on gases, but for now, you should know that you can use it to calculate the number of moles of a gas if you know some of the gas's physical properties. All you need to remember at this point is that in the equation, $PV = nRT$, n stands for moles of gas.

$$\text{Moles} = \frac{PV}{RT}$$

P = pressure (atm)
V = volume (L)
T = temperature (K)
R = the gas constant, 0.0821 L-atm/mol-K

The equation above gives the general rule for finding the number of moles of a gas. Many gas problems will take place at STP, or standard temperature and pressure, where $P = 1$ atmosphere and $T = 273$ K. At STP, the situation is much simpler and you can convert directly between the volume of a gas and the number of moles. That's because at STP, one mole of gas always occupies 22.4 liters.

$$\text{Moles} = \frac{\text{liters}}{\left(22.4 \text{ L/mol}\right)}$$

MOLES AND SOLUTIONS

We'll talk more about molarity and molality in the chapter on solutions, but for now you should realize that you can use the equations that define these common measures of concentration to find the number of moles of solute in a solution. You just rearrange the equations to isolate moles of solute.

Moles = (molarity)(liters of solution)

Moles = (molality)(kilograms of solvent)

CHEMICAL EQUATIONS

BALANCING CHEMICAL EQUATIONS

Normally, balancing a chemical equation is a trial and error process. You start with the most complicated looking compound in the equation and work from there. If the equation is an oxidation-reduction reaction, you balance the electrons first. If the equation contains a complicated hydrocarbon, you start with that.

There is, however, an old Princeton Review SAT trick that you might want to try if you see a balancing equation question on the multiple-choice section. The trick is called backsolving.

It works like this. To make a balancing equation question work in a multiple-choice format, they have to make one of the answer choices the correct coefficient for one of the species in the reaction.

So instead of starting blind in the trial and error process, you can insert the answer choices one by one to see which one works. You probably won't have to try all five and if you start in the middle and the number doesn't work, it might be obviously too small or large, eliminating other choices before you have to try them.

Let's try it.

$$...NH_3 + ...O_2 \rightarrow ...N_2 + ...H_2O$$

1. If the equation above were balanced with lowest whole number coefficients, the coefficient for NH_3 would be

   (A) 1
   (B) 2
   (C) 3
   (D) 4
   (E) 5

Start at (C) because it's the middle number.

If there are 3 NH_3s, then there can't be a whole number coefficient for N_2, so (C) is wrong, and so are the other odd number answers, (A) and (E).

Try (D).

If there are 4 NH_3s, then there must be 2 N_2s and 6 H_2Os.

If there are 6 H_2Os, then there must be 3 O_2s, and the equation is balanced with lowest whole number coefficients.

Backsolving is more efficient than the methods that you're used to using because by using the answer choices that they give you, you streamline the trial and error process and allow yourself to use process of elimination as you work the problem.

CHEMICAL EQUATIONS AND CALCULATIONS

Many of the stoichiometry problems on the test will be formatted in the following way.

You will be given a balanced chemical equation and then told that you have some number of grams (or liters of gas, or molar concentration, etc.) of reactant. Then you will be asked what number of grams (or liters of gas, or molar concentration, etc.) of products are generated.

In these cases, follow this simple series of steps.

1. Convert whatever quantity you are given into moles.

2. If you are given information about two reactants, you may have to use the equation coefficients to determine which one is the limiting reagent. Remember, the limiting reagent is not necessarily the reactant that you have the least of, it is the reactant that runs out first.

3. Use the balanced equation to determine how many moles of the desired product are generated.

4. Convert moles of product to the desired unit.

Let's try one:

$$2 \, HBr(aq) + Zn(s) \longrightarrow ZnBr_2(aq) + H_2(g)$$

2. A piece of solid zinc weighing 98 grams was added to a solution containing 324 grams of HBr. What is the volume of H_2 produced at standard temperature and pressure if the reaction above runs to completion?

   (A) 11 liters
   (B) 22 liters
   (C) 34 liters
   (D) 45 liters
   (E) 67 liters

1. Convert whatever quantity you are given into moles.

$$\text{Moles of Zn} = \frac{\text{grams}}{\text{MW}} = \frac{(98 \text{ g})}{(65.4 \text{ g/mol})} = 1.5 \text{ mol}$$

$$\text{Moles of HBr} = \frac{\text{grams}}{\text{MW}} = \frac{(324 \text{ g})}{(80.9 \text{ g/mol})} = 4.0 \text{ mol}$$

2. Use the balanced equation to find the limiting reagent.
   From the balanced equation, 2 moles of HBr are used for every mole of Zn that reacts, so when 1.5 moles of Zn react, 3 moles of HBr are consumed and there will be HBr left over when all of the Zn is gone. That makes Zn the limiting reagent.

3. Use the balanced equation to determine how many moles of the desired product are generated.
   1 mole of H_2 is produced for every mole of Zn consumed, so if 1.5 moles of Zn are consumed, then 1.5 moles of H_2 are produced.

4. Convert moles of product to the desired unit.
The H_2 gas is at STP, so we can convert directly from moles to volume.
Volume of H_2 = (moles)(22.4 L/mol) = (1.5 mol)(22.4 L/mol) = 33.6 L $\cong$ 34 L

So (C) is correct.

Let's try another one using the same reaction.

$$2 \, HBr(aq) + Zn(s) \longrightarrow ZnBr_2(aq) + H_2(g)$$

3. A piece of solid zinc weighing 13.1 grams was placed in a container. A 0.10-molar solution of HBr was slowly added to the container until the zinc was completely dissolved. What was the volume of HBr solution required to completely dissolve the solid zinc?

   (A) 1.0 L
   (B) 2.0 L
   (C) 3.0 L
   (D) 4.0 L
   (E) 5.0 L

1. Convert whatever quantity you are given into moles.

$$\text{Moles of Zn} = \frac{\text{grams}}{\text{MW}} = \frac{(13.1 \text{ g})}{(65.4 \text{ g/mol})} = 0.200 \text{ mol}$$

2. Use the balanced equation to find the limiting reagent, *and*

3. Use the balanced equation to determine how many moles of the desired product are generated.
   In this case, we're using the balanced reaction to find out how much of one reactant is required to consume the other reactant. It's a slight variation on the process described in (2) and (3).
   We can see from the balanced equation that it takes 2 moles of HBr to react completely with 1 mole of Zn, so it will take 0.400 moles of HBr to react completely with 0.200 moles of Zn.

4. Convert moles of product to the desired unit.
   Moles of HBr = (molarity)(volume)

$$\text{Volume of HBr} = \frac{\text{moles}}{\text{molarity}} = \frac{(0.400 \text{mol})}{(0.10 \text{mol/L})} = 4.0 \text{ L}$$

So (D) is correct.

When you perform calculations, always include units. Including units in your calculations will help you, and the person scoring your test, keep track of what you are doing. Including units will also get you partial credit points on the free-response section.

STOICHIOMETRY AND CHEMICAL EQUATION

QUESTIONS

Multiple choice

Questions 1–3

   (A) moles
   (B) liters
   (C) grams
   (D) atmospheres
   (E) volts

1. One mole of solid zinc has a mass of 65.39 of these.

2. These units can be calculated by dividing a quantity by 6.02×10^{23}.

3. Four grams of helium gas occupies 22.4 of these at standard temperature and pressure.

4. What is the mass ratio of fluorine to boron in a boron trifluoride molecule?

   (A) 1.8 to 1
   (B) 3.0 to 1
   (C) 3.5 to 1
   (D) 5.3 to 1
   (E) 6.0 to 1

5. A hydrocarbon sample with a mass of 6 grams underwent combustion, producing 11 grams of carbon dioxide. If all of the carbon initially present in the compound was converted to carbon dioxide, what was the percent of carbon, by mass, in the hydrocarbon sample?

   (A) 25%
   (B) 33%
   (C) 50%
   (D) 66%
   (E) 75%

6. What is the mass of oxygen in 148 grams of calcium hydroxide ($Ca(OH)_2$)?

   (A) 16 grams
   (B) 24 grams
   (C) 32 grams
   (D) 48 grams
   (E) 64 grams

7. An ion containing only oxygen and chlorine is 31% oxygen by mass. What is its empirical formula?

   (A) ClO^-
   (B) ClO_2^-
   (C) ClO_3^-
   (D) ClO_4^-
   (E) Cl_2O^-

8. A sample of propane, C_3H_8, was completely burned in air at STP. The reaction occurred as shown below.

   $$C_3H_8 + O_2 \rightarrow 3\ CO_2 + 4\ H_2O$$

   If 67 liters of CO_2 were produced and all of the carbon in the CO_2 came from the propane, what was the mass of the propane sample?

   (A) 11 grams
   (B) 22 grams
   (C) 33 grams
   (D) 44 grams
   (E) 55 grams

9. What is the percent composition by mass of the elements in the compound $NaNO_3$?

   (A) Na 20%, N 20%, O 60%
   (B) Na 23%, N 14%, O 48%
   (C) Na 23%, N 14%, O 63%
   (D) Na 27%, N 16%, O 57%
   (E) Na 36%, N 28%, O 36%

10. $$CaCO_3(s) \rightarrow CaO(s) + CO_2(g)$$

    A sample of pure $CaCO_3$ was heated and decomposed according to the reaction given above. If 28 grams of CaO were produced by the reaction, what was the initial mass of $CaCO_3$?

    (A) 14 grams
    (B) 25 grams
    (C) 42 grams
    (D) 50 grams
    (E) 84 grams

11. The composition of a typical glass used in bottles is 12.0% Na_2O, 12.0% CaO, and 76.0% SiO_2. Which of the following lists the three compounds in order of greatest to least number of moles present in a typical sample of bottle glass?

    (A) SiO_2, CaO, Na_2O
    (B) SiO_2, Na_2O, CaO
    (C) Na_2O, SiO_2, CaO
    (D) Na_2O, CaO, SiO_2
    (E) CaO, Na_2O, SiO_2

12. The concentration of sodium chloride in sea water is about 0.5 molar. How many grams of NaCl are present in 1 kg of sea water?

    (A) 30 grams
    (B) 60 grams
    (C) 100 grams
    (D) 300 grams
    (E) 600 grams

13. A sample of a hydrate of $CuSO_4$ with a mass of 250 grams was heated until all the water was removed. The sample was then weighed and found to have a mass of 160 grams. What is the formula for the hydrate?

    (A) $CuSO_4 \cdot 10\ H_2O$
    (B) $CuSO_4 \cdot 7\ H_2O$
    (C) $CuSO_4 \cdot 5\ H_2O$
    (D) $CuSO_4 \cdot 2\ H_2O$
    (E) $CuSO_4 \cdot H_2O$

14. A compound containing only sulfur and oxygen is 50% sulfur by weight. What is the empirical formula for the compound?

    (A) SO
    (B) SO_2
    (C) SO_3
    (D) S_2O
    (E) S_3O

15. $2\,Na(s) + 2\,H_2O(l) \rightarrow 2\,NaOH(aq) + H_2(g)$

    Elemental sodium reacts with water to form hydrogen gas as shown above. If a sample of sodium reacts completely to form 20 liters of hydrogen gas, measured at standard temperature and pressure, what was the mass of the sodium?

    (A) 5 grams
    (B) 10 grams
    (C) 20 grams
    (D) 30 grams
    (E) 40 grams

16. $ZnSO_3(s) \rightarrow ZnO(s) + SO_2(g)$

    What is the STP volume of SO_2 gas produced by the above reaction when 150 grams of $ZnSO_3$ are consumed?

    (A) 23 liters
    (B) 36 liters
    (C) 45 liters
    (D) 56 liters
    (E) 90 liters

17. $...CN^- + ...OH^- \rightarrow ...CNO^- + ...H_2O + ...e^-$

    When the half reaction above is balanced, what is the coefficient for OH^- if all the coefficients are reduced to the lowest whole number?

    (A) 1
    (B) 2
    (C) 3
    (D) 4
    (E) 5

18. $...MnO_4^- + ...I^- + ...H_2O \rightarrow$

    $...MnO_2 + ...IO_3^- + ...OH^-$

    The oxidation-reduction reaction above is to be balanced with lowest whole number coefficients. What is the coefficient for OH^-?

    (A) 1
    (B) 2
    (C) 3
    (D) 4
    (E) 5

19. $CaCO_3(s) + 2\,H^+(aq) \rightarrow$

    $Ca^{2+}(aq) + H_2O(l) + CO_2(g)$

    If the reaction above took place at standard temperature and pressure and 150 grams of $CaCO_3(s)$ were consumed, what was the volume of $CO_2(g)$ produced?

    (A) 11 L
    (B) 22 L
    (C) 34 L
    (D) 45 L
    (E) 56 L

20. A gaseous mixture at 25° C contained 1 mole of CH_4 and 2 moles of O_2 and the pressure was measured at 2 atm. The gases then underwent the reaction shown below.

    $CH_4(g) + 2\,O_2(g) \rightarrow CO_2(g) + 2\,H_2O(g)$

    What was the pressure in the container after the reaction had gone to completion and the temperature was allowed to return to 25° C?

    (A) 1 atm
    (B) 2 atm
    (C) 3 atm
    (D) 4 atm
    (E) 5 atm

Problems

1. A 10.0 gram sample containing calcium carbonate and an inert material was placed in excess hydrochloric acid. A reaction occurred producing calcium chloride, water, and carbon dioxide.

    (a) Write the balanced equation for the reaction.

    (b) When the reaction was complete, 900. milliliters of carbon dioxide gas were collected at 740 mmHg and 30° C. How many moles of calcium carbonate were consumed in the reaction?

    (c) If all of the calcium carbonate initially present in the sample was consumed in the reaction, what percent by mass of the sample was due to calcium carbonate?

    (d) If the inert material was silicon dioxide, what was the molar ratio of calcium carbonate to silicon dioxide in the original sample?

2. A gaseous hydrocarbon sample is completely burned in air, producing 1.80 liters of carbon dioxide at standard temperature and pressure and 2.16 grams of water.

    (a) What is the empirical formula for the hydrocarbon?

    (b) What was the mass of the hydrocarbon consumed?

    (c) The hydrocarbon was initially contained in a closed 1.00 liter vessel at a temperature of 32 °C and a pressure of 760 millimeters of mercury. What is the molecular formula of the hydrocarbon?

    (d) Write the balanced equation for the combustion of the hydrocarbon.

3. The table below shows three common forms of copper ore.

ORE #	Empirical formula	Percent by Weight		
		Copper	Sulfur	Iron
1	Cu_2S	?	?	0
2	?	34.6	34.9	30.5
3	?	55.6	28.1	16.3

    (a) What is the percent by weight of copper in Cu_2S?

    (b) What is the empirical formula of ore #2?

    (c) If a sample of ore #3 contains 11.0 grams of iron, how many grams of sulfur does it contain?

    (d) Cu can be extracted from Cu_2S by the following process:

$$3\ Cu_2S + 3\ O_2 \rightarrow 3\ SO_2 + 6\ Cu$$

    If 3.84 grams of O_2 are consumed in the process, how many grams of Cu are produced?

4. $$2\,Mg(s) + 2\,CuSO_4(aq) + H_2O(l) \rightarrow 2\,MgSO_4(aq) + Cu_2O(s) + H_2(g)$$

(a) If 1.46 grams of Mg(s) are added to 500. milliliters of a 0.200-molar solution of $CuSO_4$, what is the maximum molar yield of $H_2(g)$?

(b) When all of the limiting reagent has been consumed in (a), how many moles of the other reactant (not water) remain?

(c) What is the mass of the Cu_2O produced in (a)?

(d) What is the value of $[Mg^{2+}]$ in the solution at the end of the experiment? (Assume that the volume of the solution remains unchanged.)

Answers

Multiple choice

1. **(C)** is correct. The units for atomic weight are grams/mole.

2. **(A)** is correct. A mole is equal to 6.02×10^{23}.

3. **(B)** is correct. Four grams of helium is a mole. A mole of gas occupies 22.4 liters at STP.

4. **(D)** is correct. The empirical formula of boron trifluoride is BF_3.

   Grams = (moles)(MW)

   Grams of boron = (1 mol)(10.8 g/mol) = 10.8 g

   Grams of fluorine = (3 mol)(19.0 g/mol) = 57.0 g

   So, the mass ratio is about 57 to 11, which is about 5.3 to 1.

5. **(C)** is correct.

   $$Moles = \frac{grams}{MW}$$

   $$Moles\ of\ CO_2 = \frac{(11g)}{(44g/mol)} = 1/4\ mol$$

   If $\frac{1}{4}$ mole of CO_2 was produced, then $\frac{1}{4}$ mole of C was consumed.
   Grams = (moles)(MW)

   Grams of carbon = $(\frac{1}{4}$ mol$)(12$ g/mol$) = 3$ g

   So, the percent by mass of carbon was $\frac{3}{6} = \frac{1}{2} = 50\%$

6. **(E)** is correct.

   $$Moles = \frac{grams}{MW}$$

   $$Moles\ of\ calcium\ hydroxide = \frac{(148\ g)}{(74\ g/mol)} = 2\ moles$$

   Every mole of $Ca(OH)_2$ contains 2 moles of oxygen.

7. **(A)** is correct. Assume that we have 100 grams of the compound. That means that we have 31 grams of oxygen and 69 grams of chlorine.

$$\text{Moles} = \frac{\text{grams}}{\text{MW}}$$

$$\text{Moles of oxygen} = \frac{(31g)}{(16g/mol)} = \text{slightly less than 2 mol}$$

$$\text{Moles of chlorine} = \frac{(69g)}{(35.5g/mol)} = \text{slightly less than 2 mol}$$

So the ratio of chlorine to oxygen is 1 to 1 and the empirical formula is ClO^-.

so there are (2)(2) = 4 moles of oxygen
Grams = (moles)(MW)
So, grams of oxygen = (4 mol)(16 g/mol) = 64 grams

8. **(B)** is correct.

$$\text{Moles} = \frac{\text{liters}}{(22.4L/mol)}$$

$$\text{Moles of } CO_2 = \frac{67L}{(22.4L/mol)} = 3 \text{ mol}$$

According to the balanced equation, if 3 moles of CO_2 were produced, 1 mole of C_3H_8 was consumed.
Grams = (moles)(MW)
so, grams of C_3H_8 = (1 mol)(44 g/mol) = 44 grams

9. **(D)** is correct. The molecular weight of $NaNO_3$ is: (23) + (14) + (3)(16) = 85 g/mol
We can get the answer using pretty rough estimates.

$$\text{The percent by mass of Na} = \frac{(23)}{(85)} = \text{between 25\% } (\frac{1}{4}) \text{ and 33\% } (\frac{1}{3})$$

$$\text{The percent by mass of N} = \frac{(14)}{(85)} = \text{between 10\% } (\frac{1}{10}) \text{ and 20\% } (\frac{1}{5})$$

$$\text{The percent by mass of O} = \frac{(48)}{(85)} = \text{between 50\% } (\frac{1}{2}) \text{ and 60\% } (\frac{3}{5})$$

You can use process of elimination to get choice (D).

10. **(D)** is correct.

$$\text{Moles} = \frac{\text{grams}}{\text{MW}}$$

$$\text{Moles of CaO} = \frac{(28g)}{(56g/mol)} = 0.50 \text{ mol}$$

From the balanced equation, if 0.50 mol of CaO was produced, then 0.50 mol of $CaCO_3$ was consumed.
Grams = (moles)(MW)
Grams of $CaCO_3$ = (0.50 mol)(100 g/mol) = 50 g

11. **(A)** is correct. The molecular weights of the three compounds are:

$Na_2O - 62$ g/mol

$CaO - 56$ g/mol

$SiO_2 - 60$ g/mol

Since the molecular weights are close together, we can safely say that SiO_2, which makes up a much greater percentage by mass of bottle glass than the other two, will have far and away the most moles in a sample. So the answer must be (A) or (B).

Remember, (grams) = (moles)(MW). Since a sample of bottle glass will have the same number of grams of Na_2O and CaO, the one with the smaller molecular weight must have the greater number of moles. So there must be more moles of CaO than Na_2O.

12. **(A)** is correct. First, you have to remember that 1 liter of water has a mass of 1 kg.
Moles = (molarity)(liters)
Moles of NaCl = (0.5 M)(1 L) = 0.5 moles
Grams = (moles)(MW)
Grams of NaCl = (0.5 mol)(59 g/mol) = 30 g.

13. **(C)** is correct. The molecular weight of $CuSO_4$ is 160 g/mol, so we have only 1 mole of the hydrate. The lost mass was due to water, so 1 mole of the hydrate must have contained 90 grams of H_2O.

$$\text{Moles} = \frac{\text{grams}}{\text{MW}}$$

$$\text{Moles of water} = \frac{(90\text{ g})}{(18\text{ g/mol})} = 5 \text{ moles}$$

So, if 1 mole of hydrate contains 5 moles of H_2O, then the formula for the hydrate must be $CuSO_4 \bullet 5\ H_2O$.

14. **(B)** is correct. You might be able to do this one in your head just from knowing that sulfur's molecular weight is twice as big as oxygen's. If not, let's say you have 100 grams of the compound. So you have 50 grams of sulfur and 50 grams of oxygen.

$$\text{Moles} = \frac{\text{grams}}{\text{MW}}$$

$$\text{Moles of sulfur} = \frac{(50\text{ g})}{(32\text{ g/mol})} = \text{a little more than 1.5}$$

$$\text{Moles of oxygen} = \frac{(50\text{ g})}{(16\text{ g/mol})} = \text{a little more than 3}$$

The molar ratio of O to S is 2 to 1, so the empirical formula must be SO_2.

15. **(E)** is correct.

$$\text{Moles} = \frac{\text{liters}}{(22.4\text{L/mol})}$$

$$\text{Moles of } H_2 = \frac{(20\text{ L})}{(22.4\text{L/mol})} = \text{about 0.9 moles}$$

From the balanced equation, for every mole of H_2 produced, 2 moles of Na are consumed, so 1.8 moles of Na are consumed.

Grams = (moles)(MW)
Grams of Na = (1.8 mol)(23 g/mol) = about 40 grams
You don't really have to do the math here, you can get the answer by using rough estimates.

16. **(A)** is correct.

$$\text{Moles} = \frac{\text{grams}}{\text{MW}}$$

$$\text{Moles of } ZnSO_3 = \frac{(150\text{ g})}{(145\text{ g/mol})} = \text{about 1 mole}$$

From the balanced equation, when one mole of $ZnSO_3$ is consumed, one mole of SO_2 will be produced. So about 1 mole of SO_2 is produced.

Liters = (moles)(22.4 L/mol)
Liters of SO_2 = (about 1 mol)(22.4 L) = 23 liters

17. **(B)** is correct. Backsolve.
Start with (C). If there are 3 OH^-, there can't be a whole number coefficient for H_2O, so (C) is wrong. You should also be able to see that the answer can't be an odd number, so (A) and (E) are also wrong.
Try (D). If there are 4 OH^-, then there are 2 H_2O.
That leaves 2 more Os on the product side, so there must be 2 CNO^-.
If there are 2 CNO^- then there are 2 CN^-.
These are all whole numbers, but they are not the lowest whole numbers, so (D) is wrong.
If we divide all the coefficients by 2, we get the lowest whole number coefficients. That leaves us with 2 OH^-, which is choice (B).
By the way, N^{5-} (in CN^-) is oxidized to N^{3-} (in CNO^-), so there are 2 e^-.

18. **(B)** is correct. Backsolve.
Start at (C).

If there are 3 OH^-, there can't be a whole number coefficient for H_2O, so (C) is wrong. Also, the answer can't be an odd number, so (A) and (E) are wrong.

Notice that you don't have to test both of the remaining answers; if the one you pick works, you're done, if the one you pick doesn't work, then the one that's left must be correct. With a choice of only two answers, pick the one that looks easier to work with.

Try (B) because it's smaller. If there are 2 OH^-, then there is 1 H_2O. If you put in 1 for all the other coefficients, the equation is balanced. So (B) is correct.

19. **(C)** is correct.

$$\text{Moles} = \frac{\text{grams}}{\text{MW}}$$

$$\text{Moles of } CaCO_3 = \frac{(150\text{ g})}{(100\text{ g/mol})} = 1.5\text{ moles}$$

From the balanced equation, for every mole of $CaCO_3$ consumed, one mole of CO_2 is produced. So 1.5 moles of CO_2 are produced.
At STP, volume of gas = (moles)(22.4 L)
So, volume of CO_2 = (1.5)(22.4) = 34 L

20. **(B)** is correct. All of the reactants are consumed in the reaction and the temperature doesn't change, so the pressure will only change if the number of moles of gas changes over the course of the reaction. The number of moles of gas (3 moles) doesn't change in the balanced equation, so the pressure will remain the same (2 atm) at the end of the reaction as at the beginning.

Problems

1. (a) $CaCO_3 + 2\ HCl \rightarrow CaCl_2 + H_2O + CO_2$

   (b) Use the ideal gas equation to find the number of moles of CO_2 produced. Remember to convert to the proper units.

   $$n = \frac{PV}{RT} = \frac{\left(\frac{740}{760}\ atm\right)(0.900\ L)}{(0.0821\ )(303\ K)} = 0.035\ moles$$

   From the balanced equation, for every mole of CO_2 produced, 1 mole of $CaCO_3$ was consumed. So 0.035 moles of $CaCO_3$ were consumed.

   (c) We know the number of moles of $CaCO_3$, so we can find the mass.

   Grams = (moles)(MW)
   Grams of $CaCO_3$ = (0.035 mol)(100 g/mol) = 3.50 grams

   $$Percent\ by\ mass = \frac{mass\ of\ CaCO_3}{mass\ of\ sample} \times 100 = \frac{(3.50\ g)}{(10.0\ g)} \times 100 = 35\%$$

   (d) Mass of SiO_2 = 10.0 g – 3.5 g = 6.5 g

   $$Moles = \frac{grams}{MW}$$

   $$Moles\ of\ SiO_2 = \frac{(6.5\ g)}{(60\ g/mol)} = 0.11\ mol$$

   $$Molar\ ratio = \frac{mass\ of\ CaCO_3}{mass\ of\ sample} = \frac{(0.035)}{(0.11)} = 0.32$$

2. (a) All of the hydrogen in the water and all of the carbon in the carbon dioxide must have come from the hydrocarbon.

   $$Moles = \frac{grams}{MW}$$

   $$Moles\ of\ H_2O = \frac{(2.16\ g)}{(18.0\ g/mol)} = 0.120\ moles$$

   Every mole of water contains 2 moles of hydrogen, so there are 0.240 moles of hydrogen.

   $$Moles = \frac{(1.80\ L)}{(22.4L/mol)}$$

   $$Moles\ of\ CO_2 = \frac{(1.80\ L)}{(22.4L/mol)} = 0.080\ moles$$

   Every mole of CO_2 contains 1 mole of carbon, so there are 0.080 moles of carbon.

   There are three times as many moles of hydrogen as there are moles of carbon, so the empirical formula of the hydrocarbon is CH_3.

   (b) In (a), we found the number of moles of hydrogen and carbon consumed, so we can find the mass of the hydrocarbon.

   Grams = (moles)(MW)
   Grams of H = (0.240 mol)(1.01 g/mol) = 0.242 g
   Grams of C = (0.080 mol)(12.01 g/mol) = 0.961 g
   Grams of hydrocarbon = (0.242) + (0.961) = 1.203 g

(c) First let's find the number of moles of hydrocarbon from the ideal gas law. Don't forget to convert to the appropriate units (760 mmHg = 1 atm, 32 °C = 305 K).

$$n = \frac{PV}{RT} = \frac{(1.00\ \text{atm})(1.00\ \text{L})}{(0.0821\ )(305\ \text{K})} = 0.040\ \text{moles}$$

Now we can use the mass we found in (b) to find the molecular weight of the hydrocarbon.

$$MW = \frac{\text{grams}}{\text{moles}} = \frac{(1.203\text{g})}{(0.040\text{mol})} = 30.1\ \text{g/mole}$$

CH_3 would have a molecular weight of 15, so we can just double the empirical formula to get the molecular formula, which is C_2H_6.

(d) $2\ C_2H_6 + 7\ O_2 \rightarrow 4\ CO_2 + 6\ H_2O$

3. (a) First find the molecular weight of Cu_2S.

MW of Cu_2S = (2)(63.6) + (1)(32.1) = 159.3% by mass of Cu = $\dfrac{\text{mass of Cu}}{\text{mass of Cu}_2\text{S}} \times 100$

$= \dfrac{(2)(63.6)}{(159.3)} \times 100 = 79.8\%$

(b) Assume that we have 100 grams of ore #2. So we have 34.6 g of Cu, 30.5 g of Fe, and 34.9 g of S. To get the empirical formula, we need to find the number of moles of each element.

$\text{Moles} = \dfrac{\text{grams}}{\text{MW}}$

$\text{Moles of Cu} = \dfrac{(34.6\ \text{g})}{(63.6\ \text{g/mol})} = 0.544\ \text{moles of Cu}$

$\text{Moles of Fe} = \dfrac{(30.5\ \text{g})}{(55.9\ \text{g/mol})} = 0.546\ \text{moles of Fe}$

$\text{Moles of S} = \dfrac{(34.9\ \text{g})}{(32.1\ \text{g/mol})} = 1.09\ \text{moles of S}$

So the molar ratio of Cu:Fe:S is 1:1:2 and the empirical formula for ore #2 is $CuFeS_2$.

(c) You can use the ratio of the percents by weight.

$\text{Mass of S} = \dfrac{\%\ \text{by mass of S}}{\%\ \text{by mass of Fe}} \times (\text{mass of Fe}) = \dfrac{(28.1\,\%)}{(16.3\,\%)}\ (11.0\ \text{g}) = 19.0\ \text{g}$

(d) First find the moles of O_2 consumed.

$\text{Moles} = \dfrac{\text{grams}}{\text{MW}}$

$\text{Moles of O}_2 = \dfrac{(3.84\ \text{g})}{(32.0\ \text{g/mol})} = 0.120\ \text{moles}$

From the balanced equation, for every 3 moles of O_2 consumed, 6 moles of Cu are produced, so the number of moles of Cu produced will be twice the number of moles of O_2 consumed. So 0.240 moles of Cu are produced.

Grams = (moles)(MW)

Grams of Cu = (0.240 mol)(63.6 g/mol) = 15.3 grams

4. (a) We need to find the limiting reagent. There's plenty of water, so it must be one of the other two reactants.

$$Moles = \frac{grams}{MW}$$

$$Moles\ of\ Mg = \frac{(1.46\ g)}{(24.3\ g/mol)} = 0.060\ moles$$

$$Moles = (molarity)(volume)$$

Moles of $CuSO_4$ = (0.200 M)(0.500 L) = 0.100 moles

From the balanced equation, Mg and $CuSO_4$ are consumed in a 1:1 ratio, so we'll run out of Mg first. Mg is the limiting reagent and we'll use it to find the yield of H_2.

From the balanced equation, 1 mole of H_2 is produced for every 2 moles of Mg consumed, so the number of moles of H_2 produced will be half the number of moles of Mg consumed.

$$Moles\ of\ H_2 = \frac{1}{2}(0.060\ mol) = 0.030\ moles$$

(b) Mg is the limiting reagent, so some $CuSO_4$ will remain. From the balanced equation, Mg and $CuSO_4$ are consumed in a 1:1 ratio, so when 0.060 moles of Mg are consumed, 0.060 moles of $CuSO_4$ are also consumed.

Moles of $CuSO_4$ remaining = (0.100 mol) − (0.060 mol) = 0.040 moles

(c) From the balanced equation, 1 mole of Cu_2O is produced for every 2 moles of Mg consumed, so the number of moles of Cu_2O produced will be half the number of moles of Mg consumed.

$$Moles\ of\ Cu_2O = \frac{1}{2}(0.060\ mol) = 0.030\ moles$$

$$Grams = (moles)(MW)$$

Grams of Cu_2O = (0.030 mol)(143 g/mol) = 4.29 grams

(d) All of the Mg consumed ends up as Mg^{2+} ions in the solution.

$$Molarity = \frac{moles}{liters}$$

$$[Mg^{2+}] = \frac{(0.060\ mol)}{(0.500\ L)} = 0.120\ M$$

GASES

How often does this topic appear on the test?
In the multiple-choice section, this topic appears in about 5 out of 75 questions.
In the free-response section, you'll see this topic almost every year.

STP

You should be familiar with standard temperature and pressure (STP), which comes up fairly often
in problems involving gases.

       At STP: Pressure = 1 atmosphere = 760 millimeters of mercury (mmHg)
                    Temperature = 0 °C = 273 K

       At STP, 1 mole of gas occupies 22.4 liters

KINETIC MOLECULAR THEORY

Most of the gas problems you see on the test will assume that gases behave in what is called an ideal manner. For ideal gases, these assumptions can be made:

- The kinetic energy of an ideal gas is directly proportional to its absolute temperature: The greater the temperature, the greater the average kinetic energy of the gas molecules.

The Total Kinetic Energy of a Gas Sample

$$KE = \frac{3}{2}nRT$$

R = the gas constant; 8.31 joules/mol-K
T = absolute temperature (K)
n = number of moles (mol)

The Average Kinetic Energy of a Single Gas Molecule

$$KE = \frac{1}{2}mv^2$$

m = mass of the molecule (kg)
v = speed of the molecule (meters/sec)
KE is measured in joules

If several different gases are present in a sample at a given temperature, all the gases will have the same average kinetic energy. That is, the average kinetic energy of a gas depends only on the absolute temperature, not on the identity of the gas.

- The volume of an ideal gas particle is insignificant when compared with the volume in which the gas is contained.

- There are no forces of attraction between the gas molecules in an ideal gas.

- The time during which a collision between ideal gas molecules takes place is insignificant compared to the time between collisions.

THE IDEAL GAS EQUATION

You can use the ideal gas equation to calculate any of the four variables relating to the gas, provided that you already know the other three.

The Ideal Gas Equation

$$PV = nRT$$

P = the pressure of the gas (atm)
V = the volume of the gas (L)
n = the number of moles of gas
T = the absolute temperature of the gas (K)
R = the gas constant, 0.0821 L-atm/mol-K

You can also manipulate the ideal gas equation to figure out how changes in each of its variables affect the other variables.

$$\frac{P_1 V_1}{T_1} = \frac{P_2 V_2}{T_2}$$

P = the pressure of the gas (atm)

V = the volume of the gas (L)

T = the absolute temperature of the gas (K)

You should be comfortable with the following simple relationships:

- If the volume is constant: As pressure increases, temperature increases; and as temperature increases, pressure increases.

- If the temperature is constant: As pressure increases, volume decreases; and as volume increases, pressure decreases. That's Boyle's law.

- If the pressure is constant: As temperature increases, volume increases; and as volume increases, temperature increases. That's Charles's law.

DALTON'S LAW

Dalton's law tells us that the total pressure of a mixture of gases is just the sum of all the partial pressures of the individual gases in the mixture.

Dalton's Law

$$P_{total} = P_a + P_b + P_c + ...$$

You should also note that the partial pressure of a gas is directly proportional to the number of moles of that gas present in the mixture. So if 25 percent of the gas in a mixture is helium, then the partial pressure due to helium will be 25 percent of the total pressure.

Partial Pressure

$$P_a = (P_{total})(X_a)$$

$$X_a = \frac{\text{moles of gas A}}{\text{total moles of gas}}$$

GRAHAM'S LAW

Part of the first assumption of kinetic molecular theory was that all gases at the same temperature have the same average kinetic energy. Knowing this, we can find the average speed of a gas molecule at a given temperature.

$$u_{rms} = \sqrt{\frac{3kT}{m}} = \sqrt{\frac{3RT}{M}}$$

u_{rms} = average speed of a gas molecule (meters/sec)
T = absolute temperature (K)
m = mass of the gas molecule (kg)
M = molecular weight of the gas (kg/mol)
k = Boltzmann's constant, 1.38×10^{-23} joule/K
R = the gas constant, 8.31 joules/mol-K

By the way, you might have noticed that Boltzmann's constant, k, and the gas constant, R, differ only by a factor of Avogadro's number, N_A, the number of molecules in a mole. That is, $R = kN_A$.

Knowing that the average kinetic energy of a gas molecule is dependent only on the temperature, we can compare the average speeds (and the rates of effusion) of two different gases in a sample. The equation used to do this is called Graham's law.

Graham's Law

$$\frac{r_1}{r_2} = \sqrt{\frac{M_2}{M_1}}$$

r = rate of effusion of a gas, or average speed of the molecules of a gas
M = molecular weight

You should note that Graham's law tells us that at a given temperature, lighter molecules move faster than heavier molecules.

VAN DER WAALS EQUATION

At low temperature and/or high pressure, gases behave in a less than ideal manner. That's because under conditions where gas molecules are packed too tightly together, the assumptions made in kinetic molecular theory become invalid.

Two things happen when gas molecules are packed too tightly:

- *The volume of the gas molecules becomes significant.*
  The ideal gas equation does not take the volume of gas molecules into account, so the actual volume of a gas under non-ideal conditions will be larger than the volume predicted by the ideal gas equation.

- *Gas molecules attract each other and stick together.*
  The ideal gas equation assumes that gas molecules never stick together. When a gas is packed tightly together, van der Waals forces (dipole-dipole attractions and London dispersion forces) become significant, causing some gas molecules to stick together. When gas molecules stick together, there are fewer particles bouncing around and creating pressure, so the real pressure in a non-ideal situation will be smaller than the pressure predicted by the ideal gas equation.

The van der Waals equation is an adjustment to the Ideal Gas equation which takes non-ideal conditions into account.

Van der Waals Equation

$$(P + \frac{n^2a}{V^2})(V - nb) = nRT$$

P = the pressure of the gas (atm)

V = the volume of the gas (L)

n = the number of moles of gas (mol)

T = the absolute temperature of the gas (K)

R = the gas constant, 0.0821 L-atm/mol-K

a = a constant, different for each gas, that takes into account the attractive forces between molecules

b = a constant, different for each gas, that takes into account the volume of each molecule

DENSITY

You might be asked about the density of a gas. The density of a gas is measured in the same way as the density of a liquid or solid; in mass per unit volume.

Density of a Gas

$$D = \frac{m}{V}$$

D = density

m = mass of gas, usually grams

V = volume occupied by a gas, usually liters

GASES AND KINETIC THEORY

QUESTIONS

Multiple choice

Questions 1–5

(A) H_2
(B) He
(C) O_2
(D) N_2
(E) CO_2

1. This is the most plentiful gas in the Earth's atmosphere.

2. A 1 mole sample of this gas occupying 1 liter will have the greatest density.

3. At a given temperature, this gas will have the greatest rate of effusion.

4. The molecules of this gas contain polar bonds.

5. The molecules of this gas contain triple bonds.

6. The temperature of a sample of an ideal gas confined in a 2.0 L container was raised from 27 °C to 77 °C. If the initial pressure of the gas was 1200 mm Hg, what was the final pressure of the gas?

(A) 300 mm Hg
(B) 600 mm Hg
(C) 1400 mm Hg
(D) 2400 mm Hg
(E) 3600 mm Hg

7. A sealed container contains 0.20 moles of oxygen gas and 0.10 moles of hydrogen gas. If the temperature is 25 °C throughout the container, which of the following is true?

(A) The partial pressures of the two gases are the same.
(B) The average kinetic energy of the two gases are the same.
(C) The molecular masses of the two gases are the same.
(D) The total masses of the two gases are the same.
(E) The average molecular speeds of the two gases are the same.

8. A gas sample contains 0.1 moles of oxygen and 0.4 moles of nitrogen. If the sample is at standard temperature and pressure, what is the partial pressure due to nitrogen?

(A) 0.1 atm
(B) 0.2 atm
(C) 0.5 atm
(D) 0.8 atm
(E) 1.0 atm

9. A mixture of gases contains 1.5 moles of oxygen, 3.0 moles of nitrogen, and 0.5 moles of water vapor. If the total pressure is 700 mmHg, what is the partial pressure of the nitrogen gas?

   (A) 70 mmHg
   (B) 210 mmHg
   (C) 280 mmHg
   (D) 350 mmHg
   (E) 420 mmHg

10. A mixture of helium and neon gases has a total pressure of 1.2 atm. If the mixture contains twice as many moles of helium as neon, what is the partial pressure due to neon?

   (A) 0.2 atm
   (B) 0.3 atm
   (C) 0.4 atm
   (D) 0.8 atm
   (E) 0.9 atm

11. Nitrogen gas was collected over water at 25 °C. If the vapor pressure of water at 25 °C is 23 mmHg and the total pressure in the container is measured at 781 mmHg, what is the partial pressure of the nitrogen gas?

   (A) 23 mmHg
   (B) 46 mmHg
   (C) 551 mmHg
   (D) 735 mmHg
   (E) 758 mmHg

12. When 4.0 moles of oxygen are confined in a 24-liter vessel at 176 °C the pressure is 6.0 atm. If the oxygen is allowed to expand isothermally until it occupies 36 liters, what will be the new pressure?

   (A) 2 atm
   (B) 3 atm
   (C) 4 atm
   (D) 8 atm
   (E) 9 atm

13. A gas sample is confined in a 5-liter container. Which of the following will occur if the temperature of the container is increased?

   I. The kinetic energy of the gas will increase.
   II. The pressure of the gas will increase.
   III. The density of the gas will increase.

   (A) I only
   (B) II only
   (C) I and II only
   (D) I and III only
   (E) I, II, and III

14. A 22.0 gram sample of an unknown gas occupies 11.2 liters at standard temperature and pressure. Which of the following could be the identity of the gas?

   (A) CO_2
   (B) SO_3
   (C) O_2
   (D) N_2
   (E) He

15. A gaseous mixture at a constant temperature contains O_2, CO_2, and He. Which of the following lists the three gases in order of increasing average molecular speed?

   (A) O_2, CO_2, He
   (B) O_2, He, CO_2
   (C) He, CO_2, O_2
   (D) He, O_2, CO_2
   (E) CO_2, O_2, He

16. Which of the following conditions would be most likely to cause the ideal gas laws to fail?

   I. High pressure
   II. High temperature
   III. Large volume

   (A) I only
   (B) II only
   (C) I and II only
   (D) I and III only
   (E) II and III only

17. Which of the following expressions is equal to the density of helium gas at standard temperature and pressure?

(A) $\dfrac{1}{22.4}$ g/L

(B) $\dfrac{2}{22.4}$ g/L

(C) $\dfrac{1}{4}$ g/L

(D) $\dfrac{4}{22.4}$ g/L

(E) $\dfrac{4}{4}$ g/L

18. An ideal gas is contained in a 5.0 liter chamber at a temperature of 37 °C. If the gas exerts a pressure of 2.0 atm on the walls of the chamber, which of the following expressions is equal to the number of moles of the gas? The gas constant, R, is 0.08 (L-atm)/(mol-K).

(A) $\dfrac{(2.0)(5.0)}{(0.08)(37)}$ moles

(B) $\dfrac{(2.0)(0.08)}{(5.0)(37)}$ moles

(C) $\dfrac{(2.0)(0.08)}{(5.0)(310)}$ moles

(D) $\dfrac{(2.0)(310)}{(0.08)(5.0)}$ moles

(E) $\dfrac{(2.0)(5.0)}{(0.08)(310)}$ moles

19. Which of the following gases would be expected to have a rate of effusion that is three times as large as that of H_2?

(A) O_2
(B) N_2
(C) He
(D) H_2O
(E) CO_2

20. A gaseous mixture of oxygen and nitrogen is maintained at a constant temperature. Which of the following MUST be true regarding the two gases?

(A) Their average kinetic energies will be the same.
(B) Their average molecular speeds will be the same.
(C) Their partial pressures will be the same.
(D) Their total masses will be the same.
(E) Their densities will be the same.

21. Nitrogen gas was collected over water at a temperature of 40 °C and the pressure of the sample was measured at 796 mmHg. If the vapor pressure of water at 40 °C is 55 mmHg, what is the partial pressure of the nitrogen gas?

(A) 55 mmHg
(B) 741 mmHg
(C) 756 mmHg
(D) 796 mmHg
(E) 851 mmHg

22. A balloon occupies a volume of 1.0 liter when it contains 0.16 grams of helium at 37° C and 1 atm pressure. If helium is added to the balloon until it contains 0.80 grams while pressure and temperature are kept constant, what will be the new volume of the balloon?

(A) 0.50 liters
(B) 1.0 liters
(C) 2.0 liters
(D) 4.0 liters
(E) 5.0 liters

23. An ideal gas fills a balloon at a temperature of 27 °C and 1 atm pressure. By what factor will the volume of the balloon change if the gas in the balloon is heated to 127 °C?

(A) $\dfrac{27}{127}$

(B) $\dfrac{3}{4}$

(C) $\dfrac{4}{3}$

(D) $\dfrac{2}{1}$

(E) $\dfrac{127}{27}$

24. A gas sample with a mass of 10 grams occupies 6.0 liters and exerts a pressure of 2.0 atm at a temperature of 26 °C. Which of the following expressions is equal to the molecular mass of the gas? The gas constant, R, is 0.08 (L-atm)/(mol-K).

(A) $\dfrac{(10)(0.08)(299)}{(2.0)(6.0)}$ g/mol

(B) $\dfrac{(299)(0.08)}{(10)(2.0)(6.0)}$ g/mol

(C) $\dfrac{(2.0)(6.0)(299)}{(10)(0.08)}$ g/mol

(D) $\dfrac{(10)(2.0)(6.0)}{(299)(0.08)}$ g/mol

(E) $\dfrac{(2.0)(6.0)}{(10)(299)(0.08)}$ g/mol

25. Which of the following assumptions is (are) valid based on kinetic molecular theory?

I. Gas molecules have negligible volume.
II. Gas molecules exert no attractive forces on each other.
III. The temperature of a gas is directly proportional to its kinetic energy.

(A) I only
(B) III only
(C) I and III only
(D) II and III only
(E) I, II, and III

Problems

1.

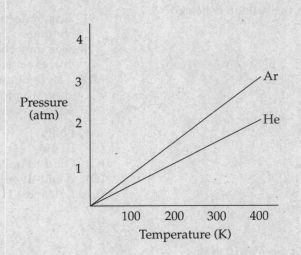

The graph above shows the changes in pressure with changing temperature of gas samples of helium and argon confined in a closed 2-liter vessel.

(a) What is the total pressure of the two gases in the container at a temperature of 200 K?

(b) How many moles of helium are contained in the vessel?

(c) How many molecules of helium are contained in the vessel?

(d) What is the ratio of the average speeds of the helium atoms to the average speeds of the argon atoms?

(e) If the volume of the container were reduced to 1 liter at a constant temperature of 300 K, what would be the new pressure of the helium gas?

2.
$$2 \ KClO_3(s) \rightarrow 2 \ KCl(s) + 3 \ O_2(g)$$

The reaction above took place and 1.45 liters of oxygen gas were collected over water at a temperature of 29 °C and a pressure of 755 millimeters of mercury. The vapor pressure of water at 29 °C is 30.0 millimeters of mercury.

(a) What is the partial pressure of the oxygen gas collected?

(b) How many moles of oxygen gas were collected?

(c) What would be the dry volume of the oxygen gas at a pressure of 760 millimeters of mercury and a temperature of 273 K?

(d) What was the mass of the $KClO_3$ consumed in the reaction?

Essays

3. Equal molar quantities of two gases, O_2 and H_2O, are confined in a closed vessel at constant temperature.

  (a) Which gas, if any, has the greater partial pressure?

  (b) Which gas, if any, has the greater density?

  (c) Which gas, if any, has the greater concentration?

  (d) Which gas, if any, has the greater average kinetic energy?

  (e) Which gas, if any, will show the greater deviation from ideal behavior?

  (f) Which gas, if any, has the greater average molecular speed?

4. Use your knowledge of chemical principles and kinetic-molecular theory to explain the following statements.

  (a) A gasoline engine stops working effectively at very high altitudes.

  (b) A glass of water left out in air can completely vaporize, even though the temperature never comes close to the boiling point of water.

  (c) The volume of a gas-filled balloon placed underwater at a constant temperature will decrease as its depth below the surface of the water is increased.

  (d) As the temperature of a gas is decreased, the measured pressure of the gas becomes less than the pressure predicted by the ideal gas law.

ANSWERS

Multiple choice

1. **(D)** is correct. Nitrogen gas makes up about 78% of the gas in the Earth's atmosphere.

2. **(E)** is correct. Density is a measure of grams per liter. CO_2 has the greatest molecular mass (44), so 1 mole of CO_2 will have the most mass in 1 liter, and therefore the greatest density.

3. **(A)** is correct. According to Graham's law, the lighter the gas, the greater the rate of effusion. H_2 is the lightest gas (MW = 2), so it will have the greatest rate of effusion.

4. **(E)** is correct. CO_2 is the only gas listed that has bonds between atoms of differing electronegativity. The carbon-oxygen bonds in CO_2 are polar, even though the linear geometry of the molecule makes the molecule nonpolar overall.

5. **(D)** is correct. N_2 is the only gas listed whose atoms are held together in a triple bond.

6. **(C)** is correct. Remember to convert Celcius to Kelvin. (°C + 273 = K)

27 °C = 300 K and 77 °C = 350 K.

From the relationship $\frac{P_1}{T_1} = \frac{P_2}{T_2}$ we get

$$\frac{(1200 \text{ mm Hg})}{(300 \text{ K})} = \frac{P_2}{(350 \text{ K})}$$

So P_2 = 1400 mm Hg

7. **(B)** is correct. According to the kinetic molecular theory, average kinetic energy is directly proportional to absolute temperature.

This relationship is given in the equation, $KE_{average} = \frac{3}{2}kT$, where k is Boltzmann's constant. Here's why the other choices are wrong:

(A) There are twice as many moles of oxygen as there are of hydrogen, so the partial pressure due to oxygen will be twice as large. That's from Dalton's law.

(C) The molecular mass of oxygen gas is 32 grams/mole and the molecular mass of hydrogen gas is 2 grams/mole.

(D) The total mass of oxygen gas is (0.20 moles)(32 grams/mole) = 6.4 grams. The total mass of hydrogen gas is (0.10 moles)(2 grams/mole) = 0.2 grams.

(E) From Graham's law, if the kinetic energies of the two gases are the same, then the molecules of the less massive gas must be moving faster, on average.

8. **(D)** is correct. If the gases are at STP, then the total pressure must be 1.0 atmosphere.

If $\frac{4}{5}$ of the gas in the sample is nitrogen, then from Dalton's law, $\frac{4}{5}$ of the pressure must be due to the nitrogen.

So the partial pressure due to nitrogen is $\frac{4}{5}$ (1.0 atm) = 0.8 atm.

9. **(E)** is correct. From Dalton's law, the partial pressure of a gas depends on the number of moles of the gas that are present.

The total number of moles of gas present is:

1.5 + 3.0 + 0.5 = 5.0 total moles.

If there are 3 moles of nitrogen, then $\frac{3}{5}$ of the pressure must be due to nitrogen.
$(\frac{3}{5})(700 \text{ mmHg}) = 420 \text{ mmHg}$

10. **(C)** is correct. From Dalton's law, the partial pressure of a gas depends on the number of moles of the gas that are present. If the mixture has twice as many moles of helium as neon, then the mixture must be $\frac{1}{3}$ neon. So $\frac{1}{3}$ of the pressure must be due to neon.
$(\frac{1}{3})(1.2 \text{ atm}) = 0.4 \text{ atm}.$

11. **(E)** is correct. From Dalton's law, the partial pressures of nitrogen and water vapor must add up to the total pressure in the container. The partial pressure of water vapor in a closed container will be equal to the vapor pressure of water, so the partial pressure of nitrogen is:

781 mmHg – 23 mmHg = 758 mmHg.

12. **(C) is correct.** From the gas laws, we know that with constant temperature:

$$P_1V_1 = P_2V_2$$

Solving for P_2, we get:

$$P_2 = \frac{P_1V_1}{V_2} = \frac{(6.0 \text{ atm})(24 \text{ L})}{(36 \text{ L})} = 4.0 \text{ atm}$$

13. **(C) is correct.** From kinetic molecular theory, we know that kinetic energy is directly proportional to temperature (think of the expression: $KE = \frac{3}{2}kT$), so (I) is true.

From the gas laws, we know that at constant volume, an increase in temperature will bring about an increase in pressure (think of $\frac{P_1}{T_1} = \frac{P_2}{T_2}$), so (II) is true.

The density of a gas is equal to mass per unit volume, which is not changed by changing temperature, so (III) is not true.

14. **(A) is correct.** Use the relationship:

$$\text{Moles} = \frac{\text{liters}}{22.4 \text{ L/mol}}$$

$$\text{Moles of unknown gas} = \frac{11.2 \text{ L}}{22.4 \text{ L/mol}} = 0.500 \text{ moles}$$

$$\text{MW} = \frac{\text{grams}}{\text{mole}}$$

$$\text{MW of unknown gas} = \frac{22.0 \text{ g}}{0.500 \text{ mole}} = 44.0 \text{ grams/mole}$$

That's the molecular weight of CO_2.

15. **(E) is correct.** According to Graham's law, at a given temperature, heavier molecules will have lower average speeds and lighter molecules will have higher speeds.

Helium is the lightest of the three molecules (MW = 4), oxygen is next (MW = 32), and carbon dioxide is the heaviest (MW = 44).

16. **(A) is correct.** The ideal gas laws fail under conditions where gas molecules are packed too tightly together. This can be brought about by high pressure (I), low temperature (not listed as a choice), or small volume (not listed as a choice).

17. **(D) is correct.** Density is measured in grams per liter. One mole of helium gas has a mass of 4 grams and occupies a volume of 22.4 liters at STP, so the density of helium gas at STP is

$$\frac{4}{22.4} \text{ g/L.}$$

18. **(E) is correct.** From the ideal gas equation, we know that $PV = nRT$.

Remember to convert 37 °C to 310 K.

Then we just rearrange the equation to solve for n:

$$n = \frac{PV}{RT} = \frac{(2.0)(5.0)}{(0.08)(310)} \text{ moles}$$

19. **(D) is correct.** Remember Graham's law, which relates the average speeds of different gases (and thus their rates of effusion) to their molecular weights:

$$\frac{v_1}{v_2} = \sqrt{\frac{MW_2}{MW_1}}$$

To get a velocity and rate of effusion that is three times as large as H_2's, we need a molecule with a molecular weight that is nine times as large. The molecular weight of H_2 is 2, so we need a molecule with a molecular weight of 18. That's H_2O.

20. **(A) is correct.** From kinetic molecular theory, if the gases are at the same temperature, then they will have the same average kinetic energies.

About the other answers:

(B) Nitrogen has a smaller molecular weight, so its molecules will have a larger average molecular speed.

(C), (D), and (E) We don't know how many moles of each gas are present, so we can't make any predictions about partial pressure, total mass, or density.

21. **(B) is correct.** From Dalton's law, the partial pressures of nitrogen and water vapor must add up to the total pressure in the container. The partial pressure of water vapor in a closed container will be equal to its vapor pressure, so the partial pressure of nitrogen is:

796 mmHg – 55 mmHg = 741 mmHg.

22. **(E) is correct.** According to the ideal gas laws, at constant temperature and pressure, the volume of a gas is directly proportional to the number of moles.

We increased the number of grams by a factor of 5 ([0.16][5] = [0.80]). That's the same as increasing the number of moles by a factor of 5. So we must have increased the volume by a factor of 5. So (5)(1 L) = 5 L.

23. **(C) is correct.** From the ideal gas laws, for a gas sample at constant pressure:

$$\frac{V_1}{T_1} = \frac{V_2}{T_2}$$

Solving for V_2 we get: $V_2 = V_1 \dfrac{V_2}{T_1}$

So V_1 is multiplied by a factor of $\dfrac{T_2}{T_1}$

Remember to convert to Kelvin, $\dfrac{127°C + 273}{27°C + 273} = \dfrac{400\ K}{300\ K} = \dfrac{4}{3}$

24. **(A) is correct.** We can find the number of moles of gas from $PV = nRT$.

Remember to convert 26 °C to 299 K.

Then solve for n:

$$n = \frac{PV}{RT} = \frac{(2.0)(6.0)}{(0.08)(299)}\ mol$$

Now, remember:

$$MW = \frac{grams}{moles} = \frac{(10\ g)}{\left(\dfrac{(2.0)(6.0)}{(0.08)(299)}\ mol\right)} = \frac{(10)(0.08)(299)}{(2.0)(6.0)}\ g/mol$$

25. **(E) is correct.** All three assumptions are included in kinetic molecular theory.

Problems

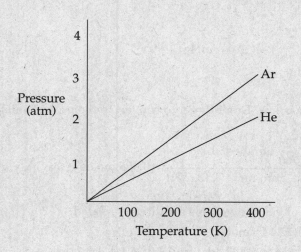

1. (a) Read the graph and add the two pressures.

$P_{Total} = P_{He} + P_{Ar}$

$P_{Total} = (1 \text{ atm}) + (1.5 \text{ atm}) = 2.5 \text{ atm}$

(b) Read the pressure (1 atm) at 200 K and use the ideal gas equation. $n = \dfrac{PV}{PT}$

$$= \frac{(1.0 \text{ atm})(2.0 \text{ L})}{(0.082 \text{ L-atm/mol-K})(200 \text{ K})} = 0.12 \text{ moles}$$

(c) Use the definition of a mole.

Molecules = (moles)(6.02×10^{23})

Molecules (atoms) of helium = $(0.12)(6.02 \times 10^{23}) = 7.2 \times 10^{22}$

(d) Use Graham's law.

$$\frac{v_1}{v_2} = \sqrt{\frac{MW_2}{MW_1}}$$

$$\frac{v_{He}}{v_{Ar}} = \sqrt{\frac{MW_{Ar}}{MW_{He}}} = \sqrt{\frac{(40)}{(4)}} = 3.2 \text{ to } 1$$

(e) Use the relationship:

$$\frac{P_1 V_1}{T_1} = \frac{P_2 V_2}{T_2}$$

With T constant:

$P_1 V_1 = P_2 V_2$

$(1.5 \text{ atm})(2.0 \text{ L}) = P_2 (1.0 \text{ L})$

$P_2 = 3.0 \text{ atm}$

2. (a) Use Dalton's law.

$P_{Total} = P_{Oxygen} + P_{Water}$

$(755 \text{ mmHg}) = (P_{Oxygen}) + (30.0 \text{ mmHg})$

$P_{Oxygen} = 725 \text{ mmHg}$

(b) Use the ideal gas law. Don't forget to convert to the proper units.

$$n = \frac{PV}{RT} = \frac{\left(\frac{725}{760} \text{ atm}\right)(1.45 \text{ L})}{(0.082 \text{ L} - \text{atm/mol} - \text{K})(302 \text{ K})} = 0.056 \text{ moles}$$

(c) At STP, moles of gas and volume are directly related.

Volume = (moles)(22.4 L/mol)

Volume of O_2 = (0.056 mol)(22.4 L/mol) = 1.25 L

(d) We know that 0.056 moles of O_2 were produced in the reaction.

From the balanced equation, we know that for every 3 moles of O_2 produced, 2 moles of $KClO_3$ are consumed. So there are $\frac{2}{3}$ as many moles of $KClO_3$ as O_2.

Moles of $KClO_3 = (\frac{2}{3})$(moles of O_2)

Moles of $KClO_3 = (\frac{2}{3})$(0.056 mol) = 0.037 moles

Grams = (moles)(MW)

Grams of $KClO_3$ = (0.037 mol)(122 g/mol) = 4.51 g

Essays

3. (a) The partial pressures depend on the number of moles of gas present. Since the number of moles of the two gases are the same, the partial pressures are the same.

(b) O_2 has the greater density. Density is mass per unit volume. Both gases have the same number of moles in the same volume, but oxygen has heavier molecules, so it has greater density.

(c) Concentration is moles per volume. Both gases have the same number of moles in the same volume, so their concentrations are the same.

(d) According to kinetic-molecular theory, the average kinetic energy of a gas depends only on the temperature. Both gases are at the same temperature, so they have the same average kinetic energy.

(e) H_2O will deviate most from ideal behavior. Ideal behavior for gas molecules assumes that there will be no intermolecular interactions.

H_2O is polar and O_2 is not. H_2O undergoes hydrogen bonding while O_2 does not. So H_2O has stronger intermolecular interactions, which will cause it to deviate more from ideal behavior.

(f) H_2O has the greater average molecular speed. From Graham's law, if two gases are at the same temperature, the one with the smaller molecular weight (MW of H_2O = 18, MW of O_2 = 32) will have the greater average molecular speed.

4. (a) A gasoline engine runs because of the combustion of hydrocarbons, which requires oxygen. At high altitudes, there is less air and less oxygen available for the combustion reaction.

(b) If the air is sufficiently dry and the water vapor is allowed to move away from the glass once it escapes from the liquid, the vapor pressure of the water will always be greater than the partial pressure of the air due to water. So water vapor will continue to slowly escape from the water until the water is gone.

(c) As depth below the surface of a fluid increases, pressure increases. According to the ideal gas law, as pressure increases at constant temperature, volume decreases.

(d) As the temperature decreases, gas molecules move closer together with less energy, causing non-ideal behavior to begin. When attractive forces between gas molecules become important, gas molecules stick together, causing there to be fewer gas molecules at any time than are supposed to be used by the ideal gas equation to predict the pressure. So attractions among molecules effectively reduce the number of molecules of gas, thus reducing the pressure.

PHASE CHANGES

How often does this topic appear on the test?
In the multiple-choice section, this topic appears in about 4 out of 75 questions.
In the free-response section, you'll see this topic occasionally.

THE PHASE DIAGRAM

You should know how to work with the following phase diagram.

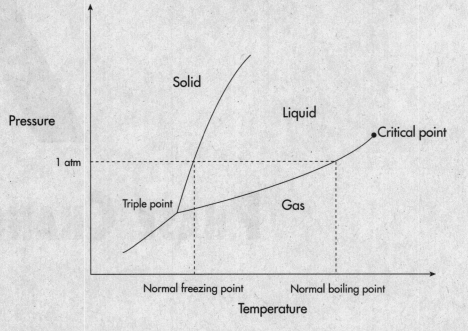

At high pressure and low temperature, a substance is in solid phase. At low pressure and high temperature, a substance is in gas phase. Liquid phase is in between.

The lines that separate the phases correspond to points at which the substance can exist simultaneously in both phases at equilibrium. The normal freezing point is the temperature at which the solid-liquid phase equilibrium line crosses the 1 atmosphere pressure line. The normal boiling point is the temperature at which the liquid-gas equilibrium line crosses the 1 atmosphere pressure line.

The **triple point** is the temperature and pressure at which all three phases can exist simultaneously in equilibrium.

The **critical point** is the temperature beyond which the molecules of a substance have too much kinetic energy to stick together and form a liquid.

PHASE CHANGES

NAMING THE PHASE CHANGES

Solid to liquid	—	Melting
Liquid to solid	—	Freezing
Liquid to gas	—	Vaporization
Gas to liquid	—	Condensation
Solid to gas	—	Sublimation
Gas to solid	—	Deposition

Phase changes occur because of changes in temperature and/or pressure. You should be able to read the phase diagram and see how a change in pressure or temperature will affect the phase of a substance.

When the liquid or solid phase of a substance is in equilibrium with the gas phase, the pressure of the gas will be equal to **vapor pressure** of the substance. As temperature increases, the vapor pressure of a liquid will increase. When the vapor pressure of a liquid increases to the point where it is equal to the surrounding atmospheric pressure, the liquid boils.

HEAT OF FUSION

The heat of fusion is the energy that must be put into a solid in order to melt it. This energy is needed to overcome the forces holding the solid together. Alternatively, the heat of fusion is the heat given off by a substance when it freezes. The intermolecular forces within a solid are more stable and therefore have lower energy than the forces within a liquid, so energy is released in the freezing process.

HEAT OF VAPORIZATION

The heat of vaporization is the energy that must be put into a liquid in order to vaporize it. This energy is needed to overcome the forces holding the liquid together. Alternatively, the heat of vaporization is the heat given off by a substance when it condenses. Intermolecular forces become stronger when a gas condenses; the gas becomes a liquid, which is more stable, and energy is released.

THE PHASE DIAGRAM FOR WATER

You should recognize how the phase diagram for water differs from the phase diagram for most other substances.

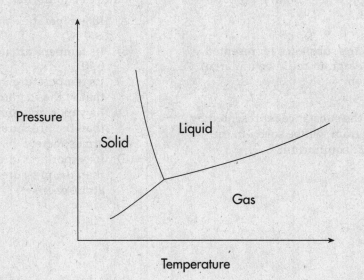

In the phase diagram for substances other than water, the solid-liquid equilibrium line slopes upward. In the phase diagram for water, the solid-liquid equilibrium line slopes downward. What this means is that when pressure is increased, a normal substance will change from liquid to solid, but water will change from solid to liquid.

Water has this odd property because its hydrogen bonds form a lattice structure when it freezes. This forces the molecules to remain farther apart in ice than in water, making the solid phase less dense than the liquid phase. That's why ice floats on water.

PHASE CHANGES

QUESTIONS

Multiple choice

Questions 1–4 refer to the phase diagram below

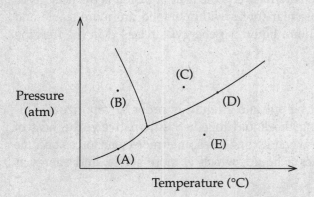

1. At this point the substance represented by the phase diagram will be solely in the solid phase at equilibrium.

2. This point represents a boiling point of the substance.

3. At this point, the substance represented by the phase diagram could be undergoing sublimation.

4. At this point the substance represented by the phase diagram will be solely in the liquid phase at equilibrium.

5. When a substance undergoes a phase change from liquid to solid, which of the following will occur?

   (A) Energy will be released by the substance because intermolecular forces are being weakened.
   (B) Energy will be released by the substance because intermolecular forces are being strengthened.
   (C) Energy will be absorbed by the substance because intermolecular forces are being weakened.
   (D) Energy will be absorbed by the substance because intermolecular forces are being strengthened.
   (E) The energy of the substance will not be changed.

6. Which of the following is true of a substance in equilibrium in the liquid phase?

   (A) Its temperature must be less than 100 °C.
   (B) Its temperature must be greater than 0 °C.
   (C) Its temperature must be lower than that of the surrounding atmosphere.
   (D) Its vapor pressure must be greater than the pressure of the surrounding atmosphere.
   (E) Its vapor pressure must be lower than the pressure of the surrounding atmosphere.

Questions 7–10 are based on the phase diagram below

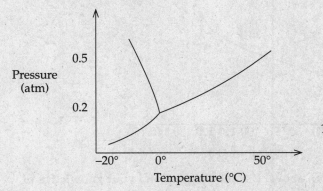

7. As pressure on the substance depicted in the diagram is increased at constant temperature, which of the following phase changes could NOT occur?

    I. Condensation
    II. Melting
    III. Freezing

    (A) I only
    (B) II only
    (C) III only
    (D) I and II only
    (E) I and III only

8. At a temperature of 50 °C and a pressure of 0.2 atmospheres, the substance depicted in the diagram is

    (A) in the gas phase
    (B) in the liquid phase
    (C) in the solid phase
    (D) at its triple point
    (E) at its critical point

9. Which of the following lists the three phases of the substance shown in the diagram in order of increasing density at –5 °C ?

    (A) solid, gas, liquid
    (B) solid, liquid, gas
    (C) gas, liquid, solid
    (D) gas, solid, liquid
    (E) liquid, solid, gas

10. When the temperature of the substance depicted in the diagram is decreased from 10 °C to –10 °C at a constant pressure of 0.3 atmosphere, which phase change will occur?

    (A) gas to liquid
    (B) liquid to solid
    (C) gas to solid
    (D) liquid to gas
    (E) solid to liquid

11. Which of the following processes can occur when the temperature of a substance is increased at constant pressure?

    I. Sublimation
    II. Melting
    III. Boiling

    (A) I only
    (B) II only
    (C) I and II only
    (D) II and III only
    (E) I, II, and III

12. The temperature above which gas molecules become too energetic to form a true liquid, no matter what the pressure, is called the

    (A) melting point
    (B) critical point
    (C) boiling point
    (D) triple point
    (E) freezing point

Essays

1.

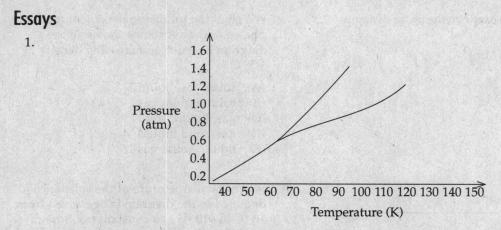

The phase diagram for a substance is shown above. Use the diagram and your knowledge of phase changes to answer the following questions.

(a) When the substance is at a pressure of 0.8 atmospheres and a temperature of 50 K, what is its phase?

(b) Describe the change in phase that the substance undergoes when the pressure is decreased from 1.2 atmospheres to 0.6 atmospheres at a constant temperature of 110 K.

(c) A constant source of heat was applied to the substance at a constant pressure of 0.8 atmospheres. The substance was initially at a temperature of 50 K. The temperature of the substance increased at a constant rate until 70 K was reached. At this point, the temperature remained constant for a period of time, and then continued to climb at a constant rate. Explain what has happened.

(d) What is the normal boiling point for this substance?

2.

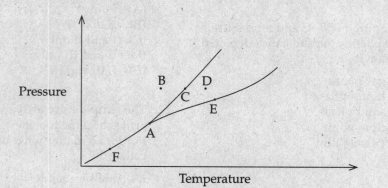

The phase diagram for a substance is shown above. Use the diagram and your knowledge of phase changes to answer the following questions.

(a) Describe the phase change that the substance undergoes as the temperature is increased from points B to C to D at constant pressure.

(b) Which of the phases are in equilibrium at point F? Give a name for one of the phase changes between these two phases.

(c) Could this phase diagram represent water? Explain why or why not.

(d) What is the name given to point A and what is the situation particular to this point?

ANSWERS

Multiple choice

1. **(B)** is correct. Point (B) is in a region of high pressure and low temperature. That corresponds to the solid phase.

2. **(D)** is correct. Point (D) is on the phase change line between liquid and gas. The temperature at point (D) is the boiling point of the substance at the pressure at point (D).

3. **(A)** is correct. Point (A) is on the phase change line between solid and gas. Sublimation is the phase change from solid directly to gas.

4. **(C)** is correct. Point (C) is in the liquid region, which is the middle region between solid and gas.

5. **(B)** is correct. The intermolecular forces in the solid phase of any substance are stronger than the intermolecular forces in the liquid phase. Whenever intermolecular forces are strengthened, energy is given off.

6. **(E)** is correct. In order for a substance to remain in the liquid phase, its vapor pressure must be lower than the atmospheric pressure. If the vapor pressure becomes equal to the atmospheric pressure, the liquid will boil.

7. **(C)** is correct. This diagram has the downward slope between the solid and liquid phases that is typical of water, so you've got to be careful in dealing with solid-liquid phase changes. The possible phase changes for increasing pressure and constant temperature are given in the diagram below.

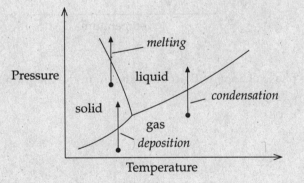

This substance will melt under increased pressure instead of freezing, so while choices (I) and (II) can occur, choice (III) cannot.

8. **(A)** is correct. At 50 °C and 0.2 atm the substance is a gas:

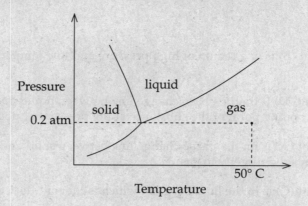

9. **(D)** is correct. As pressure is increased, density will increase; so increasing density is shown by the arrow in the diagram below.

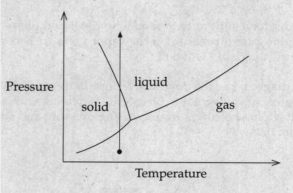

10. **(B)** is correct. The phase change will occur as shown in the diagram below.

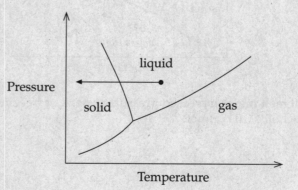

11. **(E)** is correct. All three phase changes listed can occur when temperature is increased at constant pressure. This is shown in the diagram below.

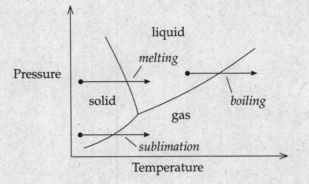

12. **(B)** is correct. At temperatures above the critical point, gases can become dense, but liquids do not form.

Essays

1. (a) Solid, which corresponds to high pressure and low temperature.

    (b) The substance starts as a liquid and changes to a gas (vaporizes) when the pressure has dropped to about 0.9 atm.

    (c) At 70 K, the substance melted. While the substance was melting, the heat from the constant source went toward overcoming the strong intermolecular forces of the solid instead of increasing the temperature. The heat that must be put into a solid to melt it is called the heat of fusion. When the heat of fusion was overcome and the substance was entirely in the liquid phase, the temperature of the liquid began to increase at a constant rate.

    (d) The normal boiling point is the boiling point at a pressure of 1 atmosphere. We can find the normal boiling point by looking for the spot at which the gas-liquid equilibrium line crosses the 1 atm line. This happens at 115 K.

2. (a) At point B, the substance is a solid.

    At point C, the substance is in equilibrium between solid and liquid phase; that is, it's melting.

    At point D, the substance is entirely in liquid phase.

    (b) At point F, the substance is in equilibrium between the gas and solid phases.

    When a substance changes from solid to gas phase, it's called sublimation.

    When a substance changes from gas to solid phase, it's called deposition.

    (c) The diagram CANNOT represent water.

    For water, the slope of the solid-liquid equilibrium line must be negative, indicating that the liquid phase of water is more dense than the solid phase.

    (d) Point A is called the triple point.

    At the triple point, all three phases can exist simultaneously in equilibrium.

THERMODYNAMICS

How often does this topic appear on the test?
In the multiple-choice section, this topic appears in about 5 out of 75 questions.
In the free-response section, you'll see this topic every year.

THE FIRST AND SECOND LAWS OF THERMODYNAMICS

The first law of thermodynamics says that the energy of the universe is constant. Energy can be neither created nor destroyed, so while energy can be *converted* in a chemical process, the total energy remains constant.

The second law of thermodynamics says that if a process is spontaneous in one direction, then it can't be spontaneous in the reverse direction.

STATE FUNCTIONS

Enthalpy change, (ΔH), entropy change (ΔS), and free-energy change (ΔG), are **state functions**. That means that they all depend only on the change between the initial and final states of a system, not on the process by which the change occurs. For a chemical reaction this means that the thermodynamic state functions are independent of reaction pathway, so for instance, the addition of a catalyst to a reaction will have no effect on the overall energy or entropy change of the reaction.

STANDARD STATE CONDITIONS

When the values of thermodynamic quantities are given on the test, they are almost always given for standard state conditions. A thermodynamic quantity under standard state conditions is indicated by the little superscript circle, so under standard state conditions:

$$\Delta H = \Delta H°$$

$$\Delta S = \Delta S°$$

$$\Delta G = \Delta G°$$

Standard State Conditions

- All gases are at 1 atmosphere pressure.
- All liquids are pure.
- All solids are pure.
- All solutions are at 1-molar (1 M) concentration.
- The energy of formation of an element in its normal state is defined as zero.
- The temperature used for standard state values is almost invariably room temperature, 25 °C (298 K). Standard state values can be calculated for other temperatures, though.

ENTHALPY

ENTHALPY CHANGE, ΔH

The enthalpy of a substance is a measure of the energy that is released or absorbed by the substance when bonds are broken and formed during a reaction.

The Basic Rules of Enthalpy

When bonds are formed, energy is released.
In order to break bonds, energy must be absorbed.

The change in enthalpy, ΔH, that takes place over the course of a reaction can be calculated by subtracting the enthalpy of the reactants from the enthalpy of the products.

Enthalpy Change

$\Delta H = H_{products} - H_{reactants}$

If the products have stronger bonds than the reactants, then the products have lower enthalpy than the reactants and are more stable; in this case energy is released by the reaction and the reaction is **exothermic**.

If the products have weaker bonds than the reactants, then the products have higher enthalpy than the reactants and are less stable; in this case energy is absorbed by the reaction and the reaction is **endothermic**.

All substances like to be in the lowest possible energy state, which gives them the greatest stability. This means that, in general, exothermic processes are more likely to occur spontaneously than endothermic processes.

HEAT OF FORMATION, ΔH_f°

Heat of formation is the change in energy that takes place when a compound is formed from its component pure elements under standard state conditions. Heats of formation are almost always calculated at a temperature of 25 °C (298 K).

Remember, ΔH_f° for a pure element is defined to be zero.

- If ΔH_f° for a compound is negative, energy is released when the compound is formed from pure elements and the product is *more* stable than its constituent elements. That is, the process is exothermic.

- If ΔH_f° for a compound is positive, energy is absorbed when the compound is formed from pure elements and the product is *less* stable than its constituent elements. That is, the process is endothermic.

If the ΔH_f°'s of the products and reactants are known, ΔH for a reaction can be calculated.

$$\Delta H^{\circ} = \sum \Delta H_f^{\circ} \text{ products} - \sum \Delta H_f^{\circ} \text{ reactants}$$

Let's find ΔH° for the following reaction.

$$2\, CH_3OH(g) + 3\, O_2(g) \rightarrow 2\, CO_2(g) + 4\, H_2O(g)$$

Compound	ΔH° (kJ/mol)
$CH_3OH(g)$	−201
$O_2(g)$	0
$CO_2(g)$	−394
$H_2O(g)$	−242

$$\Delta H^{\circ} = \sum \Delta H_f^{\circ} \text{ products} - \sum \Delta H_f^{\circ} \text{ reactants}$$

$$\Delta H^{\circ} = [(2)(\Delta H_f^{\circ}\, CO_2) + (4)(\Delta H_f^{\circ}\, H_2O)] - [(2)(\Delta H_f^{\circ}\, CH_3OH) + (3)(\Delta H_f^{\circ}\, O_2)]$$

$$\Delta H^{\circ} = [(2)(-394\text{ kJ}) + (4)(-242\text{ kJ})] - [(2)(-201\text{ kJ}) + (3)(0\text{ kJ})]$$

$$\Delta H^{\circ} = (-1756\text{ kJ}) - (-402\text{ kJ})$$

$$\Delta H^{\circ} = -1354\text{ kJ}$$

BOND ENERGY

Bond energy is the energy required to break a bond. Since the breaking of a bond is an endothermic process, bond energy is always a positive number. When a bond is formed, energy equal to the bond energy is released.

$$\Delta H° = \sum \text{Bond energies of bonds broken} - \sum \text{Bond energies of bonds formed}$$

The bonds broken will be the reactant bonds and the bonds formed will be the product bonds. Let's find $\Delta H°$ for the following reaction.

$$2\,H_2(g) + O_2(g) \rightarrow 2\,H_2O(g)$$

Bond	Bond Energy (kJ/mol)
H–H	436
O=O	499
O–H	463

$$\Delta H° = \sum \text{Bond energies of bonds broken} - \sum \text{Bond energies of bonds formed}$$

$\Delta H° = [(2)(\text{H–H}) + (1)(\text{O=O})] - [(4)(\text{O–H})]$

$\Delta H° = [(2)(436\ \text{kJ}) + (1)(499\ \text{kJ})] - [(4)(463\ \text{kJ})]$

$\Delta H° = (1371\ \text{kJ}) - (1852\ \text{kJ})$

$\Delta H° = -481\ \text{kJ}$

HESS'S LAW

Hess's law says that if a reaction can be described as a series of steps, then ΔH for the overall reaction is simply the sum of the ΔH's for all the steps.

HEAT CAPACITY AND SPECIFIC HEAT

Heat capacity, C_p, is a measure of how much the temperature of an object is raised when it absorbs heat.

Heat Capacity

$$C_p = \frac{\Delta H}{\Delta T}$$

C_p = heat capacity

ΔH = heat added (J or cal)

ΔT = temperature change (K or °C)

An object with a large heat capacity can absorb a lot of heat without undergoing much temperature change, whereas an object with a small heat capacity shows a large increase in temperature when only a small amount of heat is absorbed.

Specific heat is the amount of heat required to raise the temperature of one gram of a substance one degree Celsius.

Specific Heat

$q = mc\,\Delta T$

q = heat added (J or cal)

m = mass of the substance (g or kg)

c = specific heat

ΔT = temperature change (K or °C)

ENTROPY

The entropy, S, of a system is a measure of the randomness or disorder of the system; the greater the disorder of a system, the greater its entropy. Since zero entropy is defined to be a solid crystal at 0 K, all substances that we encounter will have some positive value for entropy. Standard entropies, $S°$, are calculated at 25 °C (298 K).

You should be familiar with several simple rules of thumb concerning entropies:

- Liquids have higher entropy values than solids.

- Gases have higher entropy values than liquids.

- Particles in solution have higher entropy values than solids.

- Two moles of a substance has a higher entropy value than one mole.

ENTROPY CHANGE, ΔS

The standard entropy change $\Delta S°$, that has taken place at the completion of a reaction is the difference between the standard entropies of the products and the standard entropies of the reactants.

$$\Delta S° = \sum S° \text{ products} - \sum S° \text{ reactants}$$

GIBBS FREE ENERGY

The Gibbs free energy, or simply free energy, G, of a process is a measure of the spontaneity of the process.

For a given reaction:

- If ΔG is negative, the reaction is spontaneous.

- If ΔG is positive, the reaction is not spontaneous.

- If $\Delta G = 0$, the reaction is at equilibrium.

FREE ENERGY CHANGE, ΔG

The standard free energy change, $\Delta G°$, for a reaction can be calculated from the standard free energies of formation, $\Delta G_f°$, of its products and reactants in the same way that $\Delta S°$ was calculated.

$$\Delta G° = \sum \Delta G_f° \text{ products} - \sum \Delta S° \text{ reactants}$$

ΔG, ΔH and ΔS

In general, nature likes to move toward two different and seemingly contradictory states, low energy and high disorder, so spontaneous processes must result in decreasing enthalpy or increasing entropy or both.

There is an important equation that relates spontaneity (ΔG), enthalpy (ΔH), and entropy (ΔS).

$$\Delta G^\circ = \Delta H^\circ - T\Delta S^\circ$$

T = absolute temperature (K)

The following chart shows how different values of enthalpy and entropy affect spontaneity.

ΔH	ΔS	T	ΔG	
–	+	Low	–	Always spontaneous
		High	–	
+	–	Low	+	Never spontaneous
		High	+	
+	+	Low	+	Not spontaneous at low temperature
		High	–	Spontaneous at high temperature
–	–	Low	–	Spontaneous at low temperature
		High	+	Not spontaneous at high temperature

You should note that at low temperature enthalpy is dominant, while at high temperature entropy is dominant.

ΔG and ΔG°

The standard free energy change, ΔG°, gives the spontaneity of a reaction when all the concentrations of reactants and products are in their standard state concentrations (1-molar). The free energy change, and thus the spontaneity, of a reaction will be different from the standard free energy change if the initial concentrations of reactants and products are not 1-molar.

The standard free energy change, ΔG°, can be related to ΔG for other conditions by the following equations.

$$\Delta G = \Delta G^\circ + RT \ln Q$$

or

$$\Delta G = \Delta G^\circ + 2.303RT \log Q$$

ΔG° = standard free energy change (J)

ΔG = free energy change under given initial conditions (J)

R = the gas constant, 8.31 J/mol-K

T = absolute temperature (K)

Q = the reaction quotient for the given initial conditions

STANDARD FREE ENERGY CHANGE AND THE EQUILIBRIUM CONSTANT

Let's look at the equation relating ΔG and $\Delta G°$.

$$\Delta G = \Delta G° + RT \ln Q$$

At equilibrium, $\Delta G = 0$ and $Q = K$.

Knowing this, we can derive an equation relating the standard free energy change, $\Delta G°$, and the equilibrium constant, K.

$$\Delta G° = -RT \ln K$$

or

$$\Delta G° = -2.303RT \log K$$

$\Delta G°$ = the gas constant, 8.31 J/mol-K
T = absolute temperature (K)
K = the equilibrium constant

Notice that if $\Delta G°$ is negative, K must be greater than 1, and products will be favored at equilibrium. Alternatively, if $\Delta G°$ is positive, K must be less than 1, and reactants will be favored at equilibrium.

ENERGY DIAGRAMS

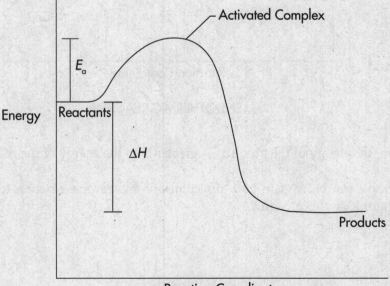

EXOTHERMIC REACTION

The diagram above shows the energy change that takes place during an exothermic reaction. The reactants start with a certain amount of energy (read the graph left to right). In order for the reaction to proceed, the reactants must have enough energy to reach the transition state, where they are part of an activated complex. This is the highest point on the graph above. The amount of energy needed to reach this point is called the activation energy, E_a. At this point, all reactant bonds have been broken, but no product bonds have been formed, so this is the point in the reaction with the highest energy and lowest stability.

Moving to the right past the activated complex, product bonds start to form and eventually we reach the energy level of the products.

This diagram represents an exothermic reaction, so the products are at a lower energy level than the reactants and ΔH is negative.

The following diagram is for an endothermic reaction.

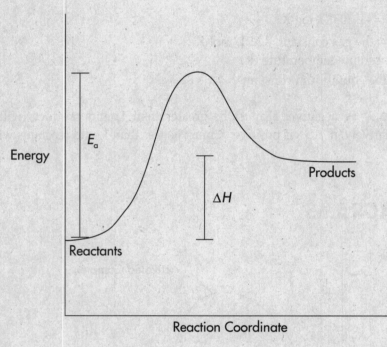

ENDOTHERMIC REACTION

In this diagram, the energy of the products is greater than the energy of the reactants, so ΔH is positive.

Reaction diagrams can be read in both directions, so the reverse reaction for an exothermic reaction is endothermic and vice versa.

CATALYSTS AND ENERGY DIAGRAMS

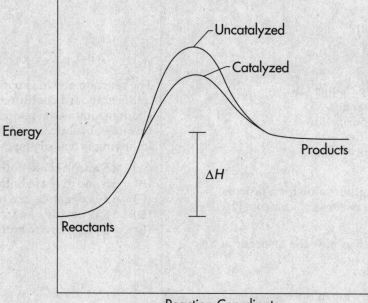

A catalyst speeds up a reaction by providing the reactants with an alternate pathway that has a lower activation energy, as shown in the diagram above.

Notice that the only difference between the catalyzed reaction and the uncatalyzed reaction is that the energy of the activated complex is lower for the catalyzed reaction. A catalyst lowers the activation energy, but it has no effect on the energy of the reactants, the energy of the products, or ΔH for the reaction.

Also note that a catalyst lowers the activation energy for both the forward and the reverse reaction, so it has no effect on the equilibrium conditions.

THERMODYNAMICS

QUESTIONS

Multiple choice

Questions 1–4

    (A) Free energy change (ΔG)
    (B) Entropy change (ΔS)
    (C) Heat of vaporization
    (D) Heat of fusion
    (E) Heat capacity

1. If this has a negative value for a process, then the process occurs spontaneously.

2. This is a measure of how the disorder of a system is changing.

3. This is the energy given off when a substance condenses.

4. This is the energy taken in by a substance when it melts.

5. $2\ Al(s) + 3\ Cl_2(g) \rightarrow 2\ AlCl_3(s)$

The reaction above is not spontaneous under standard conditions but becomes spontaneous as the temperature decreases towards absolute zero. Which of the following is true at standard conditions?

    (A) ΔS and ΔH are both negative.
    (B) ΔS and ΔH are both positive.
    (C) ΔS is negative and ΔH is positive.
    (D) ΔS is positive and ΔH is negative.
    (E) ΔS and ΔH are both equal to zero.

6.

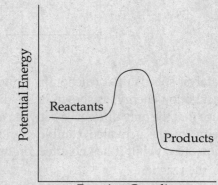

Which of the following is true of the reaction shown in the diagram above?

    (A) The reaction is endothermic because the reactants are at a higher energy level than the products.
    (B) The reaction is endothermic because the reactants are at a lower energy level than the products.
    (C) The reaction is exothermic because the reactants are at a higher energy level than the products.
    (D) The reaction is exothermic because the reactants are at a lower energy level than the products.
    (E) The reaction is endothermic because the reactants are at the same energy level as the products.

7. $$2 H_2(g) + O_2(g) \rightarrow 2 H_2O(g)$$

Based on the information given in the table below, what is $\Delta H°$ for the above reaction?

Bond	Average bond energy (kJ/mol)
H–H	500
O=O	500
O–H	500

(A) –2,000 kJ
(B) –1,500 kJ
(C) –500 kJ
(D) +1,000 kJ
(E) +2,000 kJ

8. Which of the following is true of a reaction that is spontaneous at 298 K but becomes non-spontaneous at a higher temperature?

(A) $\Delta S°$ and $\Delta H°$ are both negative.
(B) $\Delta S°$ and $\Delta H°$ are both positive.
(C) $\Delta S°$ is negative and $\Delta H°$ is positive.
(D) $\Delta S°$ is positive and $\Delta H°$ is negative.
(E) $\Delta S°$ and $\Delta H°$ are both equal to zero.

9. Which of the following will be true when a pure substance in liquid phase freezes spontaneously?

(A) ΔG, ΔH, and ΔS are all positive.
(B) ΔG, ΔH, and ΔS are all negative.
(C) ΔG and ΔH are negative, but ΔS is positive.
(D) ΔG and ΔS are negative, but ΔH is positive.
(E) ΔS and ΔH are negative, but ΔG is positive.

10.

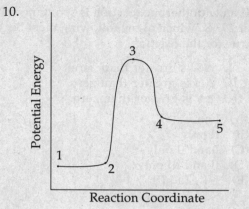

Which point on the graph shown above corresponds to activated complex, or transition state?

(A) 1
(B) 2
(C) 3
(D) 4
(E) 5

11. $C(s) + O_2(g) \rightarrow CO_2(g) \quad \Delta H° = -390 \text{ kJ/mol}$

$H_2(g) + \frac{1}{2} O_2(g) \rightarrow H_2O(l) \quad \Delta H° = -290 \text{ kJ/mol}$

$2 C(s) + H_2(g) \rightarrow C_2H_2(g) \quad \Delta H° = +230 \text{ kJ/mol}$

Based on the information given above, what is $\Delta H°$ for the following reaction?

$$C_2H_2(g) + \frac{5}{2} O_2(g) \rightarrow 2 CO_2(g) + H_2O(l)$$

(A) –1300 kJ
(B) –1070 kJ
(C) –840 kJ
(D) –780 kJ
(E) –680 kJ

12. If an endothermic reaction is spontaneous at 298 K, which of the following must be true for the reaction?

    I. ΔG is greater than zero.
   II. ΔH is greater than zero.
  III. ΔS is greater than zero.

(A) I only
(B) II only
(C) I and II only
(D) II and III only
(E) I, II, and III

13. The addition of a catalyst will have which of the following effects on a chemical reaction?

    I. The enthalpy change will decrease.
   II. The entropy change will decrease.
  III. The activation energy will decrease.

(A) I only
(B) II only
(C) III only
(D) I and II only
(E) II and III only

14.

$$C(s) + 2\,H_2(g) \rightarrow CH_4(g) \qquad \Delta H^\circ = x$$

$$C(s) + O_2(g) \rightarrow CO_2(g) \qquad \Delta H^\circ = y$$

$$H_2(g) + \frac{1}{2}\,O_2(g) \rightarrow H_2O(l) \qquad \Delta H^\circ = z$$

Based on the information given above, what is ΔH° for the following reaction?

$$CH_4(g) + 2\,O_2(g) \rightarrow CO_2(g) + 2\,H_2O(l)$$

(A) $x + y + z$
(B) $x + y - z$
(C) $z + y - 2x$
(D) $2z + y - x$
(E) $2z + y - 2x$

15. For which of the following processes will ΔS be positive?

    I. $NaCl(s) \rightarrow Na^+(aq) + Cl^-(aq)$
   II. $2\,H_2(g) + O_2(g) \rightarrow 2\,H_2O(g)$
  III. $CaCO_3(s) \rightarrow CaO(s) + CO_2(g)$

(A) I only
(B) II only
(C) I and II only
(D) I and III only
(E) I, II, and III

Problems

1.

Substance	Absolute Entropy, $S°$ (J/mol–K)	Molecular Weight
$C_6H_{12}O_2$ (s)	212.13	180
O_2 (g)	205	32
CO_2 (g)	213.6	44
H_2O (l)	69.9	18

Energy is released when glucose is oxidized in the following reaction; which is a metabolism reaction that takes place in the body.

$$C_6H_{12}O_6(s) + 6\ O_2(g) \rightarrow 6\ CO_2(g) + 6\ H_2O(l)$$

The standard enthalpy change, $\Delta H°$, for the reaction is –2801 kJ at 298 K.

(a)   Calculate the standard entropy change, $\Delta S°$, for the oxidation of glucose.

(b)   Calculate the standard free energy change, $\Delta G°$ for the reaction at 298 K.

(c)   What is the value of K_{eq} for the reaction?

(d)   How much energy is given off by the oxidation of 1.00 gram of glucose?

2.

Bond	Average bond dissociation energy (kJ/mol)
C–H	415
O=O	495
C=O	799
O–H	463

$$CH_4(g) + 2\ O_2(g) \rightarrow CO_2(g) + 2\ H_2O(l)$$

The standard free energy change, $\Delta G°$, for the reaction above is –801 kJ at 298 K.

(a)   Use the table of bond dissociation energies to find $\Delta H°$ for the reaction above.

(b)   What is the value of K_{eq} for the reaction?

(c)   What is the value of $\Delta S°$ for the reaction at 298 K?

(d)   Give an explanation for the size of the entropy change found in (c).

3. $$N_2(g) + 3\,H_2(g) \rightleftharpoons 2\,NH_3(g)$$

The heat of formation, ΔH_f°, of $NH_3(g)$ is -46.2 kJ/mol. The free energy of formation, ΔG_f°, of $NH_3(g)$ is -16.7 kJ/mol.

(a) What are the values of ΔH° and ΔG° for the reaction?

(b) What is the value of the entropy change, ΔS° for the reaction above at 298 K?

(c) As the temperature is increased, what is the effect on ΔG° for the reaction? How does this affect the spontaneity of the reaction?

(d) At what temperature can N_2, H_2, and NH_3 gases be maintained together in equilibrium, each with a partial pressure of 1 atm?

Essays

4. $$2\,H_2(g) + O_2(g) \rightarrow 2\,H_2O(l)$$

The reaction above proceeds spontaneously from standard conditions at 298 K.

(a) Predict the sign of the entropy change, ΔS°, for the reaction. Explain.

(b) How would the value of ΔS° for the reaction change if the product of the reaction was $H_2O(g)$?

(c) What is the sign of ΔG° at 298 K? Explain.

(d) What is the sign of of ΔH° at 298 K? Explain.

5. $$CaO(s) + CO_2(g) \rightarrow CaCO_3(s)$$

The reaction above is spontaneous at 298 K and the heat of reaction, ΔH° is -178 kJ.

(a) Predict the sign of the entropy change, ΔS°, for the reaction. Explain.

(b) What is the sign of ΔG° at 298 K? Explain.

(c) What change, if any, occurs to the value of ΔG° as the temperature is increased from 298 K?

(d) As the reaction takes place in a closed container what changes will occur in the concentration of CO_2 and the temperature?

6.
$$H_2O(l) \rightleftharpoons H_2O(g)$$

At 298 K, the value of the equilibrium constant, K, for the reaction above is 0.036.

(a) What is the sign of ΔS° for the reaction above at 298 K?

(b) What is the sign of ΔH° for the reaction above at 298 K?

(c) What is the sign of ΔG° for the reaction above at 298 K?

(d) At approximately what temperature will ΔG° for the reaction be equal to zero?

ANSWERS

Multiple choice

1. **(A)** is correct. A negative value for ΔG means that a process is spontaneous. A positive value for ΔG means that a process is non-spontaneous.

2. **(B)** is correct. Entropy is a measure of the disorder of a system. A positive value for ΔS means that a system has become more disordered. A negative value for ΔS means that a system has become more orderly.

3. **(C)** is correct. The heat of vaporization is the heat given off when a substance condenses. It is also the heat that must be put into a substance to make it vaporize.

4. **(D)** is correct. The heat of fusion is the heat that must be put into a substance to melt it. It is also the heat given off when a substance freezes.

   By the way, choice (E), heat capacity, is a measure of how much heat must be added to a given object in order to raise its temperature 1 °C.

5. **(A)** is correct. Remember $\Delta G = \Delta H - T \Delta S$.

   If the reaction is spontaneous only when the temperature is very low, then ΔG is only negative when T is very small. This can only happen when ΔH is negative (which favors spontaneity) and ΔS is negative (which favors non-spontaneity). A very small value for T will eliminate the influence of ΔS.

6. **(C)** is correct. In an exothermic reaction, energy is given off as the products are created because the products have less potential energy than the reactants.

7. **(C)** is correct. The bond energy is the energy that must be put into a bond in order to break it. First let's figure out how much energy must be put into the reactants in order to break their bonds.

   To break 2 moles of H–H bonds, it takes (2)(500) kJ = 1,000 kJ

   To break 1 mole of O=O bonds, it takes 500 kJ.

   So to break up the reactants, it takes +1,500 kJ.

   Energy is given off when a bond is formed; that's the negative of the bond energy. Now let's see how much energy is given off when 2 moles of H_2O are formed.

   2 moles of H_2O molecules contain 4 moles of O–H bonds, so (4)(–500) kJ = –2,000 kJ are given off.

   So the value of ΔH° for the reaction is:

   (–2,000 kJ, the energy given off) + (1,500 kJ, the energy put in) = –500 kJ.

8. **(A)** is correct. Remember $\Delta G = \Delta H - T \Delta S$. If the reaction is spontaneous at standard temperature, but becomes non-spontaneous at higher temperatures, then ΔG is negative only at lower temperatures. This can only happen when ΔH is negative (which favors spontaneity) and ΔS is negative (which favors non-spontaneity). As the value of T increases, the influence of ΔS increases, eventually making the reaction non-spontaneous.

9. **(B)** is correct. The process is spontaneous, so ΔG must be negative. The intermolecular forces become stronger and the substance moves to a lower energy level when it freezes, so ΔH must be negative. The substance becomes more orderly when it freezes, so ΔS must be negative.

10. **(C)** is correct. Point 3 represents the activated complex, which is the point of highest energy. This point is the transition state between the reactants and the products.

11. **(A)** is correct. The equations given on top give the heats of formation of all the reactants and products (remember, the heat of formation of O_2, an element in its most stable form, is zero).

    $\Delta H°$ for a reaction = ($\Delta H°$ for the products) – ($\Delta H°$ for the reactants).
    First the products:
    From CO_2, we get $(2)(-390 \text{ kJ}) = -780 \text{ kJ}$
    From H_2O, we get -290 kJ
    So $\Delta H°$ for the products = $(-780 \text{ kJ}) + (-290 \text{ kJ}) = -1,070 \text{ kJ}$
    Now the reactants:
    From C_2H_2, we get $+230 \text{ kJ}$. The heat of formation of O_2 is defined as zero, so that's it for the reactants.

    $\Delta H°$ for the reaction = $(-1.070 \text{ kJ}) - (+230 \text{ kJ}) = -1300 \text{ kJ}$.

12. **(D)** is correct.

    The reaction is spontaneous, so ΔG must be less than zero, so (I) is not true. The reaction is endothermic, so ΔH must be greater than zero, so (II) is true.

    The only way that an endothermic reaction can be spontaneous is if the entropy is increasing, so ΔS is greater than zero and (III) is true.

13. **(C)** is correct. The addition of a catalyst speeds up a reaction by lowering the activation energy. A catalyst has no effect on the entropy or enthalpy change of a reaction.

14. **(D)** is correct. The equations given above give the heats of formation of all the reactants and products (remember, the heat of formation of O_2, an element in its most stable form, is zero).

    $\Delta H°$ for a reaction = ($\Delta H°$ for the products) – ($\Delta H°$ for the reactants).
    First the products:
    From $2 H_2O$, we get $2z$
    From CO_2, we get y
    So $\Delta H°$ for the products = $2z + y$
    Now the reactants:
    From CH_4, we get x. The heat of formation of O_2 is defined to be zero, so that's it for the reactants.

    $\Delta H°$ for the reaction = $(2z + y) - (x) = 2z + y - x$.

15. **(D)** is correct.

In (I), NaCl goes from a solid to aqueous particles. Aqueous particles are more disorderly than a solid, so ΔS will be positive.

In (II), we go from 3 moles of gas to 2 moles of gas. Fewer moles and less gas means less entropy, so ΔS will be negative.

In (III), we go from a solid to a solid and a gas. More moles and the production of more gas means increasing entropy, so ΔS will be positive.

Problems

1. (a) Use the entropy values in the table.

$$\Delta S^\circ = \sum S^\circ_{products} - \sum S^\circ_{reactants}$$

$$\Delta S^\circ = [(6)(213.6) + (6)(69.9)] - [(212.13) + (6)(205)] \text{ J/K}$$

$$\Delta S^\circ = 259 \text{ J/K}$$

(b) Use the following equation. Remember that enthalpy values are given in kJ and entropy values are given in J.

$$\Delta G^\circ = \Delta H^\circ - T\,\Delta S^\circ$$

$$\Delta G^\circ = (-2801 \text{ kJ}) - (298)(0.259 \text{ kJ}) = -2880 \text{ kJ}$$

(c) Use the following equation. Remember that the gas constant is given in terms of J.

$$\log K = \frac{\Delta G^\circ}{-2.303 RT}$$

$$\log K = \frac{(-2,880,000)}{(-2.303)(8.31)(298)} = 505$$

$$K = 10^{505}$$

(d) The enthalpy change of the reaction, ΔH°, is a measure of the energy given off by 1 mole of glucose.

$$\text{Moles} = \frac{\text{grams}}{\text{MW}}$$

$$\text{Moles of glucose} = \frac{(1.00 \text{ g})}{(180 \text{ g/mol})} = 0.00556 \text{ moles}$$

$$(0.00556 \text{ mol})(2801 \text{ kJ/mol}) = 15.6 \text{ kJ}$$

2. (a) Use the following relationship.

$$\Delta H^\circ = \sum \text{Energies of the bonds broken} - \sum \text{Energies of the bonds formed}$$

$$\Delta H^\circ = [(4)(415) + (2)(495)] - [(2)(799) + (4)(463)] \text{ kJ}$$

$$\Delta H^\circ = -800 \text{ kJ}$$

(b) Use the following equation. Remember that the gas constant is given in terms of J.

$$\log K = \frac{\Delta G^\circ}{-2.303RT}$$

$$\log K = \frac{(-801{,}000)}{(-2.303)(8.31)(298)} = 140$$

$$K = 10^{140}$$

(c) Use $\Delta G^\circ = \Delta H^\circ - T\Delta S^\circ$

Remember that enthalpy values are given in kJ and entropy values are given in J.

$$\Delta S^\circ = \frac{\Delta H - \Delta G}{T} = \frac{(-800 \text{ kJ}) - (-801 \text{ kJ})}{(298 \text{ K})}$$

$$\Delta S^\circ = 0.003 \text{ kJ/K} = 3 \text{ J/K}$$

(d) ΔS° is very small, which means that the entropy change for the process is very small. This makes sense because the number of moles remains constant, the number of moles of gas remains constant, and the complexity of the molecules remains about the same.

3. (a) By definition, ΔH°_f and ΔG°_f for $N_2(g)$ and $H_2(g)$ are equal to zero.

$$\Delta H^\circ = \sum \Delta H^\circ_{f \text{ products}} - \sum \Delta H^\circ_{f \text{ reactants}}$$

$$\Delta H^\circ = [(2 \text{ mol})(-46.2 \text{ kJ/mol})] - 0 = -92.4 \text{ kJ}$$

$$\Delta G^\circ = \sum \Delta G^\circ_{f \text{ products}} - \sum \Delta G^\circ_{f \text{ reactants}}$$

$$\Delta G^\circ = [(2 \text{ mol})(-16.7 \text{ kJ/mol})] - 0 = -33.4 \text{ kJ}$$

(b) Use $\Delta G^\circ = \Delta H^\circ - T\Delta S^\circ$

Remember that enthalpy values are given in kJ and entropy values are given in J.

$$\Delta S^\circ = \frac{\Delta H - \Delta G}{T} = \frac{(-92.4 \text{ kJ}) - (-33.4 \text{ kJ})}{(298 \text{ K})}$$

$$\Delta S^\circ = -0.198 \text{ kJ/K} = -198 \text{ J/K}$$

(c) Use $\Delta G^\circ = \Delta H^\circ - T\Delta S^\circ$

From (b), ΔS° is negative, so increasing the temperature increases the value of ΔG°, making the reaction less spontaneous.

(d) Use $\Delta G^\circ = \Delta H^\circ - T\Delta S^\circ$

At equilibrium, $\Delta G^\circ = 0$

$$T = \frac{\Delta H^\circ}{\Delta S^\circ} = \frac{(-92{,}400 \text{ J})}{(-198 \text{ J/K})} = 467 \text{ K}$$

Essays

4. (a) $\Delta S°$ is negative because the products are less random than the reactants. That's because gas is converted into liquid in the reaction.

(b) The value of $\Delta S°$ would increase, becoming less negative because $H_2O(g)$ is more random than water, but remaining negative because the entropy would still decrease from reactants to products.

(c) $\Delta G°$ is negative because the reaction proceeds spontaneously.

(d) $\Delta H°$ must be negative at 298 K. For a reaction to occur spontaneously from standard conditions, either $\Delta S°$ must be positive or $\Delta H°$ must be negative. This reaction is spontaneous even though $\Delta S°$ is negative, so $\Delta H°$ must be negative.

5. (a) $\Delta S°$ is negative because the products are less random than the reactants. That's because two moles of reactants are converted to one mole of products and gas is converted into solid in the reaction.

(b) $\Delta G°$ is negative because the reaction proceeds spontaneously.

(c) Use $\Delta G° = \Delta H° - T\Delta S°$

$\Delta G°$ will become less negative because as temperature is increased, the entropy change of a reaction becomes more important in determining its spontaneity. The entropy change for this reaction is negative, which discourages spontaneity, so increasing temperature will make the reaction less spontaneous, thus making $\Delta G°$ less negative.

(d) The concentration of CO_2 will decrease as the reaction proceeds in the forward direction and the reactants are consumed. The temperature will increase as heat is given off by the exothermic reaction.

6. (a) $\Delta S°$ is positive because the product is more random than the reactant. That's because liquid is converted into gas in the reaction.

(b) $\Delta H°$ is positive because $H_2O(g)$ is less stable than water. Energy must be put into water to overcome intermolecular forces and create water vapor.

(c) Use $\Delta G° = -2.203RT \log K$

If K is less than 1, $\log K$ will be negative, making $\Delta G°$ positive.

(d) $\Delta G°$ will be equal to zero at 373 K or 100 °C. $\Delta G°$ will be equal to zero at equilibrium. The point at which water and $H_2O(g)$ are in equilibrium is the boiling point.

SOLUTIONS

How often does this topic appear on the test?
In the multiple-choice section, this topic appears in about 7 out of 75 questions.
In the free-response section, you'll see this topic almost every year.

CONCENTRATION MEASUREMENTS

MOLARITY

Molarity (M) expresses the concentration of a solution in terms of volume. It is the most widely used unit of concentration, turning up in calculations involving equilibrium, acids and bases, and electrochemistry, among others.

When you see a chemical symbol in brackets on the test, that means that they are talking about molarity. For instance "[Na^+]" is the same as "the molar concentration (molarity) of sodium ions."

$$\text{Molarity } (M) = \frac{\text{moles of solute}}{\text{liters of solution}}$$

MOLALITY

Molality (*m*) expresses concentration in terms of the mass of solvent. It is the unit of concentration used for determining the effect of most colligative properties, where the number of moles of solute is more important than the nature of the solute.

$$\text{Molality } (m) = \frac{\text{moles of solute}}{\text{kilograms of solvent}}$$

Molarity and molality differ in two ways: Molarity tells you about moles of solute per *volume* of the *entire solution* (that is, the solute and the solvent), whereas molality tells you about moles of solute per *mass* of the *solvent*. Keeping in mind that one liter of water weighs one kilogram, and that for a dilute solution, the amount of solution is about the same as the amount of solvent, you should be able to see that for dilute aqueous solutions, molarity and molality are basically the same.

MOLE FRACTION

Mole fraction (X_s) gives the fraction of moles of a given substance (S) out of the total moles present in a sample. It is used in determining how the vapor pressure of a solution is lowered by the addition of a solute.

$$\text{Mole Fraction } (X_s) = \frac{\text{moles of substance S}}{\text{total number of moles in solution}}$$

SOLUTES AND SOLVENTS

There is a basic rule for remembering what solutes will dissolve in what solvents.

Like dissolves like

That means that polar or ionic solutes (like salt) will dissolve in polar solvents (like water). That also means that nonpolar solutes (like organic compounds) are best dissolved in nonpolar solvents. When an ionic substance dissolves, it breaks up into ions. That's **dissociation**. Free ions in a solution are called electrolytes, because they can conduct electricity.

The **van't Hoff factor (*i*)** tells how many ions one unit of a substance will dissociate into in solution. For instance:

- $C_6H_{12}O_6$ does not dissociate, so $i = 1$.
- NaCl dissociates into Na^+ and Cl^-, so $i = 2$.
- HNO_3 dissociates into H^+ and NO_3^-, so $i = 2$.
- $CaCl_2$ dissociates into Ca^{2+}, Cl^-, and Cl^-, so $i = 3$.

COLLIGATIVE PROPERTIES

Colligative properties are properties of a solution that depend on the number of solute particles in the solution. For colligative properties, the identity of the particles is not important.

BOILING POINT ELEVATION

When a solute is added to a solution, the boiling point of the solution increases.

Boiling Point Elevation

$$\Delta T = i k_b m$$

i = the van't Hoff factor, the number of particles into which the added solute dissociates
k_b = the boiling point elevation constant for the solvent
m = molality

FREEZING POINT DEPRESSION

When solute is added to a solution, the freezing point of the solution decreases.

Freezing Point Depression

$$\Delta T = i k_f m$$

i = the van't Hoff factor, the number of particles into which the added solute dissociates
k_f = the freezing point depression constant for the solvent
m = molality

VAPOR PRESSURE LOWERING

When a solute is added to a solution, the vapor pressure of the solution will decrease. You might want to note that a direct result of the lowering of vapor pressure of a solution is the raising of its boiling point.

Vapor Pressure Lowering, Raoult's Law

$$P = X P^{\circ}$$

P = vapor pressure of the solution
P° = vapor pressure of the pure solvent
X = the mole fraction of the solvent

OSMOTIC PRESSURE

When a pure solvent and a solution are separated by a membrane that only allows solvent to pass through, the solvent will try to pass through the membrane to dilute the solution. The pressure that must be applied to stop this process is called the osmotic pressure. The greater the concentration of solute in the solution, the greater the osmotic pressure. The equation for osmotic pressure takes a form that is similar to the ideal gas equation, as shown below.

Osmotic Pressure

$$\lambda = \frac{nRT}{V}i = MRTi$$

λ = osmotic pressure (atm)

n = moles of solute

R = the gas constant, 0.0821 (L-atm)/(mol-K)

T = absolute temperature (K)

V = volume of the solution (L)

i = the van't Hoff factor, the number of particles into which the added solute dissociates

M = molarity of the solution ($M = \frac{n}{V}$)

DENSITY

Density is the measure of mass per unit volume. Density can be used to describe liquids, solids, or gases. Because density relates mass and volume, it is useful if you need to convert between molarity, which deals with volume, and molality, which deals with mass.

Density of a Solution

$$D = \frac{m}{V}$$

m = mass of the solution

V = volume of the solution

SOLUBILITY

Roughly speaking, a salt can be considered to be "soluble" if more than 1 gram of the salt can be dissolved in 100 milliliters of water. Soluble salts are usually assumed to dissociate completely in aqueous solution.

SOLUBILITY PRODUCT (K_{sp})

Salts that are "slightly soluble" and "insoluble" still dissociate in solution to some extent. The solubility product (K_{sp}) is a measure of the extent of a salt's dissociation in solution. The K_{sp} is one of the forms of the equilibrium expression, which we'll discuss in Chapter 10. The greater the value of the solubility product for a salt, the more soluble the salt.

Solubility Product

For the reaction:

$$A_aB_b(s) \rightleftharpoons a\ A^{b+}(aq) + b\ B^{a-}(aq)$$

The solubility expression is:
$$K_{sp} = [A^{b+}]^a[B^{a-}]^b$$

THE COMMON ION EFFECT

Let's look at the solubility expression for AgCl.

$$K_{sp} = [Ag^+][Cl^-] = 1.6 \times 10^{-10}$$

If we throw a block of solid AgCl into a beaker of water, we can tell from the K_{sp} what the concentrations of Ag^+ and Cl^- will be at equilibrium. For every unit of AgCl that dissociates, we get one Ag^+ and one Cl^-, so we can solve the equation above as follows.

$$[Ag^+][Cl^-] = 1.6 \times 10^{-10}$$

$$(x)(x) = 1.6 \times 10^{-10}$$

$$x^2 = 1.6 \times 10^{-10}$$

$$x = [Ag^+] = [Cl^-] = 1.3 \times 10^{-5}\ M$$

So there are very small amounts of Ag^+ and Cl^- in the solution.

Let's say we add 0.10 mole of NaCl to 1 liter of the AgCl solution. NaCl dissociates completely, so that's the same thing as adding 1 mole of Na^+ ions and 1 mole of Cl^- ions to the solution. The Na^+ ions will not affect the AgCl equilibrium, so we can ignore them, but the Cl^- ions must be taken into account. That's because of the common ion effect.

The common ion effect says that the newly added Cl^- ions will affect the AgCl equilibrium, even though the newly added Cl^- ions did not come from AgCl.

Let's look at the solubility expression again, but now we have 0.10 mole of Cl^- ions in 1 liter of the solution, so $[Cl^-] = 0.10$ M.

$$[Ag^+][Cl^-] = 1.6 \times 10^{-10}$$

$$[Ag^+](0.10\ M) = 1.6 \times 10^{-10}$$

$$[Ag^+] = \frac{\left(1.6 \times 10^{-10}\right)}{(0.10)} M$$

$$[Ag^+] = 1.6 \times 10^{-9}\ M$$

Now the number of Ag^+ ions in the solution has decreased drastically because of the Cl^- ions introduced to the solution by NaCl. So when solutions of AgCl and NaCl, which share a common Cl^- ion, are mixed, the more soluble salt (NaCl) can cause the less soluble salt (AgCl) to precipitate. In general, when two salt solutions that share a common ion are mixed, the salt with the lower value for K_{sp} will precipitate first.

SOLUBILITY RULES

You should have a good working knowledge of the solubilities of common salts. This is especially useful for the part in Section II, where you are asked to predict the outcome of chemical reactions.

Cations

- **Alkali Metals**: Li^+, Na^+, K^+, Rb^+, Cs^+
  All salts of the alkali metals are **soluble**.

- **Ammonium**: NH_4^+
  All ammonium salts are **soluble**.

- **Alkaline Earths and Transition Metals**
  The solubility of these elements varies depending on the identity of the anion.

Anions

These are mostly soluble.

- **Nitrate**: NO_3^-
  All nitrate salts are **soluble**.

- **Chlorate**: ClO_3^-
  All chlorate salts are **soluble**.

- **Perchlorate**: ClO_4^-
  All perchlorate salts are **soluble**.

- **Acetate**: $C_2H_3O_2^-$
  All acetate salts are **soluble**.

- **Chloride, Bromide, Iodide**: Cl^-, Br^-, I^-
  Salts containing Cl^-, Br^-, and I^- are **soluble**.
  EXCEPT for those containing: Ag^+, Pb^{2+}, and Hg_2^{2+}.

- **Sulfate**: SO_4^{2-}
  Sulfate salts are **soluble**.
  EXCEPT for those containing: Ag^+, Pb^{2+}, Hg_2^{2+}, Ca^{2+}, Sr^{2+}, and Ba^{2+}.

These are mostly insoluble.

- **Hydroxide**: OH^-
  Hydroxide salts are **insoluble**.
  EXCEPT for those containing alkali metals, which are soluble.
  AND those containing Ca^{2+}, Sr^{2+}, and Ba^{2+}, which fall in the grey area of moderate solubility.

- **Carbonate**: CO_3^{2-}
  Carbonate salts are **insoluble**.
  EXCEPT for those containing alkali metals and ammonium, which are soluble.

- **Phosphate**: PO_4^{3-}
  Phosphate salts are **insoluble**.
  EXCEPT for those containing alkali metals and ammonium, which are soluble.

- **Sulfite**: SO_3^{2-}
  Sulfite salts are **insoluble**.
  EXCEPT for those containing alkali metals and ammonium, which are soluble.

- **Chromate**: CrO_4^{2-}
  Chromate salts are **insoluble**.
  EXCEPT for those containing alkali metals and ammonium, which are soluble.

- **Sulfide**: S^{2-}
  Sulfide salts are **insoluble**.
  EXCEPT for those containing alkali metals, the alkaline earths, and ammonium, which are soluble.

SOLUTIONS

QUESTIONS

Multiple choice

Questions 1–4

    (A) Molarity (M)
    (B) Molality (m)
    (C) Density
    (D) pH
    (E) pOH

1. Has the units moles/kg.

2. This is the negative logarithm of the hydrogen ion concentration.

3. Can have the units grams/liter.

4. Has the units moles per liter.

5. Which of the following is (are) colligative properties?

    I. freezing point depression
    II. vapor pressure lowering
    III. boiling point elevation

    (A) I only
    (B) I and II only
    (C) I and III only
    (D) II and III only
    (E) I, II, and III

6. Which of the following aqueous solutions has the highest boiling point?

    (A) 0.5 m NaCl
    (B) 0.5 m KBr
    (C) 0.5 m $CaCl_2$
    (D) 0.5 m $C_6H_{12}O_6$
    (E) 0.5 m $NaNO_3$

7. When sodium chloride is added to a saturated aqueous solution of silver chloride, which of the following precipitates would be expected to appear?

    (A) Sodium
    (B) Silver
    (C) Chlorine
    (D) Sodium chloride
    (E) Silver chloride

8. A substance is dissolved in water, forming a 0.50-molar solution. If 4.0 liters of solution contains 240 grams of the substance, what is the molecular mass of the substance?

    (A) 60 grams/mole
    (B) 120 grams/mole
    (C) 240 grams/mole
    (D) 480 grams/mole
    (E) 640 grams/mole

9. The solubility product, K_{sp}, of AgCl is 1.8×10^{-10}. Which of the following expressions is equal to the solubility of AgCl?

(A) $\left(1.8 \times 10^{-10}\right)^2$ molar

(B) $\dfrac{1.8 \times 10^{-10}}{2}$ molar

(C) 1.8×10^{-10} molar

(D) $(2)\left(1.8 \times 10^{-10}\right)$ molar

(E) $\sqrt{1.8 \times 10^{-10}}$ molar

10. A 0.1-molar solution of which of the following acids will be the best conductor of electricity?

(A) $HC_2H_3O_2$
(B) H_2CO_3
(C) H_2S
(D) HF
(E) HNO_3

11. When 31 grams of a nonionic substance is dissolved in 2.00 kg of water, the observed freezing point depression of the solution is 0.93 °C. If k_f for water is 1.86 °C/m, which of the following expressions is equal to the molar mass of the substance?

(A) $\dfrac{(31.0)(0.93)(2.00)}{(1.86)}$ g/mole

(B) $\dfrac{(31.0)(1.86)}{(0.93)(2.00)}$ g/mole

(C) $\dfrac{(1.86)(2.00)}{(31.0)(0.93)}$ g/mole

(D) $\dfrac{(0.93)}{(31.0)(1.86)(2.00)}$ g/mole

(E) $(31.0)(0.93)(1.86)(2.00)$ g/mole

12. What is the boiling point of a 2 m solution of NaCl in water? (The boiling point elevation constant, k_b, for water is 0.5 °C/m)

(A) 100 °C
(B) 101 °C
(C) 102 °C
(D) 103 °C
(E) 104 °C

13. When an aqueous salt solution is compared to water, the salt solution will have

(A) a higher boiling point, a lower freezing point, and a lower vapor pressure.
(B) a higher boiling point, a higher freezing point, and a lower vapor pressure.
(C) a higher boiling point, a higher freezing point, and a higher vapor pressure.
(D) a lower boiling point, a lower freezing point, and a lower vapor pressure.
(E) a lower boiling point, a higher freezing point, and a higher vapor pressure.

14. If 46 grams of $MgBr_2$ (molar mass 184 grams) is dissolved in water to form 0.50 liters of solution, what is the concentration of bromine ions in the solution?

(A) 0.25-molar
(B) 0.50-molar
(C) 1.0-molar
(D) 2.0-molar
(E) 4.0-molar

15. A solution contains equal masses of glucose (molecular mass 180) and toluene (molecular mass 90). What is the mole fraction of glucose in the solution?

(A) $\dfrac{1}{4}$

(B) $\dfrac{1}{3}$

(C) $\dfrac{1}{2}$

(D) $\dfrac{2}{3}$

(E) $\dfrac{3}{4}$

16. When benzene and toluene are mixed together, they form an ideal solution. If benzene has a higher vapor pressure than toluene, then the vapor pressure of a solution that contains an equal number of moles of benzene and toluene will be

(A) higher than the vapor pressure of benzene
(B) equal to the vapor pressure of benzene
(C) lower than the vapor pressure of benzene and higher than the vapor pressure of toluene
(D) equal to the vapor pressure of toluene
(E) lower than the vapor pressure of toluene

17. How many moles of Na_2SO_4 must be added to 500 milliliters of water to create a solution that has a 2-molar concentration of the Na^+ ion? (Assume the volume of the solution does not change).

(A) 0.5 moles
(B) 1 mole
(C) 2 moles
(D) 4 moles
(E) 5 moles

18. Given that a solution of NaCl (molar mass 58.5 g/mole) in water (molar mass 18 g/mole) has a molality of 0.5 m, which of the following can be determined?

 I. The mass of the NaCl in the solution
 II. The total mass of the solution
 III. The mole fraction of the NaCl in the solution

(A) I only
(B) III only
(C) I and II only
(D) II and III only
(E) I, II, and III

19. How many liters of water must be added to 4 liters of a 6-molar HNO_3 solution to create a solution that is 2-molar?

(A) 2 liters
(B) 4 liters
(C) 6 liters
(D) 8 liters
(E) 12 liters

20. Which of the following expressions is equal to the K_{sp} of Ag_2CO_3?

(A) $K_{sp} = [Ag^+][CO_3^{2-}]$
(B) $K_{sp} = [Ag^+][CO_3^{2-}]^2$
(C) $K_{sp} = [Ag^+]^2[CO_3^{2-}]$
(D) $K_{sp} = [Ag^+]^2[CO_3^{2-}]^2$
(E) $K_{sp} = [Ag^+]^2[CO_3^{2-}]^3$

Problems

1. The molecular weight and formula of a hydrocarbon are to be determined through the use of the freezing-point depression method. The hydrocarbon is known to be 86% carbon and 14% hydrogen by mass. In the experiment, 3.72 grams of the unknown hydrocarbon were placed into 50.0 grams of liquid benzene, C_6H_6. The freezing point of the solution was measured to be 0.06 °C. The normal freezing point of benzene is 5.50 °C and the freezing point depression constant for benzene is 5.12 °C/m.

   (a) What is the molecular weight of the compound?

   (b) What is the molecular formula of the hydrocarbon?

   (c) What is the mole fraction of benzene in the solution?

   (d) If the density of the solution is 875 grams per liter, what is the molarity of the solution?

2. The value of the solubility product, K_{sp}, for calcium hydroxide, $Ca(OH)_2$, is 5.5×10^{-6}, at 25 °C.

   (a) Write the K_{sp} expression for calcium hydroxide.

   (b) What is the mass of $Ca(OH)_2$ in 500. ml of a saturated solution at 25 °C?

   (c) What is the pH of the solution in (b)?

   (d) If 1.0 mole of OH^- is added to the solution in (b), what will be the resulting Ca^{2+} concentration? Assume that the volume of the solution does not change.

Essays

3. Explain the following statements in terms of the chemical properties of the substances involved.

   (a) A 1-molal aqueous solution of sodium chloride has a lower freezing point than a 1-molal aqueous solution of ethanol.

   (b) NaCl is a strong electrolyte, whereas $PbCl_2$ is a weak electrolyte.

   (c) Propanol is soluble in water, but propane is not.

   (d) In a dilute aqueous solution, molarity and molality will have the same value.

4. For most salts, the solution process with water is endothermic.

   (a) Describe the change in entropy when a solid salt dissociates into aqueous particles.

   (b) Does the solubility of most salts increase or decrease at high temperatures? Explain.

   (c) The solubility product of $Ce_2(SO_4)_3$ decreases as temperature increases. Is the solution process for this salt endothermic or exothermic?

   (d) When equal molar quantities of HF and HCl are added to separate containers filled with the same amount of water, the HCl solution will freeze at a lower temperature.

ANSWERS

Multiple choice

1. **(B)** is correct. Molality is the measure of moles of solute per kilograms of solvent.

2. **(D)** is correct. $pH = -\log[H^+]$

3. **(C)** is correct. Density is a measure of mass per unit volume; for example, grams per liter.

4. **(A)** is correct. Molarity is the measure of moles of solute per liter of solution.

5. **(E)** is correct. All of the choices are colligative properties, which means that they depend only on the number of particles in solution, not on the identity of those particles.

6. **(C)** is correct. Boiling point elevation is a colligative property. That is, it depends only on the number of particles in solution, not on the specific particles.

    Remember the formula: $\Delta T = kmx$.

    All of the solutions have the same molality, so the one with the greatest boiling point elevation will be the one that breaks up into the most ions in solution. $CaCl_2$ breaks up into 3 ions, $C_6H_{12}O_6$ doesn't break up into ions, and the other three break up into 2 ions.

7. **(E)** is correct. Sodium chloride is much more soluble than silver chloride. Because of the common ion effect, the chloride ions introduced into the solution by sodium chloride will disrupt the silver chloride equilibrium, causing silver chloride to precipitate from the solution.

8. **(B)** is correct. First find the number of moles.

    Moles = (molarity)(volume)

    Moles of substance = (0.50 M)(4.0 L) = 2 moles

    $$Moles = \frac{grams}{MW}$$

    So $MW = \dfrac{240g}{2\ mol} = 120$ grams/mole

9. **(E)** is correct. The solubility of a substance is equal to its maximum concentration in solution.

    For every AgCl in solution, we get one Ag^+ and one Cl^-, so the solubility of AgCl, let's call it x, will be the same as $[Ag^+]$, which is the same as $[Cl^-]$.

    So, for AgCl, $K_{sp} = [Ag^+][Cl^-] = 1.8 \times 10^{-10} = x^2$.

    $x = \sqrt{1.8 \times 10^{-10}}$

10. **(E)** is correct. The best conductor of electricity (also called the strongest electrolyte) will be the solution that contains the most charged particles. HNO_3 is the only strong acid listed in the answer choices, so it is the only choice where the acid has dissociated completely in solution into H^+ and NO_3^- ions. So a 0.1-molar HNO_3 solution will contain the most charged particles and therefore be the best conductor of electricity.

11. **(B)** is correct. We can get the molality from the freezing point depression with the expression $\Delta T = k_1 m x$. Because the substance is nonionic, it will not dissociate and x will be equal to 1, so we can leave it out of the calculation.

$$m = \frac{\Delta T}{k_f}$$

We know the molality and the mass of the solvent, so we can calculate the number of moles of solute.

$$\text{Moles} = (\text{molality})(\text{kilograms of solvent}) = \frac{\Delta T}{k_f}(\text{kg})$$

Now we use one of our stoichiometry relationships.

$$\text{Moles} = \frac{\text{grams}}{\text{MW}}$$

So, $\text{MW} = \dfrac{\text{grams}}{\text{moles}} = \dfrac{(\text{grams})}{\left(\dfrac{(\Delta T)(\text{kg})}{k_f}\right)} = \dfrac{(\text{grams})(k_f)}{(\Delta T)(\text{kg})} = \dfrac{(31.0\text{g})(1.86\text{K}-\text{kg/mol})}{(0.93\text{ K})(2.00\text{kg})}$

$$= \frac{(31.0)(1.86)}{(0.93)(2.00)} \text{ grams/mol}$$

12. **(C)** is correct. $\Delta T = k_b m x$.

Each NaCl dissociates into two particles, so $x = 2$.
$$\Delta T = (0.5\ °\text{C}/m)(2\ m)(2) = 2\ °\text{C}.$$
So the boiling point of the solution is 102 °C.

13. **(A)** is correct. Particles in solution tend to interfere with phase changes, so the boiling point is raised, freezing point is lowered, and the vapor pressure is lowered.

14. **(C)** is correct. First we'll find the molarity of the $MgBr_2$ solution.

$$\text{Moles} = \frac{\text{grams}}{\text{MW}}$$

$$\text{Moles of } MgBr_2 \text{ added} = \frac{(46\text{g})}{(184\text{g/mol})} = 0.25 \text{ moles}$$

$$\text{Molarity} = \frac{\text{moles}}{\text{liters}} = \frac{(0.25 \text{ mol})}{(0.50 \text{ L})} = 0.50\text{-molar}$$

For every $MgBr_2$ in solution, 2 Br^- ions are produced, so a 0.50-molar $MgBr_2$ solution will have twice the concentration of Br^- ions, so the bromine ion concentration is 1.0-molar.

15. **(B)** is correct. Let's say the solution contains 180 grams of glucose and 180 grams of toluene. That's 1 mole of glucose and 2 moles of toluene. So that's 1 mole of glucose out of a total of 3 moles, for a mole fraction of $\dfrac{1}{3}$.

16. **(C)** is correct. From Raoult's law, the vapor pressure of an ideal solution depends on the mole fractions of the components of the solution. The vapor pressure of a solution with equal amounts of benzene and toluene will look like this:

$$(P_{\text{solution}}) = (\tfrac{1}{2})(P_{\text{benzene}}) + (\tfrac{1}{2})(P_{\text{toluene}})$$

That's just the average of the two vapor pressures.

17. **(A)** is correct. Let's find out how many moles of Na^+ we have to add.

Moles = (molarity)(volume)

Moles of Na^+ = (2 M)(0.5 L) = 1 mole.

Since we get 2 moles of Na^+ ions for every mole of Na_2SO_4 we add, we only need to add 0.5 moles of Na_2SO_4.

18. **(B)** is correct. We can't determine (I) and (II) because we don't know how much solution we have. We can figure out (III) because molality tells us the number of moles of NaCl found in 1 kilogram of water. We can figure out how many moles of water there are in 1 kilogram. So if we have a ratio of moles of NaCl to moles of water, we can figure out the mole fraction of NaCl.

19. **(D)** is correct. The number of moles of HNO_3 remains constant.

Moles = (molarity)(volume)

Moles of HNO_3 = (6 M)(4 L) = (2 M)(x)

x = 12 liters, but that's not the answer.

To get a 2-molar solution we need 12 liters, but the solution already has 4 liters, so we need to add 8 liters of water. That's the answer.

20. **(C)** is correct. K_{sp} is just the equilibrium constant without a denominator.

When Ag_2CO_3 dissociates, we get the following reaction:

$$Ag_2CO_3(s) \rightleftharpoons 2\ Ag^+ + CO_3^{2-}$$

In the equilibrium expression, coefficients become exponents, so we get:

$$K_{sp} = [Ag^+]^2[CO_3^{2-}]$$

Problems

1. (a) First we'll find the molality of the solution. The freezing point depression, ΔT, is:
5.50 °C − 0.06 °C = 5.44 °C.

$$\Delta T = km$$

Solve for m

$$m = \frac{\Delta T}{k} = \frac{(5.44\ ^\circ C)}{(5.12\ ^\circ C/m)} = 1.06\ m$$

From the molality of the solution, we can find the number of moles of unknown hydrocarbon.

$$Molality = \frac{moles\ of\ solute}{kg\ of\ solvent}$$

Solve for moles.

Moles = (molality)(kg of solvent)

Moles of hydrocarbon = (1.06 m)(0.050 kg) = 0.053 moles

Now we can find the molecular weight of the hydrocarbon.

$$MW = \frac{grams}{moles} = \frac{(3.72\ g)}{(0.053\ mol)} = 70.2\ g/mol$$

(b) You can use the percent by mass and the molecular weight.

For carbon:

$(86\%)(70 \text{ g/mol}) = 60 \text{ g/mol}$

Carbon has an atomic weight of 12, so there must be $\dfrac{60}{12} = 5$ moles of carbon in 1 mole of the hydrocarbon.

For hydrogen:

$(14\%)(70 \text{ g/mol}) = 10 \text{ g/mol}$

Hydrogen has an atomic weight of 1, so there must be $\dfrac{10}{1} = 10$ moles of hydrogen in 1 mole of the hydrocarbon.

So the molecular formula for the hydrocarbon is C_5H_{10}.

(c) We know that there are 0.053 moles of hydrocarbon. We need to find the number of moles of benzene.

$$\text{Moles} = \frac{\text{grams}}{\text{MW}}$$

$$\text{Moles of benzene} = \frac{(50.00 \text{ g})}{(78 \text{ g/mol})} = 0.64 \text{ mol}$$

Total moles = 0.64 mol + 0.053 mol = 0.69 mol

$$\text{Mole fraction of benzene} = \frac{0.64 \text{ mol}}{0.69 \text{ mol}}$$

(d) Remember the definition of molarity.

$$\text{Molarity} = \frac{\text{moles of solute}}{\text{liters of solution}}$$

We know that the moles of solute is 0.053. We need to find the liters of solution.

The weight of the solution is:

50.00 g + 3.72 g = 53.72 g

$$\text{Density} = \frac{\text{grams}}{\text{liters}}$$

Solve for liters.

$$\text{Liters of solution} = \frac{\text{grams}}{\text{density}} = \frac{(53.72 \text{ g})}{(875 \text{ g/L})} = 0.0614 \text{ L}$$

$$\text{Molarity} = \frac{(0.053 \text{ mol})}{(0.0614 \text{ L})} = 0.863 \text{ } M$$

2. (a) The solubility product is the same as the equilibrium expression, but since the reactant is a solid, there is no denominator.

$K_{sp} = [Ca^{2+}][OH^-]^2$

(b) Use the solubility product.

$K_{sp} = [Ca^{2+}][OH^-]^2$

$5.5 \times 10^{-6} = (x)(2x)^2 = 4x^3$

$x = 0.01 \text{ } M$ for Ca^{2+}

One mole of calcium hydroxide produces 1 mole of Ca^{2+}, so the concentration of $Ca(OH)_2$ must be 0.01 M.

Moles = (molarity)(volume)

Moles of $Ca(OH)_2$ = (0.01 M)(0.500 L) = 0.005 moles

Grams = (moles)(MW)

Grams of $Ca(OH)_2$ = (0.005 mol)(74 g/mol) = 0.37 g

(c) We can find $[OH^-]$ from (b).

If $[Ca^{2+}]$ = 0.01 M, then $[OH^-]$ must be twice that, so $[OH^-]$ = 0.02 M

pOH = $-\log[OH^-]$ = 1.7

pH = 14 − pOH = 14 − 1.7 = 12.3

(d) Find the new $[OH^-]$. The hydroxide already present is small enough to ignore, so we'll only use the hydroxide just added.

$$Molarity = \frac{moles}{liters}$$

$$[OH^-] = \frac{(1.0 \text{ mol})}{(0.500 \text{ L})} = 2.0 \ M$$

Now use the K_{sp} expression.

$K_{sp} = [Ca^{2+}][OH^-]^2$

$5.5 \times 10^{-6} = [Ca^{2+}](2.0 \ M)^2$

$[Ca^{2+}] = 1.4 \times 10^{-6} \ M$

Essays

3. (a) Freezing point depression is a colligative property, which means that it depends on the number of particles in solution, not their identity.

Sodium chloride dissociates into Na^+ and Cl^-, so every unit of sodium chloride produces two particles in solution. Ethanol does not dissociate, so sodium chloride will put twice as many particles in solution as ethanol.

(b) An electrolyte is a substance that ionizes in solution, thus causing the solution to conduct electricity.

Both of the salts dissociate into ions, but $PbCl_2$ is almost insoluble, so it will produce very few ions in solution, while NaCl is extremely soluble, and produces many ions.

(c) Water is best at dissolving polar substances.

Propanol (C_3H_7OH) has a hydroxide group, which makes it polar, and thus, soluble in water. Propane (C_3H_8) is nonpolar and is best dissolved in nonpolar solvents.

(d) Remember the definitions and remember that a dilute solution has very little solute.

$$Molarity = \frac{moles \ of \ solute}{liters \ of \ solution}$$

$$Molality = \frac{moles \ of \ solute}{kilograms \ of \ solvent}$$

For water, 1 liter weighs 1 kilogram, so for a dilute solution this distinction disappears.

If there is very little solute, the mass and volume of the solution will be indistinguishable from the mass and volume of the solvent.

4.   (a) Entropy increases when a salt dissociates because aqueous particles have more randomness than a solid.

(b) Most salt solution processes are endothermic, and endothermic processes are favored by an increase in temperature, therefore increasing temperature will increase the solubility of most salts.

(c) $Ce_2(SO_4)_3$ becomes less soluble as temperature increases, so the solution process for this salt must be exothermic.

(d) Freezing point depression is a colligative property, which means that it depends on the number of particles in solution, not their identity.

HCl is a strong acid, which means that it dissociates completely. This means that 1 mole of HCl in solution will produce 2 moles of particles. HF is a weak acid, which means that it dissociates very little. This means that 1 mole of HF in solution will remain at about 1 mole of particles in solution.

So the HCl solution will have more particles than the HF solution.

10

EQUILIBRIUM

How often does this topic appear on the test?

In the multiple-choice section, this topic appears in about 4 out of 75 questions.
In the free-response section, you'll see this topic every year.

THE EQUILIBRIUM CONSTANT, K_{EQ}

Most chemical processes are reversible. That is, reactants react to form products, but those products can also react to form reactants.

A reaction is at equilibrium when the rate of the forward reaction is equal to the rate of the reverse reaction

The relationship between the concentrations of reactants and products in a reaction at equilibrium is given by the equilibrium expression, also called the **law of mass action**.

The Equilibrium Expression

For the reaction:

$$aA + bB \rightleftharpoons cC + dD$$

$$K_{eq} = \frac{[C]^c[D]^d}{[A]^a[B]^b}$$

1. [A], [B], [C], and [D] are molar concentrations or partial pressures at equilibrium.
2. Products are in the numerator, and reactants are in the denominator.
3. Coefficients in the balanced equation become exponents in the equilibrium expression.
4. Solids and pure liquids are ignored.
5. Units are not given for K_{eq}.

Let's look at a few examples:

1. $HC_2H_3O_2(aq) \rightleftharpoons H^+(aq) + C_2H_3O_2^-(aq)$

$$K_{eq} = K_a = \frac{[H^+][C_2H_3O_2^-]}{[HC_2H_3O_2]}$$

This reaction shows the dissociation of acetic acid in water. All of the reactants and products are aqueous particles, so they are all included in the equilibrium expression. None of the reactants or products have coefficients, so there are no exponents in the equilibrium expression. This is the standard form of K_a, the acid dissociation constant.

2. $2H_2S(g) + 3O_2(g) \rightleftharpoons 2H_2O(g) + 2SO_2(g)$

$$K_{eq} = K_c = \frac{[H_2O]^2[SO_2]^2}{[H_2S]^2[O_2]^3}$$

$$K_{eq} = K_p = \frac{P^2_{H_2O}P^2_{SO_2}}{P^2_{H_2S}P^3_{O_2}}$$

All of the reactants and products in this reaction are gases, so K_{eq} can be expressed in terms of concentration (K_c, moles/liter or molarity), or in terms of partial pressure (K_p, atmospheres). In the next section, we'll see how these two different ways of looking at the same equilibrium situation are related. All of the reactants and products are included here and the coefficients in the reaction become exponents in the equilibrium expression.

3. $CaF_2(s) \rightleftharpoons Ca^{2+}(aq) + 2\,F^-(aq)$

$$K_{eq} = K_{sp} = [Ca^{2+}][F^-]^2$$

This reaction shows the dissociation of a slightly soluble salt. There is no denominator in this equilibrium expression because the reactant is a solid. Solids are left out of the equilibrium expression because the concentration of a solid is constant. There must be some solid present in order for equilibrium to exist, but you do not need to include it in your calculations. This form of K_{eq} is called the solubility product, K_{sp}, which we already saw in the chapter on solutions.

4. $NH_3(aq) + H_2O(l) \rightleftharpoons NH_4^+(aq) + OH^-(aq)$

$$K_{eq} = K_b = \frac{[NH_4^+][OH^-]}{[NH_3]}$$

This is the acid-base reaction between ammonia and water. We can leave water out of the equilibrium expression because it is a pure liquid. By pure liquid, we mean that the concentration of water is so large (about 50-molar) that nothing that happens in the reaction is going to change it significantly, so we can consider it to be constant. This is the standard form for K_b, the base dissociation constant.

Here is a roundup of the equilibrium constants you need to be familiar with for the test.

- K_c is the constant for molar concentrations.

- K_p is the constant for partial pressures.

- K_{sp} is the solubility product, which has no denominator because the reactants are solids.

- K_a is the acid dissociation constant, for weak acids.

- K_b is the base dissociation constant, for weak bases.

- K_w describes the ionization of water ($K_w = 1 \times 10^{-14}$).

The equilibrium constant has a lot of aliases, but they all take the same form and tell you the same thing: The equilibrium constant tells you the relative amounts of products and reactants at equilibrium.

A large value for K_{eq} means that products are favored over reactants at equilibrium, while a small value for K_{eq} means that reactants are favored over products at equilibrium.

K_{EQ} AND GASES

As we saw in the example above, the equilibrium constant for a gas phase reaction can be written in terms of molar concentrations, K_c, or partial pressures, K_p. These two forms of K can be related by the following equation, which is derived from the ideal gas law.

$$K_p = K_c(RT)^{\Delta n}$$

K_p = partial pressure constant (using atmospheres as units)

K_c = molar concentration constant (using molarities as units)

R = the ideal gas constant, 0.0821 (L-atm)/(mol-K)

T = absolute temperature (K)

Δn = (Moles of product gas – moles of reactant gas)

THE REACTION QUOTIENT, Q

The reaction quotient is determined in exactly the same way as the equilibrium constant, but initial conditions are used in the place of equilibrium conditions. The reaction quotient can be used to predict the direction in which a reaction will proceed from a given set of initial conditions.

The Reaction Quotient

For the reaction:

$$aA + bB \rightleftharpoons cC + dD$$

$$Q = \frac{[C]^c[D]^d}{[A]^a[B]^b}$$

[A], [B], [C], and [D] are initial molar concentrations or partial pressures.

- If Q is less than the calculated K for the reaction, the reaction proceeds forward, generating products.
- If Q is greater than K, the reaction proceeds backward, generating reactants.
- If $Q = K$, the reaction is already at equilibrium.

K_{EQ} AND MULTISTEP PROCESSES

There is a simple relationship between the equilibrium constants for the steps of a multistep reaction and the equilibrium constant for the overall reaction.

If two reactions can be added together to create a third reaction, then the K_{eq}s for the two reactions can be multiplied together to get the K_{eq} for the third reaction.

If	$A + B \rightleftharpoons C$	$K_{eq} = K_1$
and	$C \rightleftharpoons D + E$	$K_{eq} = K_2$
then	$A + B \rightleftharpoons D + E$	$K_{eq} = K_1K_2$

LE CHATELIER'S LAW

Le Chatelier's law says that whenever a stress is placed on a situation at equilibrium, the equilibrium will shift to relieve that stress.

Let's use the Haber process, which is used in the industrial preparation of ammonia, as an example:

$$N_2(g) + 3\,H_2(g) \rightleftharpoons 2\,NH_3(g) \qquad\qquad \Delta H° = -92.6 \text{ kJ}$$

CONCENTRATION

- When the concentration of a reactant or product is increased, the reaction will proceed in the direction that will use up the added substance.

If N_2 or H_2 is added, the reaction proceeds in the forward direction. If NH_3 is added, the reaction proceeds in the reverse direction.

- When the concentration of a reactant or product is decreased, the reaction will proceed in the direction that will produce more of the substance that has been removed.

If N_2 or H_2 is removed, the reaction will proceed in the reverse direction. If NH_3 is removed, the reaction will proceed in the forward direction.

VOLUME

- When the volume in which a reaction takes place is increased, the reaction will proceed in the direction that produces more moles of gas.

When the volume for the Haber process is increased, the reaction proceeds in the reverse direction because the reactants have more moles of gas (4) than the products (2).

- When the volume in which a reaction takes place is decreased, the reaction will proceed in the direction that produces fewer moles of gas.

When the volume for the Haber process is decreased, the reaction proceeds in the forward direction because the products have fewer moles of gas (2) than the reactants (4).

- If there is no gas involved in the reaction, or if the reactants and products have the same number of moles of gas, then volume changes have no effect on the equilibrium.

TEMPERATURE

- When temperature is increased, the reaction will proceed in the endothermic direction.

When the temperature for the Haber process is increased, the reaction proceeds in the reverse direction because the reverse reaction is endothermic (ΔH° is positive).

- When temperature is decreased, the reaction will proceed in the exothermic direction.

When the temperature for the Haber process is decreased, the reaction proceeds in the forward direction because the forward reaction is exothermic (ΔH° is negative).

EQUILIBRIUM

Questions

Multiple choice

Questions 1–4

    (A) K_c
    (B) K_p
    (C) K_a
    (D) K_w
    (E) K_{sp}

1. This equilibrium constant uses partial pressures of gases as units.

2. This equilibrium constant always has a value of 1×10^{-14} at 25 °C.

3. This equilibrium constant is used for the dissociation of an acid.

4. The equilibrium expression for this equilibrium constant does not contain a denominator.

5. For a particular salt, the solution process is endothermic. As the temperature at which the salt is dissolved increases, which of the following will occur?

    (A) K_{sp} will increase and the salt will become more soluble.
    (B) K_{sp} will decrease and the salt will become more soluble.
    (C) K_{sp} will increase and the salt will become less soluble.
    (D) K_{sp} will decrease and the salt will become less soluble.
    (E) K_{sp} will not change and the salt will become more soluble.

6. $2\,HI(g) + Cl_2(g) \rightleftharpoons$
$$2\,HCl(g) + I_2(g) + energy$$

A gaseous reaction occurs and comes to equilibrium as shown above. Which of the following changes to the system will serve to increase the number of moles of I_2 present at equilibrium?

    (A) Increasing the volume at constant temperature
    (B) Decreasing the volume at constant temperature
    (C) Adding a mole of inert gas at constant volume
    (D) Increasing the temperature at constant volume
    (E) Decreasing the temperature at constant volume

7. A sealed isothermal container initially contained 2 moles of CO gas and 3 moles of H_2 gas. The following reversible reaction occurred:

$$CO(g) + 2\,H_2(g) \rightleftharpoons CH_3OH(g)$$

At equilibrium, there was 1 mole of CH_3OH in the container. What was the total number of moles of gas present in the container at equilibrium?

(A) 1
(B) 2
(C) 3
(D) 4
(E) 5

8. $4\,NH_3(g) + 3\,O_2(g) \rightleftharpoons$

$$2\,N_2(g) + 6\,H_2O(g) + energy$$

Which of the following changes to the system at equilibrium shown above would cause the concentration of H_2O to increase?

(A) The volume of the system was decreased at constant temperature.
(B) The temperature of the system was increased at constant volume.
(C) NH_3 was removed from the system.
(D) N_2 was removed from the system.
(E) O_2 was removed from the system.

9. A sample of solid potassium nitrate is placed in water. The solid potassium nitrate comes to equilibrium with its dissolved ions by the endothermic process shown below:

$$KNO_3(s) + energy \rightleftharpoons K^+(aq) + NO_3^-(aq)$$

Which of the following changes to the system would increase the concentration of K^+ ions at equilibrium?

(A) The volume of the solution is increased.
(B) The volume of the solution is decreased.
(C) Additional solid KNO_3 is added to the solution.
(D) The temperature of the solution is increased.
(E) The temperature of the solution is decreased.

10. Citric acid, $H_3C_6H_5O_7$, can give up three hydrogen ions in solution. The three dissociation reactions are as follows:

$$H_3C_6H_5O_7 \rightleftharpoons H^+ + H_2C_6H_5O_7^- \qquad K_1 = x$$

$$H_2C_6H_5O_7^- \rightleftharpoons H^+ + HC_6H_5O_7^{2-} \qquad K_2 = y$$

$$HC_6H_5O_7^{2-} \rightleftharpoons H^+ + C_6H_5O_7^{3-} \qquad K_3 = z$$

Which of the following expressions gives the equilibrium constant for the reaction shown below?

$$H_3C_6H_5O_7 \rightleftharpoons 3\,H^+ + C_6H_5O_7^{3-}$$

(A) xyz

(B) $\dfrac{xy}{z}$

(C) $\dfrac{x}{yz}$

(D) $\dfrac{z}{xy}$

(E) $\dfrac{1}{xyz}$

11. $$H_2(g) + I_2(g) \rightleftharpoons 2\,HI(g)$$

At 450 °C the equilibrium constant, K_c, for the reaction shown above has a value of 50. Which of the following is true of the reaction at equilibrium?

(A) The rate of the forward reaction is greater than the rate of the reverse reaction.

(B) The rate of the forward reaction is less than the rate of the reverse reaction.

(C) The rate of the forward reaction is equal to the rate of the reverse reaction.

(D) An increase in the volume of the system will cause an increase in the value of K_c.

(E) An decrease in the volume of the system will cause an increase in the value of K_c.

12. $$2\,NOBr(g) \rightleftharpoons 2\,NO(g) + Br_2(g)$$

The reaction above came to equilibrium at a temperature of 100 °C. At equilibrium the partial pressure due to NOBr was 4 atmospheres, the partial pressure due to NO was 4 atmospheres, and the partial pressure due to Br_2 was 2 atmospheres. What is the equilibrium constant, K_p, for this reaction at 100 °C?

(A) $\dfrac{1}{4}$

(B) $\dfrac{1}{2}$

(C) 1

(D) 2

(E) 4

Problems

1.
$$BaF_2(s) \rightleftharpoons Ba^{2+}(aq) + 2\,F^-(aq)$$

The value of the solubility product , K_{sp}, for the reaction above is 1.0×10^{-6} at 25 °C.

(a)   Write the K_{sp} expression for BaF_2.

(b)   What is the concentration of F^- ions in a saturated solution of BaF_2 at 25 °C?

(c)   500 milliliters of a 0.0060-molar NaF solution is added to 400 ml of a 0.0060-molar $Ba(NO_3)_2$ solution. Will there be a precipitate?

(d)   What is the value of $\Delta G°$ for the dissociation of BaF_2 at 25 °C?

2.
$$H_2CO_3 \rightleftharpoons H^+ + HCO_3^- \qquad K_1 = 4.3 \times 10^{-7}$$
$$HCO_3^- \rightleftharpoons H^+ + CO_3^{2-} \qquad K_2 = 5.6 \times 10^{-11}$$

The acid dissociation constants for the reactions above are given at 25 °C.

(a)   What is the pH of a 0.050-molar solution of H_2CO_3 at 25 °C?

(b)   What is the concentration of CO_3^{2-} ions in the solution in (a)?

(c)   How would the addition of each of the following substances affect the pH of the solution in (a)?

   (i)   HCl

   (ii) $NaHCO_3$

   (iii)   NaOH

   (iv)   NaCl

(d)   What is the value of K_{eq} for the following reaction?

$$H_2CO_3 \rightleftharpoons 2\,H^+ + CO_3^{2-}$$

3.
$$N_2(g) + 3 H_2(g) \rightleftharpoons 2 NH_3(g) \qquad\qquad \Delta H = -92.4 \text{ kJ}$$

When the reaction above took place at a temperature of 570 K, the following equilibrium concentrations were measured.

$[NH_3] = 0.20 \text{ mol/L}$

$[N_2] = 0.50 \text{ mol/L}$

$[H_2] = 0.20 \text{ mol/L}$

(a) Write the expression for K_c and calculate its value.

(b) What is the value of K_p for the reaction?

(c) Describe how the concentration of H_2 will be affected by each of the following changes to the system at equilibrium.

    (i) The temperature is increased.

    (ii) The volume of the reaction chamber is increased.

    (iii) N_2 gas is added to the reaction chamber.

    (iv) He gas is added to the reaction chamber.

4.
$$CaCO_3(s) \rightleftharpoons Ca^{2+}(aq) + CO_3^{2-}(aq) \qquad K_{sp} = 2.8 \times 10^{-9}$$
$$CaSO_4(s) \rightleftharpoons Ca^{2+}(aq) + SO_4^{2-}(aq) \qquad K_{sp} = 9.1 \times 10^{-6}$$

The values for the solubility products for the two reactions above are given at 25 °C.

(a) What is the concentration of CO_3^{2-} ions in a saturated 1.00 liter solution of $CaCO_3$ at 25 °C?

(b) Excess $CaSO_4(s)$ is placed in the solution in (a). Assume that the volume of the solution does not change.

    (i) What is the concentration of the SO_4^{2-} ion?

    (ii) What is the concentration of the CO_3^{2-} ion?

(c) A 0.20 mole sample of $CaCl_2$ is placed in the solution in (b). Assume that the volume of the solution does not change.

    (i) What is the concentration of the Ca^{2+} ion?

    (ii) What is the concentration of the SO_4^{2-} ion?

    (iii) What is the concentration of the CO_3^{2-} ion?

ANSWERS

Multiple choice

1. **(B)** is correct. K_p is used for gaseous reactions and the units used are partial pressures.

2. **(D)** is correct. K_w is the dissociation constant for water.

   At 25 °C, $K_w = [H^+][OH^-] = 1 \times 10^{-14}$.

3. **(C)** is correct. K_a is known as the acid dissociation constant.

4. **(E)** is correct. K_{sp} is the solubility product. It always has a solid as the reactant. Since the reactant is always in the denominator and solids are ignored in the equilibrium expression, K_{sp} never has a denominator.

5. **(A)** is correct. From Le Chatelier's law, the equilibrium will shift to counteract any stress that is placed on it. Increasing temperature favors the endothermic direction of a reaction because the endothermic reaction absorbs the added heat. So the salt becomes more soluble, increasing the number of dissociated particles, thus increasing the value of K_{sp}.

6. **(E)** is correct. According to Le Chatelier's law, the equilibrium will shift to counteract any stress that is placed on it. If the temperature is decreased, the equilibrium will shift towards the side that produces energy, or heat. That's the product side, where I_2 is produced.

   Choices (A) and (B) are wrong because there are equal numbers of moles of gas (3 moles) on each side, so changing the volume will not affect the equilibrium. Choice (C) is wrong because the addition of a substance that does not affect the reaction will not affect the equilibrium conditions.

7. **(C)** is correct. From the balanced equation:

   If 1 mole of CH_3OH was created, then 1 mole of CO was consumed and 1 mole of CO remains, and if 1 mole of CH_3OH was created, then 2 moles of H_2 were consumed and 1 mole of H_2 remains. So at equilibrium, there are:

   (1 mol CH_3OH) + (1 mol CO) + (1 mol H_2) = 3 moles of gas.

8. **(D)** is correct. According to Le Chatelier's law, equilibrium will shift to relieve any stress placed on a system. If N_2 is removed, the equilibrium will shift to the right to produce more N_2 with the result that more H_2O will also be produced.

   If the volume is decreased (A) the equilibrium will shift towards the left, where there are fewer moles of gas. If the temperature is increased (B) the equilibrium will shift to the left. That's the endothermic reaction, which absorbs the added energy of the temperature increase. If NH_3 (C) or O_2 (E) is removed, the equilibrium will shift to the left to replace the substance removed.

9. **(D)** is correct. According to Le Chatelier's law, equilibrium will shift to relieve any stress placed on a system. If the temperature is increased, the equilibrium will shift to favor the endothermic reaction because it absorbs the added energy. In this case, the equilibrium will be shifted to the right, increasing the concentration of both K^+ and NO_3^- ions.

   Changing the volume of the solution, (A) and (B), will change the *number* of K^+ ions in solution, but not the *concentration* of K^+ ions. Since solids are not considered in the equilibrium expression, adding more solid KNO_3 to the solution (C) will not change the equilibrium. Decreasing the temperature (E) will favor the exothermic reaction, driving the equilibrium toward the left and decreasing the concentration of K^+ ions.

10. **(A)** is correct. The three dissociation reactions can be added to get the desired reaction as shown below:

$$
\begin{aligned}
&(H_3C_6H_5O_7 \rightleftharpoons H^+ + H_2C_6H_5O_7^-) \\
+&(H_2C_6H_5O_7^- \rightleftharpoons H^+ + HC_6H_5O_7^{2-}) \\
+&\underline{(HC_6H_5O_7^{2-} \rightleftharpoons H^+ + C_6H_5O_7^{3-})} \\
&\,H_3C_6H_5O_7 \rightleftharpoons 3\,H^+ + C_6H_5O_7^{3-}
\end{aligned}
$$

When two or more reactions can be added to get a resulting reaction, their equilibrium constants can be multiplied to get the equilibrium constant of the resulting reaction.

So $K_{eq} = K_1 K_2 K_3 = xyz$

11. **(C)** is correct. From the definition of equilibrium, the rates of the forward and reverse reactions must be equal. The volume of a system has no affect on the equilibrium constant.

12. **(D)** is correct.

$$
K_p = \frac{[NO]^2[Br_2]}{[NOBr]^2} = \frac{(4)^2(2)}{(4)^2} = 2
$$

Problems

1. (a) $K_{sp} = [Ba^{2+}][F^-]^2$

(b) Use the K_{sp} expression.

$K_{sp} = [Ba^{2+}][F^-]^2$

2 F⁻s are produced for every Ba^{2+}, so $[F^-]$ will be twice as big as $[Ba^{2+}]$.

Let $x = [F^-]$

$$
1.0 \times 10^{-6} = \left(\frac{x}{2}\right)(x)^2 = \frac{x^3}{2}
$$

$x = [F^-] = 0.01\ M$

(c) First we need to find the concentrations of the Ba^{2+} and F⁻ ions.

Moles = (molarity)(volume)

Moles of Ba^{2+} = (0.0060 M)(0.400 L) = 0.0024 mol

Moles of F⁻ = (0.0060 M)(0.500 L) = 0.0030 mol

Remember to add the two volumes: (0.400 L) + (0.500 L) = 0.900 L

$$
\text{Molarity} = \frac{\text{moles}}{\text{liters}}
$$

$$
\left[Ba^{2+}\right] = \frac{(0.0024\ \text{mol})}{(0.900\ \text{L})} = 0.0027\ M
$$

$$
\left[F^-\right] = \frac{(0.0030\ \text{mol})}{(0.900\ \text{L})} = 0.0033\ M
$$

Now test the solubility expression using the initial values, to find the reaction quotient.

$Q = [Ba^{2+}][F^-]^2$

$Q = (0.0027)(0.0033)^2 = 2.9 \times 10^{-8}$

Q is less than K_{sp}, so no precipitate forms.

(d) Use the standard free energy expression.

$\Delta G^\circ = -2.303RT \ \log K$

$\Delta G^\circ = (-2.303)(8.31 \ \text{J/mol} - \text{K})(298\text{K})\left(\log 1.0 \times 10^{-6}\right) = 34{,}000 \ \text{J/mol}$

The positive value of ΔG° means that the reaction is not spontaneous under standard conditions.

2. (a) Use the equilibrium expression.

$$K_1 = \frac{\left[H^+\right]\left[HCO_3^-\right]}{\left[H_2CO_3\right]}$$

$$\left[H^+\right] = \left[HCO_3^-\right] = x$$

$$\left[H_2CO_3\right] = (0.050 \ M - x)$$

Assume that x is small enough so that we can use $\left[H_2CO_3\right] = (0.050 \ M)$

$$4.3 \times 10^{-7} = \frac{x^2}{(0.050)}$$

$$x = \left[H^+\right] = 1.5 \times 10^{-4}$$

$$pH = -\log\left[H^+\right] = -\log\left(1.5 \times 10^{-4}\right) = 3.8$$

(b) Use the equilibrium expression.

$$K_2 = \frac{\left[H^+\right]\left[CO_3^{2-}\right]}{\left[HCO_3^-\right]}$$

From (a) we know: $\left[H^+\right] = \left[HCO_3^-\right] = 1.5 \times 10^{-4}$

$$5.6 \times 10^{-11} = \frac{\left(1.5 \times 10^{-4}\right)\left[CO_3^{2-}\right]}{\left(1.5 \times 10^{-4}\right)} = \left[CO_3^{2-}\right]$$

$$\left[CO_3^{2-}\right] = 5.6 \times 10^{-11} \ M$$

(c) (i) Adding HCl will increase [H+], lowering the pH.

(ii) From Le Chatelier's rule, you can see that adding $NaHCO_3$ will cause the first equilibrium to shift to the left to try to use up the excess HCO_3^-. This will cause a decrease in [H+], raising the pH.

You might notice that adding $NaHCO_3$ will also cause the second equilibrium to shift towards the right, which should increase [H+], but because K_2 is much smaller than K_1, this shift is insignificant.

(iii) Adding NaOH will neutralize hydrogen ions, decreasing [H+], and raising the pH.

(iv) Adding NaCl will have no effect on the pH.

(d) The reaction in (d) is just the sum of the two reactions given. When two reactions can be added to give a third reaction, the equilibrium constants for those reactions can be multiplied to give K_{eq} for the third reaction.

$$K_{eq} = (K_1)(K_2) = (4.3 \times 10^{-7})(5.6 \times 10^{-11}) = 2.4 \times 10^{-17}$$

3. (a) $K_c = \dfrac{[NH_3]^2}{[N_2][H_2]^3}$

$$K_c = \frac{(0.20)^2}{(0.50)(0.20)^3} = 10$$

(b) Use the formula that relates the two constants.

$$K_p = K_c(RT)^{\Delta n}$$

Δn is the change in the number of moles of gas from reactants to products. So $\Delta n = -2$.

$$K_p = (10)[(0.082)(570)]^{-2} = (10)(46.7)^{-2} = 4.7 \times 10^{-3}$$

(c) (i) An increase in temperature favors the endothermic direction. In this case that's the reverse reaction, so the concentration of H_2 will increase.

(ii) An increase in volume favors the direction that produces more moles of gas. In this case that's the reverse direction, so the concentration of H_2 will increase.

(iii) According to Le Chatelier's rule, increasing the concentration of the reactants forces the reaction to proceed in the direction that will use up the added reactants. In this case, adding the reactant N_2 will shift the reaction to the right and decrease the concentration of H_2.

(iv) The addition of He, a gas that takes no part in the reaction, will have no effect on the concentration of H_2.

4. (a) Use the solubility product.

$$K_{sp} = [Ca^{2+}][CO_3^{2-}]$$

$$[Ca^{2+}] = [CO_3^{2-}] = x$$

$$2.8 \times 10^{-9} = x^2$$

$$x = [CO_3^{2-}] = 5.3 \times 10^{-5} M$$

(b) Use the solubility product.

(i) $K_{sp} = [Ca^{2+}][SO_4^{2-}]$

$$[Ca^{2+}] = [SO_4^{2-}] = x$$

$$K_{sp} = 9.1 \times 10^{-6} = x^2$$

$$x = [SO_4^{2-}] = 3.0 \times 10^{-3} M$$

(ii) $K_{sp} = \left[Ca^{2+}\right]\left[CO_3^{2-}\right]$

Now use the value of $[Ca^{2+}]$ that you found in (b)(i).

$\left[Ca^{2+}\right] = x = 3.0 \times 10^{-3}\,M$

$K_{sp} = 2.8 \times 10^{-9} = \left(3.0 \times 10^{-3}\right)\left[CO_3^{2-}\right]$

$\left[CO_3^{2-}\right] = 9.3 \times 10^{-7}\,M$

(c) (i) The $CaCl_2$ dissociates completely, so the solution can be assumed to contain 0.2 moles of Ca^{2+} ions. We can ignore the ions from $CaCO_3$ and $CaSO_4$ because there are so few of them.

$$\text{Molarity} = \frac{\text{moles}}{\text{volume}}$$

$\left[Ca^{2+}\right] = \dfrac{(0.20\ \text{mol})}{(1\ \text{L})} = 0.20M$

(ii) Use K_{sp} again with the new value of $[Ca^{2+}]$.

$K_{sp} = \left[Ca^{2+}\right]\left[SO_4^{2-}\right]$

$9.1 \times 10^{-6} = (0.20)\left[SO_4^{2-}\right]$

$\left[SO_4^{2-}\right] = 4.6 \times 10^{-5}\,M$

(iii) Use K_{sp} again with the new value of $[Ca^{2+}]$.

$K_{sp} = \left[Ca^{2+}\right]\left[CO_3^{2-}\right]$

$2.8 \times 10^{-9} = (0.20)\left[CO_3^{2-}\right]$

$\left[CO_3^{2-}\right] = 1.4 \times 10^{-8}\,M$

11
ACIDS AND BASES

How often does this topic appear on the test?
In the multiple-choice section, this topic appears in about 10 out of 75 questions.
In the free-response section, you'll see this topic every year.

DEFINITIONS

ARRHENIUS

Arrhenius defined an acid as a substance that ionizes in water and produces hydrogen ions (H^+ ions).
For instance, HCl is an acid:

$$HCl \rightarrow H^+ + Cl^-$$

He defined a base as a substance that ionizes in water and produces hydroxide ions (OH^- ions).
For instance, NaOH is a base:

$$NaOH \rightarrow Na^+ + OH^-$$

BRØNSTED-LOWRY

Brønsted and Lowry defined an acid as a substance that is capable of donating a proton, which is the same as donating an H^+ ion, and they defined a base as a substance that is capable of accepting a proton.

Look at the reversible reaction below:

$$HC_2H_3O_2 + H_2O \leftrightarrow C_2H_3O_2^- + H_3O^+$$

According to Brønsted-Lowry:

$HC_2H_3O_2$ and H_3O^+ are acids.

$C_2H_3O_2^-$ and H_2O are bases.

Now look at this reversible reaction:

$$NH_3 + H_2O \leftrightarrow NH_4^+ + OH^-$$

According to Brønsted-Lowry:

NH_3 and OH^- are bases.
H_2O and NH_4^+ are acids.

So, in each case, the species with the H^+ ion is the acid and the same species without the H^+ ion is the base; the two species are called a **conjugate pair**. These are the acid-base conjugate pairs in the reactions above:

$HC_2H_3O_2$ and $C_2H_3O_2^-$

NH_4^+ and NH_3

H_3O^+ and H_2O

H_2O and OH^-

Notice that water can act as either an acid or a base.

LEWIS

Lewis focused on electrons, and his definitions are the most broad of the acid-base definitions. Lewis defined a base as an electron pair donor and an acid as an electron pair acceptor; according to Lewis' rule, all of the Brønsted-Lowry bases above are also Lewis bases and all of the Brønsted-Lowry acids are Lewis acids.

The following reaction is exclusively a Lewis acid-base reaction.

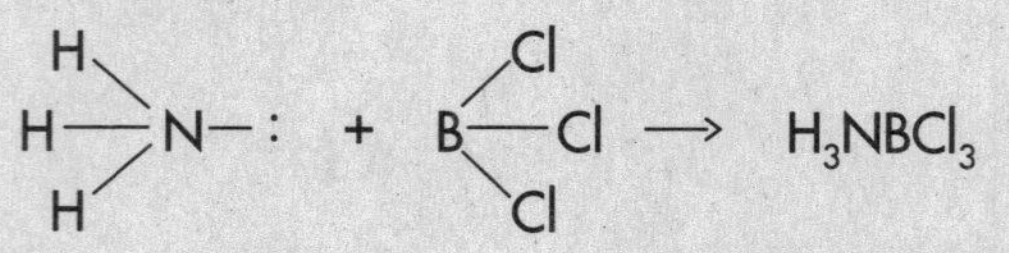

NH_3 is the Lewis base, donating its electron pair, and BCl_3 is the Lewis acid, accepting the electron pair.

pH

Many of the concentration measurements in acid-base problems are given to us in terms of pH and pOH.

$$p \text{ (anything)} = -\log \text{ (anything)}$$

$$pH = -\log [H^+]$$
$$pOH = -\log [OH^-]$$
$$pK_a = -\log K_a$$
$$pK_b = -\log K_b$$

In a solution:

- When $[H^+] = [OH^-]$, the solution is neutral, and pH = 7.

- When $[H^+]$ is greater than $[OH^-]$, the solution is acidic, and pH is less than 7.

- When $[H^+]$ is less than $[OH^-]$, the solution is basic, and pH is greater than 7.

It is important to remember that *increasing* pH means *decreasing* $[H^+]$, which means that there are fewer H^+ ions floating around and the solution is *less acidic*. Alternatively, *decreasing* pH means *increasing* $[H^+]$, which means that there are more H^+ ions floating around and the solution is *more acidic*.

WEAK ACIDS

When a weak acid is placed in water, a small fraction of its molecules will dissociate into hydrogen ions (H^+) and conjugate base ions (B^-). Most of the acid molecules will remain in solution as undissociated aqueous particles.

The dissociation constants, K_a and K_b, are measures of the strengths of weak acids and bases. K_a and K_b are just the equilibrium constants specific to acids and bases.

Acid Dissociation Constant

$$K_a = \frac{[H^+][B^-]}{[HB]}$$

$[H^+]$ = molar concentration of hydrogen ions (M)
$[B^-]$ = molar concentration of conjugate base ions (M)
$[HB]$ = molar concentration of undissociated acid molecules (M)

Base Dissociation Constant

$$K_b = \frac{[HB^+][OH^-]}{[B]}$$

$[HB^+]$ = protonated base ions (M)

$[OH^-]$ = molar concentration of hydroxide ions (M)

$[B]$ = unprotonated base molecules (M)

The greater the value of K_a, the greater the extent of the dissociation of the acid, and the stronger the acid. The same thing goes for K_b.

WEAK ACIDS AND CALCULATIONS

If you know the K_a for an acid and the concentration of the acid, you can find the pH. For instance, let's look at 0.20-molar solution of $HC_2H_3O_2$, with $K_a = 1.8 \times 10^{-5}$.

First we set up the K_a equation, plugging in values.

$$K_a = \frac{[H^+][C_2H_3O_2^-]}{[HC_2H_3O_2]}$$

Since every acid molecule that dissociates produces one H^+ and one $C_2H_3O_2^-$,

$$[H^+] = [C_2H_3O_2^-] = x$$

and since, strictly speaking, the molecules that dissociate should be subtracted from the initial concentration of $HC_2H_3O_2$, $[HC_2H_3O_2]$ should be $(0.20\,M - x)$. In practice, however, x is almost always insignificant compared to the initial concentration of acid, so we just use the initial concentration in the calculation.

$$[HC_2H_3O_2] = 0.20\,M$$

Now we can plug our values and variable into the K_a expression:

$$1.8 \times 10^{-5} = \frac{x^2}{0.20}$$

Solve for x:

$$x = [H^+] = 1.9 \times 10^{-3}$$

Now that we know $[H^+]$, we can calculate the pH:

$$pH = -\log [H^+] = -\log (1.9 \times 10^{-3}) = 2.7$$

This is the basic approach to solving many of the weak acid/base problems that will be on the test.

STRONG ACIDS

Strong acids dissociate completely in water, so the reaction goes to completion and they never reach equilibrium with their conjugate bases. Because there is no equilibrium, there is no equilibrium constant, so there is no dissociation constant for strong acids or bases.

Important Strong Acids

HCl, HBr, HI, HNO_3, $HClO_4$, H_2SO_4

Important Strong Bases

$LiOH$, $NaOH$, KOH, $Ba(OH)_2$, $Sr(OH)_2$

Because the dissociation of a strong acid goes to completion, there is no tendency for the reverse reaction to occur, which means that the conjugate base of a strong acid must be extremely weak.

Oxoacids are acids that contain oxygen. The greater the number of oxygen atoms attached to the central atom in an oxoacid, the stronger the acid. For instance, $HClO_4$ is stronger than $HClO_3$, which is stronger than $HClO_2$. That's because increasing the number of oxygen atoms that are attached to the central atom weakens the attraction that the central atom has for the H^+ ion.

STRONG ACIDS AND CALCULATIONS

It's much easier to find the pH of a strong acid solution than it is to find the pH of a weak acid solution. That's because strong acids dissociate completely, so the final concentration of H^+ ions will be the same as the initial concentration of the strong acid.

Let's look at a 0.040-molar solution of HCl:

HCl dissociates completely, so $[H^+] = 0.040\ M$

$pH = -\log [H^+] = -\log (0.040) = 1.4$

So, you can always find the pH of a strong acid solution directly from its concentration.

K_w

Water comes to equilibrium with its ions according to the following reaction.

$$H_2O(l) \rightleftharpoons H^+(aq) + OH^-(aq) \qquad K_w = 1 \times 10^{-14} \text{ at } 25\ ^\circ C.$$
$$K_w = 1 \times 10^{-14} = [H^+][OH^-]$$
$$pH + pOH = 14$$

The common ion effect tells us that the hydrogen ion and hydroxide ion concentrations for any acid or base solution must be consistent with the equilibrium for the ionization of water. That is, no matter where the H^+ and OH^- ions came from, when you multiply $[H^+]$ and $[OH^-]$, you must get 1×10^{-14}. So, for any aqueous solution, if you know the value of $[H^+]$, you can find out the value of $[OH^-]$, and vice versa.

The acid and base dissociation constants for conjugates must also be consistent with the equilibrium for the ionization of water.

$$K_w = 1 \times 10^{-14} = K_a K_b$$
$$pK_a + pK_b = 14$$

So if you know K_a for a weak acid, you can find K_b for its conjugate base, and vice versa.

ACID AND BASE SALTS

A salt solution can be acidic or basic, depending on the identities of the anion and cation in the salt.

- *If a salt is composed of the conjugates of a strong base and a strong acid, its solution will be neutral.*
  For example, let's look at NaCl:
  Na^+ is the conjugate acid of NaOH (a strong base) and Cl^- is the conjugate base of HCl (a strong acid).

  $$NaCl(s) \rightarrow Na^+(aq) + Cl^-(aq) \qquad\qquad pH = 7$$

  That's because neither ion will react in water. This is because, as you may recall, the conjugates of strong acids and bases are very weak and unreactive.

- *If a salt is composed of the conjugates of a weak base and a strong acid, its solution will be acidic.*
  For example, look at NH_4Cl:
  NH_4^+ is the conjugate acid of NH_3 (a weak base) and Cl^- is the conjugate base of HCl (a strong acid).

  $$NH_4Cl(s) \rightarrow NH_4^+(aq) + Cl^-(aq) \qquad\qquad pH \text{ is less than } 7$$

  When NH_4Cl ionizes in water, the Cl^- ions won't react at all, but the NH_4^+ will dissociate to some extent to produce some H^+ ions, making the solution acidic.

- *If a salt is composed of the conjugates of a strong base and a weak acid, its solution will be basic.*
  For instance, look at $NaC_2H_3O_2$:
  Na^+ is the conjugate acid of NaOH (a strong base) and $C_2H_3O_2^-$ is the conjugate base of $HC_2H_3O_2$ (a weak acid).

  $$NaC_2H_3O_2(s) \rightarrow Na^+(aq) + C_2H_3O_2^-(aq) \qquad pH \text{ is greater than } 7$$

  When $NaC_2H_3O_2$ ionizes in water, the Na^+ ions don't react at all, but the $C_2H_3O_2^-$ ions will react with water according to the following reaction:

  $$C_2H_3O_2^-(aq) + H_2O(l) \rightarrow HC_2H_3O_2(aq) + OH^-(aq)$$

  This is an acid-base reaction, which produces some OH^- ions, and increases the pH.

- *If a salt is composed of the conjugates of a weak base and a weak acid, the pH of its solution will depend on the relative strengths of the conjugate acid and base of the specific ions in the salt.*

ACID-BASE SALTS AND CALCULATIONS

Calculations with salts aren't much different than regular acid-base calculations, except that you might need to convert between K_a and K_b, and pH and pOH.
   Remember:

$$K_a K_b = 1 \times 10^{-14}, \text{ and } pH + pOH = 14$$

Let's find the pH of a 0.10-molar solution of $NaC_2H_3O_2$. K_a for $HC_2H_3O_2$ is 1.8×10^{-5}. The solution will be basic, so let's find K_b for $C_2H_3O_2^-$.

$$K_b = \frac{\left(1.0 \times 10^{-14}\right)}{K_a} = \frac{\left(1.0 \times 10^{-14}\right)}{\left(1.8 \times 10^{-5}\right)} = 5.6 \times 10^{-10}$$

Now we can use the base dissociation expression.

$$K_b = \frac{\left[HC_2H_3O_2\right]\left[OH^-\right]}{\left[C_2H_3O_2^-\right]}$$

Every $C_2H_3O_2^-$ polyatomic ion that reacts with a water molecule produces one $HC_2H_3O_2$ and one OH^-, so

$$[HC_2H_3O_2] = [OH^-] = x$$

Again, we assume that x is insignificant compared to the initial concentration of $C_2H_3O_2^-$; $0.10\ M$, so:

$$[C_2H_3O_2^-] = (0.10\ M - x) = 0.10\ M$$

Now we can plug our values and variable into the K_b expression:

$$5.6 \times 10^{-10} = \frac{x^2}{0.10}$$

Solve for x:

$$x = [OH^-] = 7.5 \times 10^{-6}$$

Once we know the value of $[OH^-]$, we can calculate the pOH:

$$pOH = -\log [OH^-] = -\log (7.5 \times 10^{-6}) = 5.1$$

Now we use pOH to find pH.

$$pH = 14 - pOH = 14 - 5.1 = 8.9$$

BUFFERS

A **buffer** is a solution with a very stable pH. You can add acid or base to a buffer solution without greatly affecting the pH of the solution.

A buffer is created by placing a large amount of a weak acid or base into a solution along with its conjugate. A weak acid and its conjugate base can remain in solution together without neutralizing each other.

When both the acid and the conjugate base are together in the solution, any hydrogen ions that are added will be neutralized by the base while any hydroxide ions that are added will be neutralized by the acid without this having much of an effect on the solution's pH.

When dealing with buffers, it is useful to rearrange the equilibrium constant to create the Henderson-Hasselbach equation.

The Henderson-Hasselbach Equation

$$pH = pK_a + \log \frac{[A^-]}{[HA]}$$

[HA] = molar concentration of undissociated weak acid (M)

[A$^-$] = molar concentration of conjugate base (M)

$$pOH = pK_b + \log \frac{[HB^+]}{[B]}$$

[B] = molar concentration of weak base

[HB$^+$] = molar concentration of conjugate acid

Let's say we have a buffer solution with concentrations of 0.20 M HC$_2$H$_3$O$_2$ and 0.50 M C$_2$H$_3$O$_2^-$. The acid dissociation constant for HC$_2$H$_3$O$_2$ is 1.8×10^{-5}. Let's find the pH of the solution. We can just plug the values we have into the Henderson-Hasselbach equation for acids:

$$pH = pK_a + \log \frac{\left[C_2H_3O_2^-\right]}{\left[HC_2H_3O\right]}$$

$$pH = -\log (1.8 \times 10^{-5}) + \log \frac{(0.50M)}{(0.20)}$$

$$pH = -\log (1.8 \times 10^{-5}) + \log (2.5)$$

$$pH = (4.7) + (0.40) = 5.1$$

Now let's see what happens when [HC$_2$H$_3$O$_2$] and [C$_2$H$_3$O$_2^-$] are both equal to 0.20 M.

$$pH = pK_a + \log \frac{\left[C_2H_3O_2^-\right]}{\left[HC_2H_3O\right]}$$

$$pH = -\log (1.8 \times 10^{-5}) + \log \frac{(0.20M)}{(0.20M)}$$

$$pH = -\log (1.8 \times 10^{-5}) + \log (1)$$

$$pH = (4.7) + (0) = 4.7$$

Notice that when the concentrations of acid and conjugate base in a solution are the same, pH = pK_a (and pOH = pK_b). When you choose an acid for a buffer solution, it is best to pick an acid with a pK_a that is close to the desired pH. That way you can have almost equal amounts of acid and conjugate base in the solution, which will make the buffer as flexible as possible in neutralizing both added H$^+$ and OH$^-$.

POLYPROTIC ACIDS AND AMPHOTERIC SUBSTANCES

Some acids, such as H_2SO_4 and H_3PO_4, can give up more than one hydrogen ion. These are called **polyprotic** acids.

Polyprotic acids are always more willing to give up their first protons than later protons. For example, H_3PO_4 gives up an H^+ ion (proton) more easily than does $H_2PO_4^-$, so H_3PO_4 is a stronger acid. In the same way, $H_2PO_4^-$ is a stronger acid than HPO_4^{2-}.

Substances that can act as either acids or bases are called **amphoteric** substances.

For instance:

- $H_2PO_4^-$ can act as an acid, giving up a proton to become HPO_4^{2-}, or it can act as a base, accepting a proton to become H_3PO_4.

- HSO_4^- can act as an acid, giving up a proton to become SO_4^{2-}, or it can act as a base, accepting a proton to become H_2SO_4.

- H_2O can act as an acid, giving up a proton to become OH^-, or it can act as a base, accepting a proton to become H_3O^+.

ANHYDRIDES

An **acid anhydride** is a substance that combines with water to form an acid. Generally, oxides of nonmetals are acid anhydrides:

$$CO_2 + H_2O \rightarrow H_2CO_3$$

$$SO_3 + H_2O \rightarrow H^+ + HSO_4^-$$

A **basic anhydride** is a substance that combines with water to form a base. Generally, oxides of metals are basic anhydrides:

$$CaO + H_2O \rightarrow Ca(OH)_2$$

$$Na_2O + H_2O \rightarrow 2\,Na^+ + 2\,OH^-$$

TITRATION

When an acid and a base are mixed, a neutralization reaction occurs. Neutralization reactions can be written in this form:

$$Acid + Base \rightarrow Water + Salt$$

Neutralization reactions are generally performed by titration, where a base of known concentration is slowly added to an acid (or vice versa). The progress of a neutralization reaction can be shown in a titration curve. The diagram below shows the titration of a strong acid by a strong base.

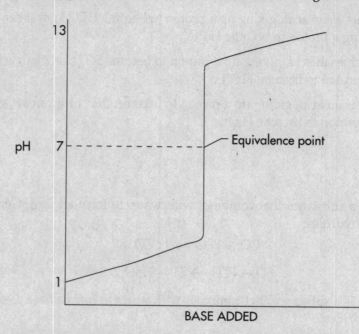

In the diagram above, the pH increases slowly but steadily from the beginning of the titration until just before the equivalence point. The **equivalence point**, or **end point**, is the point in the titration when exactly enough base has been added to neutralize all the acid that was initially present. Just before the equivalence point, the pH increases sharply as the last of the acid is neutralized.

For this titration, the pH at the equivalence point is exactly 7 because the titration of a strong acid by a strong base produces a neutral salt solution.

The following diagram shows the titration of a weak acid by a strong base.

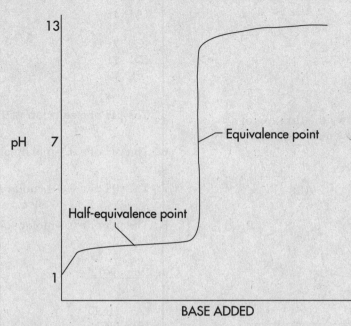

In this diagram, the pH increases more quickly at first and then levels out into a buffer region. At the center of the buffer region is the **half-equivalence point**. At this point, enough base has been added to convert exactly half of the acid into conjugate base; here the concentration of acid is equal to the concentration of conjugate base (pH = pK_a). The curve remains fairly flat until just before the equivalence point, when the pH increases sharply. For this titration, the pH at the equivalence point is greater than 7 because the titration of a weak acid by a strong base produces a basic salt solution.

The following diagram shows the titration curve of a polyprotic acid.

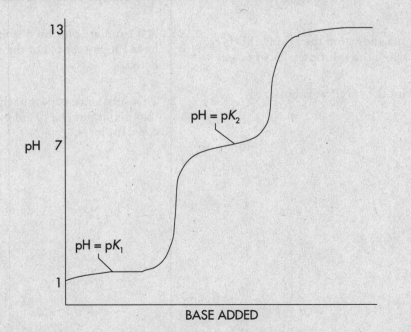

For a polyprotic acid, the titration curve will have as many bumps as there are hydrogen ions to give up. The curve above has two bumps, so it represents the titration of a diprotic acid.

ACID-BASE

Questions

Multiple choice

Questions 1–4

The diagram below shows the titration of a weak monoprotic acid by a strong base.

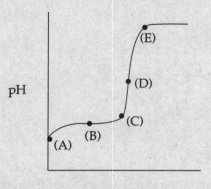

Base added

1. At this point in the titration, the pH of the solution is equal to the pK_a of the acid.

2. This is the equivalence point of the titration.

3. Of the points shown on the graph, this is the point when the solution is most basic.

4. At this point the solution is buffered.

Questions 5–8

   (A) 1
   (B) 3
   (C) 7
   (D) 11
   (E) 13

5. The pH of a solution with a pOH of 11

6. The pH of a 0.1-molar solution of HCl

7. The pH of a 0.001-molar solution of HNO_3

8. The pH of a 0.1-molar solution of NaOH

Questions 9–12

   (A) HNO_3
   (B) HCN
   (C) H_2CO_3
   (D) HF
   (E) H_2O

9. This is a strong electrolyte.

10. This substance can act as a Lewis base.

11. A 0.1-molar solution of this substance will have the lowest pH of the substances listed.

12. This substance is part of the buffer system that maintains the pH of blood at a constant level.

13. What is the pH of a 0.01-molar solution of NaOH?

   (A) 1
   (B) 2
   (C) 8
   (D) 10
   (E) 12

14. What is the volume of 0.05-molar HCl that is required to neutralize 50 ml of a 0.10-molar $Mg(OH)_2$ solution?

   (A) 100 ml
   (B) 200 ml
   (C) 300 ml
   (D) 400 ml
   (E) 500 ml

15. Which of the following best describes the pH of a 0.01-molar solution of HBrO? (For HBrO, $K_a = 2 \times 10^{-9}$)

   (A) Less than or equal to 2
   (B) Between 2 and 7
   (C) 7
   (D) Between 7 and 11
   (E) Greater than or equal to 11

16. A 0.5-molar solution of which of the following salts will have the lowest pH?

   (A) KCl
   (B) $NaC_2H_3O_2$
   (C) NaI
   (D) KNO_3
   (E) NH_4Cl

17. Which of the following salts will produce a solution with a pH of greater than 7 when placed in distilled water?

   (A) NaCN
   (B) KCl
   (C) $NaNO_3$
   (D) NH_4NO_3
   (E) KI

18. A laboratory technician wishes to create a buffered solution with a pH of 5. Which of the following acids would be the best choice for the buffer?

   (A) $H_2C_2O_4$, $K_a = 5.9 \times 10^{-2}$
   (B) H_3AsO_4, $K_a = 5.6 \times 10^{-3}$
   (C) $H_2C_2H_3O_2$, $K_a = 1.8 \times 10^{-5}$
   (D) HOCl, $K_a = 3.0 \times 10^{-8}$
   (E) HCN, $K_a = 4.9 \times 10^{-10}$

19. Which of the following species is amphoteric?

   (A) H^+
   (B) CO_3^{2-}
   (C) HCO_3^-
   (D) H_2CO_3
   (E) H_2

20. How many liters of distilled water must be added to 1 liter of an aqueous solution of HCl with a pH of 1 in order to create a solution with a pH of 2?

   (A) 0.1 L
   (B) 0.9 L
   (C) 2 L
   (D) 9 L
   (E) 100 L

21. A 1-molar solution of a very weak monoprotic acid has a pH of 5. What is the value of K_a for the acid?

   (A) $K_a = 1 \times 10^{-10}$
   (B) $K_a = 1 \times 10^{-7}$
   (C) $K_a = 1 \times 10^{-5}$
   (D) $K_a = 1 \times 10^{-2}$
   (E) $K_a = 1 \times 10^{-1}$

22. The value of K_a for HSO_4^- is 1×10^{-2}. What is the value of K_b for SO_4^{2-}?

   (A) $K_b = 1 \times 10^{-12}$
   (B) $K_b = 1 \times 10^{-8}$
   (C) $K_b = 1 \times 10^{-2}$
   (D) $K_b = 1 \times 10^2$
   (E) $K_b = 1 \times 10^5$

23. How much 0.1-molar NaOH solution must be added to 100 milliliters of a 0.2-molar H_2SO_3 solution in order to neutralize all of the hydrogen ions in H_2SO_3?

    (A) 100 ml
    (B) 200 ml
    (C) 300 ml
    (D) 400 ml
    (E) 500 ml

24. The concentrations of which of the following species will be increased when HCl is added to a solution of $HC_2H_3O_2$ in water?

    I. H^+
    II. $C_2H_3O_2^-$
    III. $HC_2H_3O_2$

    (A) I only
    (B) I and II only
    (C) I and III only
    (D) II and III only
    (E) I, II, and III

25. Which of the following species is amphoteric?

    (A) HNO_3
    (B) $HC_2H_3O_2$
    (C) HSO_4^-
    (D) H_3PO_4
    (E) ClO_4^-

Problems

1. A beaker contains 100. milliliters of a solution of hypochlorous acid, HOCl, of unknown concentration.

   (a) The solution was titrated with 0.100 molar NaOH solution and the equivalence point was reached when 40.0 milliliters of NaOH solution was added. What was the original concentration of the HOCl solution?

   (b) If the original HOCl solution had a pH of 4.46, what is the value of K_a for HOCl?

   (c) What percent of the HOCl molecules were ionized in the original solution?

   (d) What is the concentration of OCl$^-$ ions in the solution at the equivalence point reached in (a)?

2. A vessel contains 500. milliliters of a 0.100-molar H_2S solution. For H_2S, $K_1 = 1.0 \times 10^{-7}$ and $K_2 = 1.3 \times 10^{-13}$.

   (a) What is the pH of the solution?

   (b) How many milliliters of 0.100-molar NaOH solution must be added to the solution to create a solution with a pH of 7?

   (c) What will be the pH when 800 milliliters of 0.100-molar NaOH has been added?

   (d) What is the value of K_{eq} for the following reaction?

3. A 100. milliliter sample of 0.100-molar NH_4Cl solution was added to 80 milliliters of a 0.200-molar solution of NH_3. The value of K_b for ammonia is 1.79×10^{-5}.

   (a) What is the value of pK_b for ammonia?

   (b) What is the pH of the solution described in the question?

   (c) If 0.200 grams of NaOH were added to the solution, what would be the new pH of the solution? (Assume that the volume of the solution does not change.)

   (d) If equal molar quantities of NH_3 and NH_4^+ were mixed in solution, what would be the pH of the solution?

Essays

4.
$$H_3PO_4 \rightleftharpoons H^+ + H_2PO_4^- \qquad K_1 = 7.5 \times 10^{-3}$$
$$H_2PO_4^- \rightleftharpoons H^+ + HPO_4^{2-} \qquad K_2 = 6.2 \times 10^{-8}$$
$$HPO_4^{2-} \rightleftharpoons H^+ + PO_4^{3-} \qquad K_3 = 2.2 \times 10^{-13}$$

(a) Choose an amphoteric species from the reactions listed above and give its conjugate acid and its conjugate base.

(b) Explain why the dissociation constant decreases with each hydrogen ion lost.

(c) Of the acids listed above, which would be most useful in creating a buffer solution with a pH of 7.5?

(d) Sketch the titration curve that results when H_3PO_4 is titrated with excess NaOH and label the two axes.

5. Use the principles of acid-base theory to answer the following questions.

(a) Predict whether a 0.1-molar solution of sodium acetate, $NaC_2H_3O_2$, will be acidic or basic and give a reaction occurring with water that supports your conclusion.

(b) Predict whether a 0.1-molar solution of ammonium chloride, NH_4Cl, will be acidic or basic and give a reaction occurring with water that supports your conclusion.

(c) Explain why buffer solutions are made with weak acids instead of strong acids.

(d) Explain why, although oxygen occupies the same position in both KOH and HBrO, KOH is a base and HBrO is an acid.

6. Tell which one of the acids listed in pairs below is the stronger of the two and explain why.

(a) HF and HCl

(b) H_2SO_3 and HSO_3^-

(c) HNO_3 and HNO_2

(d) $HClO_4$ and $HBrO_4$

ANSWERS

Multiple choice

1. **(B)** is correct. At this point, sometimes called the half-equivalence point, enough base has been added to neutralize half of the weak acid. That means that at this point, the concentration of the acid, let's call it HA, will be equal to the concentration of the conjugate base, A^-.

    Now let's look at the equilibrium expression:

    $$K_a = \frac{\left[H^+\right]\left[A^-\right]}{[HA]}$$

    If [HA] = [A–], then they cancel and K_a = [H$^+$].

    So pH = pK_a.

2. **(D)** is correct. The point in the middle of the steep rise in a titration curve is the equivalence point. That's the point when exactly enough base has been added to neutralize all of the acid that was originally in the solution.

3. **(E)** is correct. This is the point with the highest pH, so at this point, the solution is most basic.

4. **(B)** is correct. A buffered solution resists changes to its pH, so the flat part of the titration curve is the buffer region because the pH of the solution is changing very little even when base is being added.

    At (B), the solution contains a large quantity of both the acid HA, which absorbs added base, and its conjugate base, A^-, which absorbs added acid.

5. **(B)** is correct. In any aqueous solution at 25 °C, pH + pOH = 14.

    So pH + 3 = 14 and pH = 3.

6. **(A)** is correct. HCl is a strong acid and dissociates completely, so the hydrogen ion concentration is equal to the molarity.

    So [H$^+$] = 0.1 M

    pH = –log[H$^+$] = –log(0.1) = 1

7. **(B)** is correct. HNO_3 is a strong acid and dissociates completely, so the hydrogen ion concentration is equal to the molarity.

    So [H$^+$] = 0.001 M

    pH = –log[H$^+$] = –log(0.001) = 3

8. **(E)** is correct. NaOH is a strong acid and dissociates completely, so the hydroxide ion concentration [OH$^-$] is equal to the molarity.

    So [OH$^-$] = 0.1 M

    pOH = –log[OH$^-$] = –log(0.1) = 1

    Now, pH + pOH = 14

    So pH + 1 = 14 and pH = 13

9. **(A)** is correct. A strong electrolyte is a substance that dissociates to form a lot of ions. HNO_3 is the only substance listed that ionizes completely in solution.

10. **(E)** is correct. Water can act as a Lewis base by donating an electron pair to a hydrogen ion to form H_3O^+.

11. **(A)** is correct. HNO_3 is the only strong acid listed, meaning that it is the only acid listed that ionizes completely, so it will have the lowest pH. By the way, in a 0.1 M solution of a strong acid, the hydrogen ion concentration will be 0.1 M, so the pH will be equal to 1.

12. **(C)** is correct. H_2CO_3, carbonic acid, is part of the buffer system in blood which maintains the pH at about 7.4.

13. **(E)** is correct. NaOH is a strong base, so it can be assumed to dissociate completely. That means that the OH^- concentration will also be 0.01 M.

    pOH = $-\log[OH^-]$, so pOH = 2, but we're looking for the pH.

    In an aqueous solution, pH + pOH = 14, so pH = 12.

14. **(B)** is correct. Every mole of $Mg(OH)_2$ molecules dissociates to produce 2 moles of OH^- ions, so a 0.10 M $Mg(OH)_2$ solution will be a 0.20 M OH^- solution.

    The solution will be neutralized when the number of moles of H^+ ions added is equal to the number of OH^- ions originally in the solution.

    Moles = (molarity)(volume)

    Moles of OH^- = (0.20 M)(50 ml) = 10 millimoles = moles of H^+ added

    $$\text{Volume} = \frac{\text{moles}}{\text{molarity}}$$

    $$\text{Volume of HCl} = \frac{(10 \text{ millimoles})}{(0.05 M)} = 200 \text{ ml}$$

15. **(B)** is correct. You can eliminate (C), (D), and (E) by using common sense. HBrO is a weak acid, so an HBrO solution will be acidic, with a pH of less than 7.

    To choose between (A) and (B) you have to remember that HBrO is a weak acid. If HBrO were a strong acid, it would dissociate completely and $[H^+]$ would be equal to 0.01-molar, for a pH of exactly 2. Since HBrO is a weak acid, it will not dissociate completely and $[H^+]$ will be less than 0.01-molar, which means that the pH will be greater than 2. So, by process of elimination, (B) is the answer.

16. **(E)** is correct. To find the lowest pH, we should look for the salt that produces an acidic solution.

    The salt composed of the conjugate of a weak base (NH_4^+ is the conjugate of NH_3) and the conjugate of a strong acid (Cl^- is the conjugate of HCl) will produce an acidic solution.

    As for the other choices, (A), (C), and (D) are composed of conjugates of strong acids and bases and will produce neutral solutions.

    (B) is composed of the conjugate of a strong base (Na^+) and the conjugate of a weak acid ($C_2H_3O_2^-$) and will produce a basic solution.

17. **(A)** is correct. A pH of greater than 7 means that the solution is basic.

    The salt composed of the conjugate of a strong base (Na^+ is the conjugate of NaOH) and the conjugate of a weak acid (CN^- is the conjugate of HCN) will produce a basic solution.

    As for the other choices, (B), (C), and (E) are composed of conjugates of strong acids and bases and will produce neutral solutions.

    (D) is composed of the conjugate of a weak base (NH_4^+) and the conjugate of a strong acid (NO_3^-) and will produce an acidic solution.

18. **(C) is correct.** The best buffered solution occurs when $pH = pK_a$. That happens when the solution contains equal amounts of acid and conjugate base. If you want to create a buffer with a pH of 5, the best choice would be an acid with a pK_a that is as close to 5 as possible. You shouldn't have to do a calculation to see that the pK_a for choice (C) is much closer to 5 than that of any of the others.

19. **(C) is correct.** An amphoteric species can act as either an acid or a base, gaining or losing a proton.

     HCO_3^- can act as an acid, losing a proton to become CO_3^{2-}, or it can act as a base, gaining a proton to become H_2CO_3.

20. **(D) is correct.** We want to change the hydrogen ion concentration from 0.1 M (pH of 1) to 0.01 M (pH of 2).

     The HCl is completely dissociated, so the number of moles of H^+ will remain constant as we dilute the solution.

     Moles = (molarity)(volume) = Constant

     $(M_1)(V_1) = (M_2)(V_2)$

     $(0.1\ M)(1\ L) = (0.01\ M)(V_2)$

     So, $V_2 = 10$ L, which means that 9 L must be added.

21. **(A) is correct.** A pH of 5 means that $[H^+] = 1 \times 10^{-5}$

     $$K_a = \frac{[H^+][A^-]}{[HA]}$$

     For every HA that dissociates, we get one H^+ and one A^-, so $[H^+] = [A^-] = 1 \times 10^{-5}$

     The acid is weak, so we can assume that very little HA dissociates and that the concentration of HA remains 1-molar.

     $$K_a = \frac{[H^+][A^-]}{[HA]} = \frac{(1 \times 10^{-5})(1 \times 10^{-5})}{(1)} = 1 \times 10^{-10}.$$

22. **(A) is correct.** For conjugates, $(K_a)(K_b) = K_w = 1 \times 10^{-14}$

     $$K_b = \frac{K_w}{K_a} = \frac{(1 \times 10^{-14})}{(1 \times 10^{-2})} = 1 \times 10^{-12}$$

23. **(D) is correct.** First let's find out how many moles of H^+ ions we need to neutralize.

     Every H_2SO_3 will produce 2 H^+ ions, so for our purposes, we can think of the solution as a 0.4-molar H^+ solution.

     Moles = (molarity)(volume)

     Moles of H^+ = (molarity)(volume) = (0.4 M)(100 ml) = 40 millimoles = moles of OH^- required.

     $$\text{Volume of NaOH} = \frac{\text{moles}}{\text{molarity}} = \frac{(40\ \text{millimoles})}{(0.1M)} = 400\ \text{ml}$$

24. **(C) is correct.** Let's look at the equilibrium expression for the dissociation of $HC_2H_3O_2$.

     $$K_a = \frac{[H^+][C_2H_3O_2^-]}{[HC_2H_3O_2^-]}$$

     When HCl is added to the solution, H^+ ions are added and $[H^+]$ will increase, so (I) is correct.

     Because of Le Chatelier's principle, the equilibrium will shift to consume some of the added H^+ ions, so some of the H^+ ions will combine with $C_2H_3O_2^-$ ions to form more $HC_2H_3O_2$.

So $[C_2H_3O_2^-]$ will decrease, making (II) wrong, and $[HC_2H_3O_2]$ will increase, making (III) correct.

25. **(C)** is correct. An amphoteric species can either act as a base and gain an H^+ or act as an acid and lose an H^+.

    HSO_4^- can lose an H^+ to become SO_4^{2-} or it can gain an H^+ to become H_2SO_4.

    HNO_3 (A), $HC_2H_3O_2$ (B), and H_3PO_4 (D) can only lose an H^+.

    ClO_4^- (E) can only gain an H^+.

Problems

1. (a) First let's find out how many moles of NaOH were added.

   Moles = (molarity)(volume)

   Moles of NaOH = (0.100 M)(.040 L) = 0.004 moles

   Every OH^- ion neutralizes one H^+ ion, so at the equivalence point, the number of moles of NaOH added is equal to the number of moles of HOCl originally present.

   (moles of NaOH) = (moles of HOCl) = 0.004 moles

   Now we can find the original concentration of the HOCl solution.

   $$\text{Molarity} = \frac{\text{moles}}{\text{volume}}$$

   $$[\text{HOCl}] = \frac{(0.004 \text{ mol})}{(0.100 \text{ L})} = 0.040 \ M$$

   (b) Use the equilibrium expression.

   $$K_a = \frac{[H^+][OCl^-]}{[HOCl^-]}$$

   $[H^+] = 10^{-pH} = 10^{-4.46} = 3.47 \times 10^{-5} \ M$

   $[H^+] = [OCl^-] = 3.47 \times 10^{-5} \ M$

   $[HOCl] = 0.40 \ M$

   $$K_a = \frac{\left(3.47 \times 10^{-5} M\right)^2}{\left(0.040 M - 3.47 \times 10^{-5} M\right)}$$

   0.040 is much larger than 3.47×10^{-5}, so we can simplify the expression.

   $$K_a = \frac{\left(3.47 \times 10^{-5} M\right)^2}{(0.040 M)} = \frac{\left(1.20 \times 10^{-9}\right)}{(0.040 M)} M = 3.00 \times 10^{-8} \ M$$

   (c) The percent of molecules ionized is given by the following expression.

   $$\% \text{ ionized} = \frac{[H^+]}{[HOCl]} \times 100\% = \frac{\left(3.47 \times 10^{-5} M\right)}{(0.040 M)} \times 100\% = 0.087\%$$

   (d) At the equivalence point, all of the HOCl initially present has been converted into OCl^- ions.

   From (a), we know that there were initially 0.004 moles of HOCl, so at equivalence, there are 0.004 moles of OCl^-.

At equivalence, we have added 40 ml to the 100 ml of solution originally present, so we must take this into account in our concentration calculation.

$$Molarity = \frac{moles}{volume}$$

$$[OCl^-] = \frac{(0.004\ mol)}{(0.100\ L + 0.040\ L)} = \frac{(0.004\ mol)}{(0.140\ L)} = 0.029\ M$$

2. (a) Use the equilibrium expression for H_2S to find $[H^+]$.

$$K_1 = \frac{[H^+][HS^-]}{[H_2S]}$$

$[H^+] = [HS^-] = x$

$[H_2S] = 0.100\ M$

$K_1 = 1.0 \times 10^{-7}$

$$1.0 \times 10^{-7} = \frac{x^2}{(0.100\ M - x)}$$

Let's assume that 0.100 is much larger than x. That simplifies the expression.

$$1.0 \times 10^{-7} = \frac{x^2}{(0.100\ M)}$$

$x^2 = (1.0 \times 10^{-7})(0.100)\ M^2 = 1.0 \times 10^{-8}\ M^2$

$x = 1.0 \times 10^{-4}\ M = [H^+]$

$pH = -\log[H^+] = -\log(1.0 \times 10^{-4}) = 4.0$

(b) At pH = 7, $pH = pK_1$

Let's look at the Henderson-Hasselbach expression.

$$pH = pK + \log \frac{[HS^-]}{[H_2S]}$$

When $pH = pK$, $[HS^-]$ must be equal to $[H_2S]$, making $\frac{[HS^-]}{[H_2S]}$ equal to one and log $\frac{[HS^-]}{[H_2S]}$ equal to zero.

For every molecule of H_2S neutralized, one unit of HS^- is generated, so we must add enough NaOH to neutralized half of the HS^- initially present. (We are assuming that the further dissociation of HS^- into H^+ and S_2^- is negligible and can be ignored.)

Let's find out how many moles of H_2S were initially present.

Moles = (molarity)(volume)

Moles of H_2S = (0.100 M)(0.500 L) = 0.050 moles

We need to neutralize half of that, or 0.025 moles, so we need 0.025 moles of NaOH.

$$Volume = \frac{moles}{molarity}$$

$$Volume\ of\ NaOH = \frac{(0.025\ mol)}{(0.100\ M)} = 0.250\ L = 250\ ml$$

(c) The concentrations of the H_2S solution and NaOH solution are both 0.100 M so the first 500 ml of NaOH solution will completely neutralize the H_2S. The final 300 ml of NaOH solution will neutralize HS^- molecules.

Initially, there were 0.050 moles of H_2S, so after 500 ml of NaOH solution was added, there were 0.050 moles of HS^-.

By adding 300 ml more of NaOH solution, we added (0.100 M)(0.300 L) = 0.030 moles of NaOH. [Moles = (molarity)(volume)]

Every unit of NaOH added neutralizes one unit of HS^-, so when all the NaOH has been added, we have 0.030 moles of S^{2-} and (0.050 moles) – (0.030 moles) = 0.020 moles of HS^-.

Now we can use the Henderson-Hasselbach expression to find the pH. We can use the number of moles we just calculated (0.030 for S^{2-} and 0.020 for HS^-) instead of concentrations because in a solution the concentrations are proportional to the number of moles.

$$pH = pK + \log \frac{[S^{2-}]}{[HS^-]}$$

$$pK = -\log(1.3 \times 10^{-13}) = 12.9$$

$$\log \frac{[S^{2-}]}{[HS^-]} = \log \frac{(0.030)}{(0.020)} = \log(1.5) = 0.18$$

$$pH = 12.9 + 0.18 = 13.1.$$

(d) The reaction ($H_2S \rightleftharpoons 2 H^+ + S^{2-}$) is the sum of the two acid dissociation reactions below.

$$H_2S \rightleftharpoons H^+ + HS^-$$
$$HS^- \rightleftharpoons H^+ + S^{2-}$$

If one reaction is the sum of two other reactions, then its equilibrium constant will be the product of the equilibrium constants for the other two reactions.

So $K_{eq} = K_1 K_2 = (1.0 \times 10^{-7})(1.3 \times 10^{-13}) = 1.3 \times 10^{-20}$

3. (a) $pK_b = -\log K_b = -\log(1.79 \times 10^{-5}) = 4.75$

(b) This is a buffered solution, so we'll use the Henderson-Hasselbach expression.

First let's find $[NH_4^+]$ and $[NH_3]$.

Moles = (molarity)(volume)

Moles of NH_4^+ = (0.100 M)(0.100 L) = 0.010 moles

Moles of NH_3 = (0.200)(0.080 L) = 0.016 moles

When we mix the solutions, the volume becomes (0.100 L) + (0.080 L) = 0.180 L.

$$Molarity = \frac{moles}{volume}$$

$$[NH_4^+] = \frac{(0.010 \text{ mol})}{(0.180 \text{ L})} = 0.056 \ M$$

$$[NH_3] = \frac{(0.016 \text{ mol})}{(0.180 \text{ mol})} = 0.089 \ M$$

Now we can use the Henderson-Hasselbach expression for bases.

$$pOH = pK + \log \frac{[NH_4^+]}{[NH_3]}$$

$pK = 4.75$

$$\log \frac{[NH_4{}^+]}{[NH_3]} = \log \frac{(0.056\ M)}{(0.089\ M)} = -0.20$$

$pOH = 4.75 + (-0.20) = 4.55$

$pH = 14 - pOH = 14 - 4.55 = 9.45$

(c) First let's find out how many moles of NaOH were added.

$$Moles = \frac{moles}{MW}$$

$$Moles\ of\ NaOH = \frac{(0.200\ g)}{(40.0\ g/m)} = 0.005\ mol$$

When NaOH is added to the solution, the following reaction occurs.

$NH_4{}^+ + OH^- \rightarrow NH_3 + H_2O$

So for every unit of NaOH added, one ion of $NH_4{}^+$ disappears and one molecule of NH_3 appears. We can use the results of the molar calculations we did in part (b).

Moles of $NH_4{}^+ = (0.010) - (0.005) = 0.005$ moles

Moles of $NH_3 = (0.016) + (0.005) = 0.021$ moles

Now we can use the Henderson-Hasselbach expression. We can use the number of moles we just calculated (0.005 for $NH_4{}^+$ and 0.021 for NH_3) instead of concentrations because in a solution the concentrations will be proportional to the number of moles.

$$pOH = pK + \log \frac{[NH_4{}^+]}{[NH_3]}$$

$pK = 4.75$

$$\log \frac{[NH_4{}^+]}{[NH_3]} = \log \frac{(0.005\ mol)}{(0.021\ mol)} = -0.62$$

$pOH = 4.75 + (-0.62) = 4.13$

$pH = 14 - pOH = 9.87$

(d) When equal quantities of a base (NH_3) and its conjugate acid ($NH_4{}^+$) are mixed in a solution, the pOH will be equal to the pK_b.

From (a), $pOH = pK_b = 4.75$

$pH = 14 - pOH = 9.25$.

Essays

4. (a) An amphoteric species can act as either an acid or base.

    $H_2PO_4{}^-$ is amphoteric.

    Conjugate base: $HPO_4{}^{2-}$

    Conjugate acid: H_3PO_4

    OR

    $HPO_4{}^{2-}$ is amphoteric.

    Conjugate base: $PO_4{}^{3-}$

    Conjugate acid: $H_2PO_4{}^-$

(b) The smaller the dissociation constant, the more tightly the acid holds its hydrogen ions and the weaker the acid becomes.

After a hydrogen ion has been removed, the remaining species has a negative charge that attracts the remaining hydrogen ions more strongly.

(c) $H_2PO_4^- \rightleftharpoons H^+ + HPO_4^{2-}$ $K_2 = 6.2 \times 10^{-8}$

For $H_2PO_4^-$, $pK_a = -\log(6.2 \times 10^{-8}) = 7.2$

The best buffer solution is made with an acid whose pK_a is approximately equal to the desired pH.

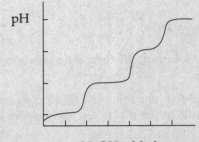

NaOH added

The axes should have the correct labelling (pH and NaOH added).

The curve should show rising pH and it should have three bumps.

5.   (a) The solution will be basic. A salt composed of the conjugate of a strong base (Na^+) and the conjugate of a weak acid ($C_2H_3O_2^-$) will create a basic solution in water.

$NaC_2H_3O_2$ dissociates into Na^+ and $C_2H_3O_2^-$.

Na^+ does not react with water but $C_2H_3O_2^-$ does.

$C_2H_3O_2^- + H_2O \rightleftharpoons HC_2H_3O_2 + OH^-$

(b) The solution will be acidic. A salt composed of the conjugate of a strong acid (Cl^-) and the conjugate of a weak base (NH_4^+) will create an acidic solution in water.

NH_4Cl dissociates into NH_4^+ and Cl^-.

Cl^- does not react with water but NH_4^+ does.

$NH_4^+ + H_2O \rightleftharpoons NH_3 + H_3O^+$

(c) For a buffer solution, it is necessary for both an acid (HA) and its conjugate base (A^-) to be present in the solution.

By definition, strong acids dissociate completely, so while there will be plenty of conjugate base (A^-), there will never be enough acid (HA) for a buffer.

Weak acids do not dissociate completely, so it is possible to have a solution that contains both undissociated acid (HA) and conjugate base (A^-).

(d) KOH separates into K^+ and OH^- in water because the ionic bond between O and K in the unit can be broken by water, which is a polar solvent.

HBrO separates into H^+ and BrO^- because the O–Br bond pulls electrons away from the O–H bond, making it easier to break.

6. (a) HCl is stronger. The bond between H and Cl is weaker than the bond between H and F, so HCl dissociates more easily.

By the way, the fact that HF is more polar than HCl does NOT make it a weaker acid; in general, greater polarity of the H–X bond makes for greater acid strength. HF is an anomaly in that it has high polarity and low acid strength.

(b) H_2SO_3 is stronger. As a polyprotic acid gives up hydrogen ions, it becomes negatively charged, causing it to hang on to its remaining hydrogen ions more tightly, which weakens it as an acid.

(c)

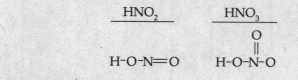

HNO_3 is stronger. As more oxygens are added to the central atom of an oxyacid, the oxidation number of the central atom increases.

In HNO_2, the central atom, N, has an oxidation state of +3.

In HNO_3, N has an oxidation state of +5.

The increased oxidation state of N makes the N–O bond stronger, which in turn makes the O–H bond weaker. The weakness of the O–H bond makes the acid stronger.

(d)

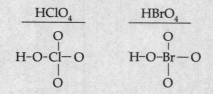

$HClO_4$ is stronger. Cl has greater electronegativity than Br, so Cl draws electrons away from O in the Cl–O bond, making the O more positive. This weakens O's attraction for the H^+ ion and thus weakens the O–H bond. A weak O–H bond makes for a strong acid.

12

KINETICS

How often does this topic appear on the test?

In the multiple-choice section, this topic appears in about 3 out of 75 questions.
In the free-response section, you'll see this topic almost every year.

THE RATE LAW

The rate law for a reaction describes the dependence of the initial rate of a reaction on the concentrations of its reactants. It includes a rate constant, k. The rate of a reaction is described in terms of the rate of appearance of a product or the rate of disappearance of a reactant. The rate law for a reaction can not be determined from a balanced equation; it must be determined from experimental data, which is presented on the test in table form.

Here's how it's done

The data below were collected for the following hypothetical reaction:

$$A + 2B + C \rightarrow D$$

Experiment	Initial Concentration of Reactants (M)			Initial rate of Formation of D (M/min)
	[A]	[B]	[C]	
1	0.10	0.10	0.10	0.01
2	0.10	0.10	0.20	0.01
3	0.10	0.20	0.20	0.02
4	0.20	0.20	0.20	0.08

The rate law always takes the following form, using the concentrations of the reactants:

$$\text{Rate} = k[A]^x[B]^y[C]^z$$

The greater the value of a reactant's exponent, the more a change in the concentration of that reactant will affect the rate of the reaction. To find the values for the exponents x, y, and z, we need to examine how changes in the individual reactants affect the rate. The easiest way to find the exponents is to see what happens to the rate when the concentration of an individual reactant is doubled.

Let's look at [A]

From experiment 3 to experiment 4, [A] doubles while the other reactant concentrations remain constant. For this reason, it is useful to use the rate values from these two experiments to calculate x (the order of the reaction with respect to reactant A).

As you can see from the table, the rate quadruples from experiment 3 to experiment 4, going from 0.02 M/sec to 0.08 M/sec.

We need to find a value for the exponent x that relates the doubling of the concentration to the quadrupling of the rate. The value of x can be calculated in this way:

$$(2)^x = 4, \text{ so } x = 2$$

Because the value of x is 2, the reaction is said to be second order with respect to A.

$$\text{Rate} = k[A]^2[B]^y[C]^z$$

Let's look at [B]

From experiment 2 to experiment 3, [B] doubles while the other reactant concentrations remain constant. For this reason it is useful to use the rate values from these two experiments to calculate y (the order of the reaction with respect to reactant B).

As you can see from the table, the rate doubles from experiment 2 to experiment 3, going from 0.01 M/sec to 0.02 M/sec.

We need to find a value for the exponent y that relates the doubling of the concentration to the doubling of the rate. The value of y can be calculated in this way:

$$(2)^y = 2, \text{ so } y = 1$$

Because the value of y is 1, the reaction is said to be first order with respect to B.

$$\text{Rate} = k[A]^2[B][C]^z$$

Let's look at [C]

From experiment 1 to experiment 2, [C] doubles while the other reactant concentrations remain constant.

The rate remains the same at 0.01 M.

The rate change is $(2)^z = 1$, so $z = 0$.

Because the value of z is 0, the reaction is said to be zero order with respect to C.

$$\text{Rate} = k[A]^2[B]$$

Because the sum of the exponents is 3, the reaction is said to be third order overall.

Once the rate law has been determined, the value of the rate constant can be calculated using any of the lines of data on the table. The units of the rate constant are dependent on the order of the reaction, so it's important to carry along units throughout all rate constant calculations.

Let's use experiment 3:

$$k = \frac{\text{Rate}}{[A]^2[B]} = \frac{(0.02\,M/\text{sec})}{(0.10\,M)^2(0.20\,M)} = 10\left(\frac{(M)}{(M)^3(\text{sec})}\right) = 10\ M^{-2}\text{-sec}^{-1}$$

You should note that we can tell from the coefficients in the original balanced equation that the rate of appearance of D is equal to the rate of disappearance of A and C because the coefficients of all three are the same. The coefficient of D is half as large as the coefficient of B, however, so the rate at which D appears is half the rate at which B disappears.

COLLISION THEORY

According to collision theory, chemical reactions occur because reactants are constantly moving around and colliding with each other.

When reactants collide with sufficient energy (**activation energy, E_a**), a reaction occurs. At any given time during a reaction, a certain fraction of the reactant molecules will collide with sufficient energy to cause a reaction between them.

Reaction rate increases with increasing concentration of reactants because if there are more reactant molecules moving around in a given volume, then more collisions will occur.

Reaction rate increases with increasing temperature because increasing temperature means that the molecules are moving faster, which means that the molecules have greater average kinetic energy. The higher the temperature, the greater the number of reactant molecules colliding with each other with enough energy (E_a) to cause a reaction.

The diagram below is often used to show that increasing temperature increases the fraction of reactant molecules above the activation energy.

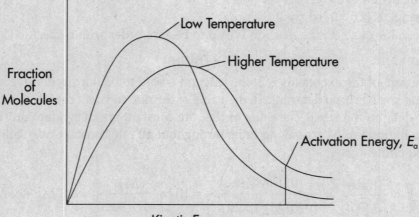

REACTION MECHANISMS

Many chemical reactions are not one-step processes. Rather, the balanced equation is the sum of a series of simple steps. Three molecules will not collide simultaneously very often, so steps of a reaction mechanism involve only one or two reactants at a time.

For instance, the following hypothetical reaction:

$$2\,A + 2\,B \rightarrow C + D \qquad\qquad Rate = k[A]^2[B]$$

could take place by the following three-step mechanism:

I. $A + A \rightleftharpoons X$ (fast)

II. $X + B \rightarrow C + Y$ (slow)

III. $Y + B \rightarrow D$ (fast)

Species X and Y are called **intermediates** because they appear in the mechanism, but they cancel out of the balanced equation. The steps of a reaction mechanism must add up to equal the balanced equation, with all intermediates canceling out.

Let's show that the mechanism above is consistent with the balanced equation by adding up all the steps.

I. $A + A \rightleftharpoons X$

II. $X + B \rightarrow C + Y$

III. $Y + B \rightarrow D$

___

$A + A + X + B + Y + B \rightarrow X + C + Y + D$

Cancel species that appear on both sides.

$2\,A + 2\,B \rightarrow C + D$

By adding up all the steps, we get the balanced equation for the overall reaction, so this mechanism is consistent with the balanced equation.

As in any process where many steps are involved, the speed of the whole process can't go faster than the speed of the slowest step in the process, so the slowest step of a reaction is the **rate-determining step**. Because the slowest step is the most important step in determining the rate of a reaction, the slowest step and the steps leading up to it are used to see if the mechanism is consistent with the rate law for the overall reaction.

Let's look at the reaction and the three-step mechanism again:

$$2\,A + 2\,B \rightarrow C + D \qquad\qquad\qquad \text{Rate} = k[A]^2[B]$$

The reaction above takes place by the following three-step mechanism:

I. $A + A \rightleftharpoons X$ (fast)

II. $X + B \rightarrow C + Y$ (slow)

III. $Y + B \rightarrow D$ (fast)

Let's show that the reaction mechanism is consistent with the rate law (Rate = $k[A]^2[B]$).
The slowest step is the rate-determining step, so we should start with the rate law for step II:

$$\text{Rate} = k_2[X][B]$$

But X is an intermediate, which means that it can't appear in the overall rate law. To eliminate X from the rate law, we need to look at the equilibrium reaction in step I. We can assume that the reaction in step I comes to equilibrium quickly. At equilibrium the rate of the forward reaction is equal to the rate of the reverse reaction, so we get:

$$k_f[A][A] = k_r[X]$$

Now we can solve for [X].

$$[X] = \frac{k_f}{k_r}[A]^2$$

Once we have solved our equilibrium rate expression for [X] in terms of [A], we can substitute for [X] in our step II rate law:

$$\text{Rate} = k_2\frac{k_f}{k_r}[A]^2[B] = k[A]^2[B]$$

Now we have a rate law containing only reactants from the overall equation and which is consistent with the experimentally derived rate law that we were given. You can always eliminate intermediates from the rate-determining step by this process.

CATALYSTS

A catalyst increases the rate of a chemical reaction without being consumed in the process; catalysts do not appear in the balanced equation. In some cases, a catalyst is a necessary part of a reaction because in its absence, the reaction would proceed at too slow a rate to be at all useful.

A catalyst increases the rate of a chemical reaction by providing an alternate reaction pathway with a lower activation energy.

KINETICS AND EQUILIBRIUM

There is a relationship between the rate constants for the forward and reverse directions of a particular reaction and the equilibrium constant for that reaction.

$$K_{eq} = \frac{k_f}{k_r}$$

K_{eq} = the equilibrium constant

k_f = the rate constant for the forward reaction

k_r = the rate constant for the reverse reaction

KINETICS

QUESTIONS

Multiple choice

Questions 1–3

$$A + B \rightarrow C$$

The following are possible rate laws for the hypothetical reaction given above.

(A) Rate = $k[A]$
(B) Rate = $k[A]^2$
(C) Rate = $k[A][B]$
(D) Rate = $k[A]^2[B]$
(E) Rate = $k[A]^2[B]^2$

1. This is the rate law for a first order reaction.

2. This is the rate law for a reaction that is second order with respect to B.

3. This is the rate law for a third order reaction.

Questions 4–6

$$A + B \rightarrow C$$

The following are possible rate laws for the hypothetical reaction given above.

(A) Rate = $k[A]$
(B) Rate = $k[B]^2$
(C) Rate = $k[A][B]$
(D) Rate = $k[A]^2[B]$
(E) Rate = $k[A]^2[B]^2$

4. When [A] and [B] are doubled, the initial rate of reaction will increase by a factor of eight.

5. When [A] and [B] are doubled, the initial rate of reaction will increase by a factor of two.

6. When [A] is doubled and [B] is held constant, the initial rate of reaction will not change.

7. A multistep reaction takes place by the following mechanism.

$$A + B \rightarrow C + D$$
$$A + C \rightarrow D + E$$

Which of the species shown above is an intermediate in the reaction?

(A) A
(B) B
(C) C
(D) D
(E) E

8.
$$2\ NOCl \rightarrow 2\ NO + Cl_2$$

The reaction above takes place with all of the reactants and products in the gaseous phase. Which of the following is true of the relative rates of disappearance of the reactants and appearance of the products?

(A) NO appears at twice the rate that NOCl disappears.
(B) NO appears at the same rate that NOCl disappears.
(C) NO appears at half the rate that NOCl disappears.
(D) Cl_2 appears at the same rate that NOCl disappears.
(E) Cl_2 appears at twice the rate that NOCl disappears.

9.
$$H_2(g) + I_2(g) \rightarrow 2\ HI(g)$$

When the reaction given above takes place in a sealed isothermal container, the rate law is:

$$Rate = k[H_2][I_2]$$

If a mole of H_2 gas is added to the reaction chamber, which of the following will be true?

(A) The rate of reaction and the rate constant will increase.
(B) The rate of reaction and the rate constant will not change.
(C) The rate of reaction will increase and the rate constant will decrease.
(D) The rate of reaction will increase and the rate constant will not change.
(E) The rate of reaction will not change and the rate constant will increase.

10.
$$A + B \rightarrow C$$

When the reaction given above takes place, the rate law is:

$$Rate = k[A]$$

If the temperature of the reaction chamber were increased, which of the following would be true?

(A) The rate of reaction and the rate constant will increase.
(B) The rate of reaction and the rate constant will not change.
(C) The rate of reaction will increase and the rate constant will decrease.
(D) The rate of reaction will increase and the rate constant will not change.
(E) The rate of reaction will not change and the rate constant will increase.

11. $A + B \rightarrow C$

Based on the following experimental data, what is the rate law for the hypothetical reaction given above?

Experiment	[A] (M)	[B] (M)	Initial Rate of Formation of C (mol/L-sec)
1	0.20	0.10	3×10^{-2}
2	0.20	0.20	6×10^{-2}
3	0.40	0.20	6×10^{-2}

(A) Rate = $k[A]$
(B) Rate = $k[A]^2$
(C) Rate = $k[B]$
(D) Rate = $k[B]^2$
(E) Rate = $k[A][B]$

12. $A + B \rightarrow C + D$

The rate law for the hypothetical reaction shown above is as follows:

$$Rate = k[A]$$

Which of the following changes to the system will increase the rate of the reaction?

  I. An increase in the concentration of A
 II. An increase in the concentration of B
III. An increase in the temperature

(A) I only
(B) I and II only
(C) I and III only
(D) II and III only
(E) I, II, and III

Problems

1.

$$A + 2B \rightarrow 2C$$

The following results were obtained in experiments designed to study the rate of the reaction above.

Experiment	Initial Concentration (mol/L)		Initial rate of disappearance of A (M/sec)
	[A]	[B]	
1	0.05	0.05	3.0×10^{-3}
2	0.05	0.10	6.0×10^{-3}
3	0.10	0.10	1.2×10^{-2}
4	0.20	0.10	2.4×10^{-2}

(a) Determine the order of the reaction with respect to each of the reactants and write the rate law for the reaction.

(b) Calculate the value of the rate constant, k, for the reaction. Include the units.

(c) If another experiment is attempted with [A] and [B] both 0.02-molar, what will be the initial rate of disappearance of A?

(d) The following reaction mechanism was proposed for the reaction above.

$$A + B \rightarrow C + D$$
$$D + B \rightarrow C$$

(i) Show that the mechanism is consistent with the balanced reaction.

(ii) Show which step is the rate-determining step and explain your choice.

2.

$$2\,NO(g) + Br_2(g) \rightarrow 2\,NOBr(g)$$

The following results were obtained in experiments designed to study the rate of the reaction above.

Experiment	Initial Concentration (mol/L)		Initial rate of Appearance of NOBr (M/sec)
	[NO]	[Br_2]	
1	0.02	0.02	9.6×10^{-3}
2	0.04	0.02	3.8×10^{-1}
3	0.02	0.04	1.9×10^{-1}

(a) Write the rate law for the reaction.

(b) Calculate the value of the rate constant, k, for the reaction. Include the units.

(c) In experiment 2, what was the concentration of NO remaining when half of the original amount of Br_2 was consumed?

(d)   Which of the following reaction mechanisms is consistent with the rate law established in (a)? Explain your choice.

  I. $NO + NO \rightleftharpoons N_2O_2$ (fast)

       $N_2O_2 + Br_2 \rightarrow 2\ NOBr$ (slow)

  II. $Br_2 \rightarrow Br + Br$ (slow)

       $2(NO + Br \rightarrow NOBr)$ (fast)

3. $2\ A + B \rightarrow C + D$

The following results were obtained in experiments designed to study the rate of the reaction above.

Experiment	Initial Concentration (moles/L) [A] [B]		Initial rate of Formation of D (M/min)
1	0.10	0.10	1.5×10^{-3}
2	0.20	0.20	3.0×10^{-3}
3	0.20	0.40	6.0×10^{-3}

(a)   Write the rate law for the reaction.

(b)   Calculate the value of the rate constant, k, for the reaction. Include the units.

(c)   If experiment 2 goes to completion, what will be the final concentration of D? Assume that the volume is unchanged over the course of the reaction and that no D was present at the start of the experiment.

(d)   Which of the following possible reaction mechanisms is consistent with the rate law found in (a)?

  I. $A + B \rightarrow C + E$ (slow)

       $A + E \rightarrow D$ (fast)

  II. $B \rightarrow C + E$ (slow)

       $A + E \rightarrow F$ (fast)

       $A + F \rightarrow D$ (fast)

Essays

4. $$A(g) + B(g) \rightarrow C(g)$$

The reaction above is second order with respect to A and zero order with respect to B. Reactants A and B are present in a closed container. Predict how each of the following changes to the reaction system will affect the rate and rate constant.

(a) More gas A is added to the container.

(b) More gas B is added to the container.

(c) The temperature is increased.

(d) An inert gas D is added to the container.

(e) The volume of the container is decreased.

5. Use your knowledge of kinetics to answer the following questions.

(a)

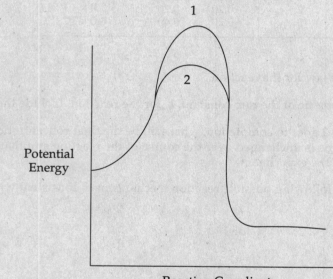

The two lines in the diagram above show different reaction pathways for the same reaction. Which of the two lines shows the reaction when a catalyst has been added? Explain.

(b)

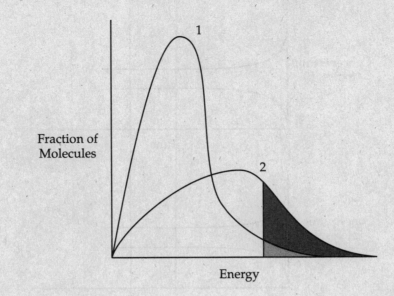

Which of the two lines in the energy distribution diagram shows the conditions at a higher temperature?

(c)

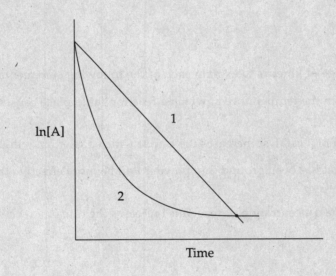

Which of the two lines in the diagram above shows the relationship of ln[A] to time for a first order reaction with the following rate law.

$$Rate = k[A]$$

(d)

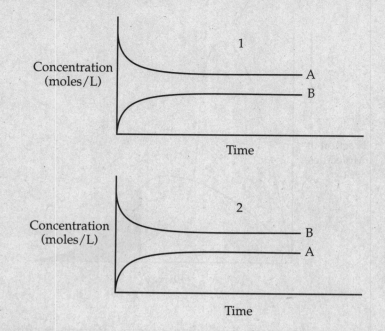

Which of the two graphs above shows the changes in concentration over time for the following reaction?

$$A \rightarrow B$$

6. Use your knowledge of kinetics to explain each of the following statements.

   (a) An increase in the temperature at which a reaction takes place causes an increase in reaction rate.

   (b) The addition of a catalyst increases the rate at which a reaction will take place.

   (c) A catalyst that has been ground into powder will be more effective than a solid block of the same catalyst.

   (d) Increasing the concentration of reactants increases the rate of a reaction.

ANSWERS

Multiple choice

1. **(A)** is correct. In a first order reaction, the exponents of all the reactants present in the rate law add up to 1.

$$Rate = k[A]^1$$

2. **(E)** is correct. The exponent for B in this rate law is 2, so the reaction is second order with respect to B.

$$Rate = k[A]^2[B]^2$$

3. **(D)** is correct. In a third order reaction, the exponents of all the reactants present in the rate law add up to 3.

$$Rate = k[A]^2[B]^1$$

4. **(D)** is correct. Let's say that [A] = [B] = 1. Then Rate = k

Now if we double [A] and [B], that is, we make [A] = [B] = 2, here's what we get for each of the answer choices:

(A) Rate = $k(2) = 2k$

(B) Rate = $k(2)^2 = 4k$

(C) Rate = $k(2)(2) = 4k$

(D) Rate = $k(2)^2(2) = 8k$

(E) Rate = $k(2)^2(2)^2 = 16k$

So in (D), the rate increases by a factor of 8.

5. **(A)** is correct. Let's say that [A] = [B] = 1. Then Rate = k

Now if we double [A] and [B], that is, we make [A] = [B] = 2, here's what we get for each of the answer choices:

(A) Rate = $k(2) = 2k$

(B) Rate = $k(2)^2 = 4k$

(C) Rate = $k(2)(2) = 4k$

(D) Rate = $k(2)^2(2) = 8k$

(E) Rate = $k(2)^2(2)^2 = 16k$

So in (A), the rate increases by a factor of 2.

6. **(B)** is correct. We need to find the rate law that is independent of changes in [A].

The only choice listed that does not include [A] is choice (B), Rate = $k[B]^2$.

7. **(C)** is correct. C is created and used up in the reaction, so it will not be present in the balanced equation.

8. **(B)** is correct. For every two NO molecules that form, two NOCl molecules must disappear, so NO is appearing at the same rate that NOCl is disappearing. Choices (D) and (E) are wrong because for every mole of Cl_2 that forms, two moles of NOCl are disappearing, so Cl_2 is appearing at *half* the rate that NOCl is disappearing.

9. **(D)** is correct. From the rate law given in the question (Rate = $k[H_2][I_2]$), we can see that increasing the concentration of H_2 will increase the rate of reaction. The rate constant k is not affected by changes in the concentration of the reactants.

10. **(A)** is correct. When temperature increases, the rate constant increases to reflect the fact that more reactant molecules are likely to have enough energy to react at any given time. So both the rate constant and the rate of reaction will increase.

11. **(C)** is correct.

From a comparison of experiments 1 and 2, when [B] is doubled while [A] is held constant, the rate doubles. That means that the reaction is first order with respect to B.

From a comparison of experiments 2 and 3, when [A] is doubled while [B] is held constant, the rate doesn't change. That means that the reaction is zero order with respect to A and that A will not appear in the rate law.

So the rate law is: Rate = $k[B]$

12. **(C) is correct.**

An increase in the concentration of A will increase the rate, as shown in the rate law for the reaction, so (I) is correct. Reactant B is not included in the rate law, so an increase in the concentration of B will not affect the rate, so (II) is wrong. An increase in temperature causes more collisions with greater energy among reactants and always increases the rate of a reaction, so (III) is correct.

Problems

1. (a) When we compare the results of experiments 3 and 4, we see that when [A] doubles, the rate doubles, so the reaction is first order with respect to A.

    When we compare the results of experiments 1 and 2, we see that when [B] doubles, the rate doubles, so the reaction is first order with respect to B.

    Rate = k[A][B]

    (b) Use the values from experiment 3, just because they look the most simple.

    $$k = \frac{\text{Rate}}{[A][B]} = \frac{\left(1.2 \times 10^{-2} \ M/\text{sec}\right)}{(0.10 \ M)(0.10 \ M)} = 1.2 \ M^{-1}\text{sec}^{-1} = 1.2 \ \text{L/mol-sec}$$

    (c) Use the rate law.

    Rate = k[A][B]

    Rate = $(1.2 \ M^{-1}\text{sec}^{-1})(0.02 \ M)(0.02 \ M) = 4.8 \times 10^{-4} \ M/\text{sec}$

    (d) (i) $A + B \rightarrow C + D$

    $D + B \rightarrow C$

    The two reactions add up to:

    $A + 2B + D \rightarrow 2C + D$

    D's cancel and we're left with the balanced equation.

    $A + 2B \rightarrow 2C$

    (ii) $A + B \rightarrow C + D$ (slow)

    $D + B \rightarrow C$ (fast)

    The first part of the mechanism is the slow, rate determining step because its reactants (A and B) are the ones present in the rate law.

2. (a) When we compare the results of experiments 1 and 2, we see that when [NO] doubles, the rate quadruples, so the reaction is second order with respect to NO.

    When we compare the results of experiments 1 and 3, we see that when [Br$_2$] doubles, the rate doubles, so the reaction is first order with respect to Br$_2$.

    Rate = k[NO]^2[Br$_2$]

    (b) Use the values from experiment 1, just because they look the most simple.

    $$k = \frac{\text{Rate}}{[NO]^2[Br_2]} = \frac{\left(9.6 \times 10^{-2} \ M/\text{sec}\right)}{(0.02 \ M)^2(0.02 \ M)} = 1.2 \times 10^4 \ M^{-2}\text{sec}^{-1} = 1.2 \times 10^4 \ \text{L}^2/\text{mol}^2\text{-sec}$$

    (c) In experiment 2, we started with [Br$_2$] = 0.02 M, so 0.01 M was consumed.

    From the balanced equation, 2 moles of NO are consumed for every mole of Br$_2$ consumed. So 0.02 M of NO are consumed.

    [NO] remaining = 0.04 M − 0.02 M = 0.02 M

(d) Choice (I) agrees with the rate law.

$$NO + NO \leftrightarrow N_2O_2 \qquad (fast)$$

$$N_2O_2 + Br_2 \rightarrow 2\,NOBr \quad (slow)$$

The slow step is the rate-determining step, with the following rate law:

Rate = $k[N_2O_2][Br_2]$

We can replace the intermediate (N_2O_2) by assuming that the first step reaches equilibrium instantaneously and remembering that at equilibrium, the rates of the forward and reverse reactions are equal.

$k_f[NO]^2 = k_r[N_2O_2]$

Now solve for $[N_2O_2]$:

$[N_2O_2] = \dfrac{k_f}{k_r}[NO]^2$

Now we can substitute in the rate law for the rate determining step.

Rate = $k\dfrac{k_f}{k_r}[NO]^2[Br_2]$

By the way, the mechanism in choice (II) would have a rate law of Rate = $k[Br_2]$.

3. (a) When we compare the results of experiments 2 and 3, we see that when [B] doubles, the rate doubles, so the reaction is first order with respect to B.

Experiments 2 and 3 prove that the rate must double when [B] doubles. Knowing this, we can see that when the rate doubles from experiment 1 to 2, it must be because of B, and the change in A has no effect. So the reaction is zero order with respect to A.

Rate = $k[B]$

(b) Take the values from experiment 1.

$$k = \frac{\text{Rate}}{[B]} = \frac{\left(1.5 \times 10^{-3}\ M/sec\right)}{\left(0.10\ M\right)} = 1.5 \times 10^{-2}\ sec^{-1}$$

(c) In experiment 2, there are equal concentrations of A and B, but A is consumed twice as fast, so A is the limiting reagant.

0.2 M of A is consumed.

According to the balanced equation, for every 2 moles of A consumed, 1 mole of D is produced.

So if 0.2 M of A is consumed, 0.1 M of D is produced.

(d) The reaction mechanism in choice (II) is consistent with the rate law.

$$B \rightarrow C + E \qquad (slow)$$
$$A + E \rightarrow F \qquad (fast)$$
$$A + F \rightarrow D \qquad (fast)$$

The slow, rate-determining step gives the proper rate law:

Rate = $k[B]$

By the way, choice (I) gives a rate law of Rate = $k[A][B]$

Essays

4. (a) The rate of the reaction will increase because the rate depends on the concentration of A as given in the rate law: Rate = $k[A]^2$.

    The rate constant is independent of the concentration of the reactants and will not change.

    (b) The rate of the reaction will not change. If the reaction is zero order with respect to B, then the rate is independent of the concentration of B.

    The rate constant is independent of the concentration of the reactants and will not change.

    (c) The rate of the reaction will increase with increasing temperature because the rate constant increases with increasing temperature.

    The rate constant increases with increasing temperature because at higher temperature more gas molecules will collide with enough energy to overcome the activation energy for the reaction.

    (d) Neither the rate nor the rate constant will be affected by the addition of an inert gas.

    (e) The rate of the reaction will increase because decreasing the volume of the container will increase the concentration of A. Rate = $k[A]^2$

    The rate constant is independent of the concentration of the reactants and will not change.

5. (a) Line 2 is the catalyzed reaction. Adding a catalyst lowers the activation energy of the reaction, making it easier for the reaction to occur.

    (b) Line 2 shows the higher temperature distribution. At a higher temperature, more of the molecules will be at higher energies, causing the distribution to flatten out and shift to the right.

    (c) Line 1 is correct. ln[reactant] for a first order reaction changes in a linear fashion over time, as shown in the following equation.

    $\ln[A]_t = -kt + \ln[A]_o$

    $y = mx + b$

    Notice the similarity to the slope-intercept form for a linear equation.

    (d) Graph 1 is correct, showing a decrease in the concentration of A as it is consumed in the reaction and a corresponding increase in the concentration of B as it is produced.

6. (a) An increase in temperature means an increase in the energy of the molecules present. If the molecules have more energy, then more of them will collide more often with enough energy to overcome the activation energy required for a reaction to take place, causing the reaction to proceed more quickly.

    (b) A catalyst offers a reaction an alternate pathway with a lower activation energy. If the activation energy is lowered, then more molecular collisions will occur with enough energy to overcome the activation energy, causing the reaction to go more quickly.

    (c) The effectiveness of a solid catalyst depends on the surface area of the catalyst that is exposed to the reactants. Grinding a solid into powder greatly increases its surface area.

    (d) Increasing the concentration of reactants crowds the reactants more closely together, making it more likely that they will collide with each other. The more collisions that occur, the more likely that collisions that will result in a reaction will occur.

13

OXIDATION-REDUCTION AND ELECTROCHEMISTRY

How often does this topic appear on the test?
In the multiple-choice section, this topic appears in about 5 out of 75 questions.
In the free-response section, you'll see this topic every year.

OXIDATION STATES

The **oxidation state** (or oxidation number) of an atom indicates the number of electrons that it gains or loses when it forms a bond. For instance, upon forming a bond with another atom, oxygen generally gains two electrons, which are negatively charged, so the oxidation state of oxygen in a bond is –2. Similarly, sodium generally loses one electron when it bonds to another atom, so its oxidation state in a bond is +1.

Here are three important things you have to keep in mind when dealing with oxidation numbers:

- The oxidation state of an atom that is not bonded to an atom of another element is zero. That means either an atom that is not bonded to any other atom, or an atom that is bonded to another atom of the same element (like the oxygen atoms in O_2).

- The oxidation numbers for all the atoms in a molecule must add up to zero.

- The oxidation numbers for all the atoms in a polyatomic ion must add up to the charge on the ion.

Most elements have different oxidation numbers that can vary depending on the molecule that they are a part of. The following chart shows some elements that consistently take the same oxidation numbers.

Element	Oxidation Number
Alkali metals (Li, Na, ...)	+1
Alkaline earths (Be, Mg, ...)	+2
Group 3A (B, Al, ...)	+3
Oxygen	–2
Halogens (F, Cl, ...)	–1

Transition metals can have several oxidation states, which are differentiated from one another by a Roman numeral in the name of the compound. For example, in copper (II) sulfate ($CuSO_4$), the oxidation state for copper is +2, and in lead (II) oxide (PbO), the oxidation state for lead is +2.

You should be familiar with the following polyatomic ions and their charges.

Hydroxide	OH^-
Nitrate	NO_3^-
Perchlorate	ClO_4^-
Acetate	$C_2H_3O_2^-$
Carbonate	CO_3^{2-}
Sulfate	SO_4^{2-}
Phosphate	PO_4^{3-}

OXIDATION-REDUCTION REACTIONS

In an oxidation-reduction (or redox, for short) reaction, electrons are exchanged by the reactants and the oxidation states of some of the reactants are changed over the course of the reaction. Look at the following reaction.

$$Fe + 2\,HCl \rightarrow FeCl_2 + H_2$$

The oxidation state of Fe changes from 0 to +2.
The oxidation state of H changes from +1 to 0.
When an atom gains electrons, its oxidation number decreases and it is said to have been reduced. In the reaction above, H was reduced.
When an atom loses electrons, its oxidation number increases and it is said to have been oxidized. In the reaction above, Fe was oxidized.
Here's a mnemonic device that might be useful.

> LEO the lion says GER
> **LEO**: you **L**ose **E**lectrons in **O**xidation
> **GER**: you **G**ain **E**lectrons in **R**eduction

Oxidation and reduction go hand in hand. If one atom is losing electrons, another atom must be gaining them.

- If an atom is losing electrons and being oxidized, it must be giving the electrons to another atom, which is being reduced. So if an atom is being oxidized, it is a **reducing agent** or **reductant**.

- If an atom is taking electrons and being reduced, it must be taking electrons away from another atom, which is being oxidized. So if an atom is being reduced, it is an **oxidizing agent** or **oxidant**.

An oxidation-reduction reaction can be written as two **half-reactions**; one for the reduction and one for the oxidation. For example, the reaction:

$$Fe + 2\,HCl \rightarrow FeCl_2 + H_2$$

can be written as:

$$Fe \rightarrow Fe^{2+} + 2\,e^- \qquad \text{Oxidation}$$
$$2\,H^+ + 2\,e^- \rightarrow H_2 \qquad \text{Reduction}$$

REDUCTION POTENTIALS

Every half-reaction has a potential, or voltage, associated with it. For Section II of the test, you'll be given a table of standard reduction potentials like the one below. The potentials are given as reduction half-reactions, but you can read them in reverse and change the sign on the voltage to get oxidation potentials.

STANDARD REDUCTION POTENTIALS, E , IN WATER SOLUTION AT 25 °C (in V)		
$Li^+ + e^-$	$\longrightarrow$ $Li(s)$	−3.05
$Cs^+ + e^-$	$\longrightarrow$ $Cs(s)$	−2.92
$K^+ + e^-$	$\longrightarrow$ $K(s)$	−2.92
$Rb^+ + e^-$	$\longrightarrow$ $Rb(s)$	−2.92
$Ba^2 + 2\,e^-$	$\longrightarrow$ $Ba(s)$	−2.90
$Sr^+ + 2\,e^-$	$\longrightarrow$ $Sr(s)$	−2.89
$Ca^{2+} + 2\,e^-$	$\longrightarrow$ $Ca(s)$	−2.87
$Na^+ + e^-$	$\longrightarrow$ $Na(s)$	−2.71
$Mg^{2+} + 2\,e^-$	$\longrightarrow$ $Mg(s)$	−2.37
$Be^{2+} + 2\,e^-$	$\longrightarrow$ $Be(s)$	−1.70
$Al^{3+} + 3\,e^-$	$\longrightarrow$ $Al(s)$	−1.66
$Mn^{2+} + 2\,e^-$	$\longrightarrow$ $Mn(s)$	−1.18
$Zn^{2+} + 2\,e^-$	$\longrightarrow$ $Zn(s)$	−0.76
$Cr^{3+} + 3\,e^-$	$\longrightarrow$ $Cr(s)$	−0.74
$Fe^{2+} + 2\,e^-$	$\longrightarrow$ $Fe(s)$	−0.44
$Cr^{3+} + e^-$	$\longrightarrow$ Cr^{2+}	−0.41
$Cd^{2+} + 2\,e^-$	$\longrightarrow$ $Cd(s)$	−0.40
$Tl^+ + e^-$	$\longrightarrow$ $Tl(s)$	−0.34
$Co^{2+} + 2\,e^-$	$\longrightarrow$ $Co(s)$	−0.28
$Ni^{2+} + 2\,e^-$	$\longrightarrow$ $Ni(s)$	−0.25
$Sn^{2+} + 2\,e^-$	$\longrightarrow$ $Sn(s)$	−0.14
$Pb^{2+} + 2\,e^-$	$\longrightarrow$ $Pb(s)$	−0.13
$2\,H^+ + 2\,e^-$	$\longrightarrow$ $H_2(g)$	0.00
$S(s) + 2\,H^+ + 2\,e^-$	$\longrightarrow$ H_2S	0.14
$Sn^{4+} + 2\,e^-$	$\longrightarrow$ Sn^{2+}	0.15
$Cu^{2+} + e^-$	$\longrightarrow$ Cu^+	0.15
$Cu^{2+} + 2\,e^-$	$\longrightarrow$ $Cu(s)$	0.34
$Cu^+ + e^-$	$\longrightarrow$ $Cu(s)$	0.52
$I_2(s) + 2\,e^-$	$\longrightarrow$ $2\,I^-$	0.53
$Fe^{3+} + e^-$	$\longrightarrow$ Fe^{2+}	0.77
$Hg_2^{2+} + 2\,e^-$	$\longrightarrow$ $2\,Hg(l)$	0.79
$Ag^+ + e^-$	$\longrightarrow$ $Ag(s)$	0.80
$Hg^{2+} + 2\,e^-$	$\longrightarrow$ $Hg(l)$	0.85
$2\,Hg^{2+} + 2\,e^-$	$\longrightarrow$ Hg_2^{2+}	0.92
$Br_2(l) + 2\,e^-$	$\longrightarrow$ $2\,Br^-$	1.07
$O_2(g) + 4\,H^+ + 4\,e^-$	$\longrightarrow$ $2\,H_2O$	1.23
$Cl_2(g) + 2\,e^-$	$\longrightarrow$ $2\,Cl^-$	1.36
$Au^{3+} + 3\,e^-$	$\longrightarrow$ $Au(s)$	1.50
$Co^{3+} + e^-$	$\longrightarrow$ Co^{2+}	1.82
$F_2(g) + 2\,e^-$	$\longrightarrow$ $2\,F^-$	2.87

Look at the reduction potential for Zn^{2+}:

$$Zn^{2+} + 2\ e^- \rightarrow Zn \qquad\qquad E^\circ = -0.76\ V$$

Read the reduction half-reaction in reverse and change the sign on the voltage to get the oxidation potential for Zn.

$$Zn \rightarrow Zn^{2+} + 2\ e^- \qquad\qquad E^\circ = +0.76\ V$$

The larger the potential for a half-reaction, the more likely it is to occur, for instance, let's look at the bottom of the table of half-reactions:

$$F_2(g) + 2e^- \rightarrow 2\ F^- \qquad\qquad E^\circ = +2.87\ V$$

$F_2(g)$ has a very large reduction potential, so it is likely to gain electrons and be reduced, making it a strong oxidizing agent.

Now let's look at the top of the table. We need to look at the reverse (oxidation) reaction to get a positive potential.

$$Li(s) \rightarrow Li^+ + e^- \qquad\qquad E^\circ = +3.05\ V$$

$Li(s)$ has a very large oxidation potential, making it very likely to lose electrons and be oxidized, so $Li(s)$ is a very strong reducing agent.

You can calculate the potential of a redox reaction if you know the potentials for the two half-reactions that constitute it. There are two important things to remember when calculating the potential of a redox reaction:

- Add the potential for the oxidation half-reaction to the potential for the reduction half-reaction.

- Never multiply the potential for a half-reaction by a coefficient.

Let's look at the following reaction:

$$Zn + 2\ Ag^+ \rightarrow Zn^{2+} + 2\ Ag$$

The two half reactions are:

Oxidation:	$Zn \rightarrow Zn^{2+} + 2\ e^-$	$E^\circ = +0.76\ V$
Reduction:	$Ag^+ + e^- \rightarrow Ag$	$E^\circ = +0.80\ V$

$E = E_{oxidation} + E_{reduction}$

$E = 0.76\ V + 0.80\ V = 1.56\ V$

Notice that we ignored the fact that silver has a coefficient of 2 in the balanced equation.

VOLTAGE AND SPONTANEITY

A redox reaction will occur spontaneously if its potential has a positive value. We also know from thermodynamics that a reaction that occurs spontaneously has a negative value for free-energy change. The relationship between reaction potential and free energy for a redox reaction is given by the following equation, which serves as a bridge between thermodynamics and electrochemistry.

$\Delta G° = -nFE°$

$\Delta G°$ = Standard Gibbs free energy change (kJ/mol)

n = the number of moles of electrons exchanged in the reaction (mol)

F = Faraday's constant, 96,500 coulombs/mole (that is, 1 mole of electrons has a charge of 96,500 coulombs).

$E°$ = Standard reaction potential (V)

From this equation we can see a few important things. *If $E°$ is positive, $\Delta G°$ is negative and the reaction is spontaneous, and if $E°$ is negative, $\Delta G°$ is positive and the reaction is non-spontaneous.*

Look at the reaction we saw above:

$$Zn + 2\ Ag^+ \rightarrow Zn^{2+} + 2\ Ag \qquad\qquad E° = +1.56\ V$$

The reaction potential is positive, so the free energy change is negative and the reaction is spontaneous.

VOLTAGE AND EQUILIBRIUM

The standard reaction potential is related to the equilibrium constant for a reaction by the following equation, which is another bridge between two important concepts.

$$E° = \frac{RT}{nF}\ln K$$

R = the gas constant, 8.31 (volt-coulomb)/(mol-K)

T = absolute temperature (K)

n = the number of moles of electrons exchanged in the reaction (mol)

F = Faraday's constant, 96,500 coulombs/mole

At 25 °C (298 K), this simplifies to:

$$\log K = \frac{nE°}{0.0592}$$

If $E°$ is positive, then K is greater than 1 and the forward reaction is favored, and if $E°$ is negative, then K is less than 1 and the reverse reaction is favored.

GALVANIC CELLS

In a **galvanic cell** (also called a voltaic cell), a spontaneous redox reaction is used to generate a flow of current.

Look at the following spontaneous redox reaction:

$$Zn(s) + Cu^{2+}(aq) \rightarrow Zn^{2+}(aq) + Cu(s) \qquad E° = 1.10 \text{ V}$$

Oxidation:	$Zn(s) \rightarrow Zn^{2+}(aq) + 2 \text{ e}^-$	$E° = 0.76 \text{ V}$
Reduction:	$Cu^{2+}(aq) + 2 \text{ e}^- \rightarrow Cu(s)$	$E° = 0.34 \text{ V}$

A galvanic cell using this reaction is shown below.

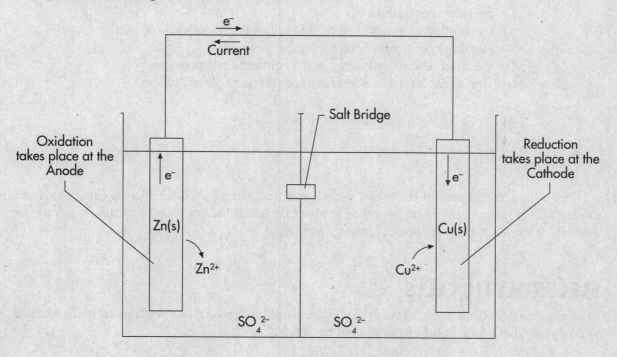

In a galvanic cell, the two half-reactions take place in separate chambers and the electrons that are released by the oxidation reaction pass through a wire to the chamber where they are consumed in the reduction reaction. That's how the current is created. Current, by the way, is defined as the flow of positive charge, so current is always in the opposite direction from the flow of electrons.

In any electric cell (either a galvanic cell or an electrolytic cell, which we'll discuss in a moment) oxidation takes place at the electrode called the **anode**. Reduction takes place at the electrode called the **cathode**.

There's a mnemonic device to remember that.

AN OX
RED CAT

The salt bridge maintains electrical neutrality in the system by providing enough negative ions to equal the positive ions being created at the anode (during oxidation) and providing positive ions to replace the Cu^{2+} ions being used up at the cathode (during reduction). The salt bridge can be an actual salt, or it can be a slim passage that allows ions to move between the two chambers.

Under standard conditions (when all concentrations are 1 M) the voltage of the cell is the same as the total voltage of the redox reaction. Under nonstandard conditions, the cell voltage can be computed by using the Nernst equation.

The Nernst Equation

$$E_{cell} = E°_{cell} - \frac{RT}{nF} \ln Q$$

E_{cell} = cell potential under nonstandard conditions (V)
$E°_{cell}$ = cell potential under standard conditions (V)
R = the gas constant, 8.31 (volt-coulomb)/(mol-K)
T = absolute temperature (K)
n = the number of moles of electrons exchanged in the reaction (mol)
F = Faraday's constant, 96,500 coulombs/mole
Q = the reaction quotient (same as the equilibrium expression, but with initial concentrations instead of equilibrium concentrations)

At 25 °C, the Nernst equation reduces to:

$$E_{cell} = E°_{cell} - \frac{0.0592}{n} \log Q$$

Here's the most important thing that you should understand from the Nernst equation: *As the concentration of the products of a redox reaction increases, the voltage decreases; and as the concentration of the reactants in a redox reaction increases, the voltage increases.*

ELECTROLYTIC CELLS

In an electrolytic cell, an outside source of voltage is used to force a non-spontaneous redox reaction to take place. Let's look at the electrolysis of molten NaCl.

2 Na$^+$(*molten*) + 2 Cl$^-$(*molten*) →2 Na(l) + Cl$_2$(g)		$E°$ = –4.07 V
Oxidation:	2 Cl$^-$(*molten*) → Cl$_2$(g) + 2 e$^-$	$E°$ = –1.36 V
Reduction:	2 Na$^+$(*molten*) + 2 e$^-$ → 2 Na(l)	$E°$ = –2.71 V

An electrolytic cell that forces this reaction to take place is shown below.

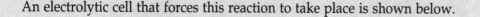

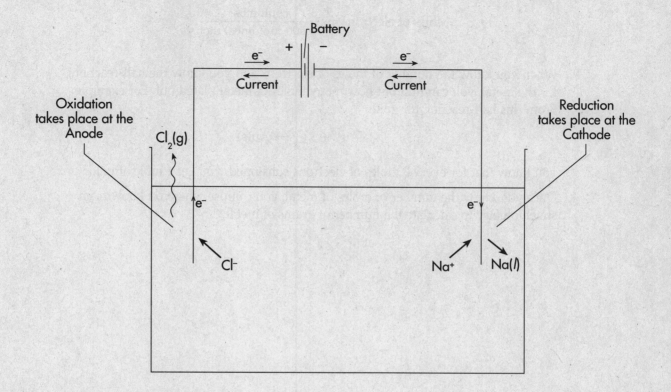

In this process, pure liquid sodium and pure chlorine gas are generated from molten sodium chloride. Notice that the process does not take place in aqueous solution. That's because water is more easily reduced than Na^+, so water would be reduced instead of sodium ions in an aqueous solution.

The AN OX/RED CAT rule applies to the electrolytic cell in the same way that it applies to the galvanic cell.

Electrolytic cells are used for electroplating. You might see a question on the test that gives you an electrical current and asks you how much metal "plates out."

There are roughly four steps for figuring out electolysis problems.

1. If you know the current and the time, you can calculate the charge in coulombs.

Current

$$I = \frac{q}{t}$$

I = current (amperes, A)
q = charge (coulombs, C)
t = time (sec)

2. Once you know the charge in coulombs, you know how many electrons were involved in the reaction.

$$\text{Moles of electrons} = \frac{\text{coulombs}}{96{,}500 \text{ coulombs/mol}}$$

3. When you know the number of moles of electrons and you know the half-reaction for the metal, you can find out how many moles of metal plated out. For example: From this half-reaction for gold:

$$Au^{3+} + 3\ e^- \rightarrow Au(s)$$

you know that for every 3 moles of electrons consumed, you get 1 mole of gold.

4. Once you know the number of moles of metal, you can use what you know from stoichiometry to calculate the number of grams of metal.

OXIDATION-REDUCTION AND ELECTROCHEMISTRY

Questions

Multiple choice

Questions 1–3

    (A) MnO_4^-
    (B) H^+
    (C) H_2
    (D) Na
    (E) Na^+

1. This is a very strong reducing agent.

2. By definition, the reduction potential for this species is equal to zero.

3. This is a very strong oxidizing agent.

Questions 4–7

The choices listed below refer to n, the number of moles of electrons transferred in a reaction.

    (A) $n = 4$
    (B) $n = 3$
    (C) $n = 2$
    (D) $n = 1$
    (E) $n = 0$

4. $2\,Fe^{3+} + Mg \rightarrow 2\,Fe^{2+} + Mg^{2+}$

5. $F_2 + 2\,Br^- \rightarrow 2\,F^- + Br_2$

6. $NH_3 + H_2O \rightarrow NH_4^+ + OH^-$

7. $MnO_4^- + Cr + 2\,H_2O \rightarrow$
$$MnO_2 + Cr^{3+} + 4OH^-$$

8. $Cr_2O_7^{2-} + 6I^- + 14 H^+ \rightarrow 2Cr^{3+} + 3I_2 + 7H_2O$

Which of the following statements about the reaction given above is NOT true?

(A) The oxidation number of chromium changes from +6 to +3.
(B) The oxidation number of iodine changes from −1 to 0.
(C) The oxidation number of hydrogen changes from +1 to 0.
(D) The oxidation number of oxygen remains the same.
(E) The reaction takes place in acidic solution.

9. $Al^{3+} + 3e^- \rightarrow Al(s)$ $E° = -1.66$ V

     $Cr^{3+} + 3e^- \rightarrow Cr(s)$ $E° = -0.74$ V

The standard reduction potentials for two half reactions are shown above. Which of the statements listed below will be true for the following reaction taking place under standard conditions?

     $Al(s) + Cr_3+ \rightarrow Al_3+ + Cr(s)$

(A) $E° = 2.40$ V and the reaction is not spontaneous.
(B) $E° = 0.92$ V and the reaction is spontaneous.
(C) $E° = -0.92$ V and the reaction is not spontaneous.
(D) $E° = -0.92$ V and the reaction is spontaneous.
(E) $E° = -2.40$ V and the reaction is not spontaneous.

10. In which of the following molecules does hydrogen have an oxidation state of −1?

(A) H_2O
(B) NH_3
(C) CaH_2
(D) CH_4
(E) H_2

11. Oxygen takes the oxidation state −1 in hydrogen peroxide, H_2O_2. The equation for the decomposition of H_2O_2 is shown below.

     $2 H_2O_2 \rightarrow 2 H_2O + O_2$

Which of the following statements about the reaction above is true?

(A) Oxygen is reduced and hydrogen is oxidized.
(B) Oxygen is oxidized and hydrogen is reduced.
(C) Oxygen is both oxidized and reduced.
(D) Hydrogen is both oxidized and reduced.
(E) Neither oxygen nor hydrogen changes oxidation state.

12. When solid iron is brought into contact with water and oxygen, it undergoes the following half-reaction:

     $Fe(s) \rightarrow Fe^{2+}(aq) + 2e^-$

This half reaction is instrumental in the corrosion of iron. When iron is coated with solid zinc, the half-reaction above is impeded, even if the zinc coating is incomplete. This is most likely because

(A) $Zn(s)$ is more easily reduced than $Fe(s)$.
(B) $Zn(s)$ is more easily oxidized than $Fe(s)$.
(C) $Zn^{2+}(aq)$ is more easily reduced than $Fe(s)$.
(D) $Zn^{2+}(aq)$ is more easily reduced than $Fe(s)$.
(E) $Zn(s)$ is more easily reduced than $Fe^{2+}(aq)$.

13. $2 H_2O(l) + 2e^- \rightarrow$

   $H_2(g) + 2 OH^-(aq)$ $E° = -0.8 V$

   $Na^+(aq) + e^- \rightarrow Na(s)$ $E° = -2.7 V$

   $Cl_2(g) + 2e^- \rightarrow Cl^-(aq)$ $E° = +1.4 V$

   Based on the reduction potentials given above, which of the following would be expected to occur when electrodes connected to the terminals of a 2.0 V battery are immersed in a solution of sodium chloride in water?

   (A) Solid sodium will appear at the anode and chlorine gas will appear at the cathode.
   (B) Chlorine gas will appear at the anode and solid sodium will appear at the cathode.
   (C) Hydrogen gas will appear at the cathode and solid sodium will appear at the anode.
   (D) Hydrogen gas will appear at the anode and chlorine gas will appear at the cathode.
   (E) Chlorine gas will appear at the anode and hydrogen gas will appear at the cathode.

14. $Cu^{2+} + 2e^- \rightarrow Cu$ $E° = +0.3 V$

   $Fe^2+ + 2e^- \rightarrow Fe$ $E° = -0.4 V$

   Based on the reduction potentials given above, what is the reaction potential for the following reaction?

   $Fe^{2+} + Cu \rightarrow Fe + Cu^{2+}$

   (A) -0.7 V
   (B) -0.1 V
   (C) +0.1 V
   (D) +0.7 V
   (E) +1.4 V

15. $Cu^{2+} + 2e^- \rightarrow Cu$ $E° = +0.3 V$

   $Zn^{2+} + 2e^- \rightarrow Zn$ $E° = -0.8 V$

   $Mn^{2+} + 2e^- \rightarrow Mn$ $E° = -1.2 V$

   Based on the reduction potentials given above, which of the following reactions will occur spontaneously?

   (A) $Mn^{2+} + Cu \rightarrow Mn + Cu^{2+}$
   (B) $Mn^{2+} + Zn \rightarrow Mn + Zn^{2+}$
   (C) $Zn^{2+} + Cu \rightarrow Zn + Cu^{2+}$
   (D) $Zn^{2+} + Mn \rightarrow Zn + Mn^{2+}$
   (E) $Cu^{2+} + Zn^{2+} \rightarrow Cu + Zn$

16. Which of the following is true of the oxidation-reduction reaction that takes place in a galvanic cell under standard conditions?

   (A) $G°$ and $E°$ are positive and K_{eq} is greater than 1.
   (B) $G°$ is negative, $E°$ is positive, and K_{eq} is greater than 1.
   (C) $G°$ is positive, $E°$ is negative, and K_{eq} is less than 1.
   (D) $G°$ and $E°$ are negative and K_{eq} is greater than 1.
   (E) $G°$ and $E°$ are negative and K_{eq} is less than 1.

17. $$Ni(s) + Cu^{2+}(aq) \rightarrow Ni^{2+}(aq) + Cu(s)$$

The oxidation-reduction reaction above takes place in a galvanic cell. If the initial concentration of Ni^{2+} ions is increased while the initial concentration of Cu^{2+} ions remains constant, what will be the effect on the reaction quotient Q and the cell potential, E ?

(A) Q and E will increase.
(B) Q and E will decrease.
(C) Q will increase and E will decrease.
(D) Q will decrease and E will increase.
(E) Q and E will not change.

18.   When solid copper shavings are placed in a solution of dilute HNO_3, Cu^{2+} ions appear and NO gas bubbles form. Which of the following has occurred?

(A)   Cu has been oxidized by H^+.
(B)   Cu has been oxidized by NO_3^-.
(C)   Cu has been reduced by NO_3^-.
(D) NO_3^- has been oxidized by H^+.
(E) NO_3^- has been reduced by H^+.

19.   Molten $AlCl_3$ is electrolyzed with a constant current of 5.00 amperes over a period of 600. seconds. Which of the following expressions is equal to the maximum mass of $Al(s)$ that plates out? (1 faraday = 96,500 coulombs)

(A) $\dfrac{(600)(5.00)}{(96,500)(3)(27.0)}$ grams

(B) $\dfrac{(600)(5.00)(3)(27.0)}{(96,500)}$ grams

(C) $\dfrac{(600)(5.00)(27.0)}{(96,500)(3)}$ grams

(D) $\dfrac{(96,500)(3)(27.0)}{(600)(5.00)}$ grams

(E) $\dfrac{(96,500)(3)}{(600)(5.00)(27.0)}$ grams

20.   The half reaction at the anode of a galvanic cell is as follows:

$$Zn(s) \rightarrow Zn^{2+} + 2e^-$$

What is the maximum charge, in coulombs, that can be delivered by a cell with an anode composed of 6.54 grams of zinc? (1 faraday = 96,500 coulombs)

(A)   4,820 coulombs
(B)   9,650 coulombs
(C)   19,300 coulombs
(D)   38,600 coulombs
(E)   48,200 coulombs

Problems

1. An electrochemical cell is created by placing a zinc electrode in a 1.00-molar solution of $ZnSO_4$ and placing a copper electrode in a 1.00-molar solution of $CuSO_4$. The two compartments were connected by a salt bridge and the following reaction occurred at 25 °C.

$$Zn(s) + Cu^{2+} \rightarrow Zn^{2+} + Cu(s)$$

   (a)   What is the standard potential for the cell?

   (b)   What is the value of $G°$ for the cell?

   (c)   What is the value of K_{eq} for the reaction?

   (d)   At a certain point in the progress of the reaction, $[Cu^{2+}]$ drops to 0.10-molar and $[Zn^{2+}]$ increases to 1.90-molar. What is the cell potential at this point?

2. An 800. milliliter sample of 0.080-molar Ag^+ solution was electrolyzed, resulting in the formation of solid silver and oxygen gas. The solution was subjected to a current of 2.00 amperes for 10.0 minutes. The solution became progressively more acidic as the reaction progressed.

   (a)   Write the two half reactions that occur, stating which takes place at the anode and which at the cathode.

   (b)   If the oxygen gas produced in the electrolysis was collected at standard temperature and pressure, what was its volume?

   (c)   What was the mass of solid silver produced in the electrolysis?

   (d)   If the solution was neutral at the start of the electrolysis, what was the pH of the solution when the process was completed?

Essays

3. Use the principles of electrochemistry to answer each of the following.

   (a)   Explain why a salt bridge connecting the two compartments of a galvanic cell is necessary for the operation of the cell.

   (b)   Explain why when an iron nail is placed in hydrochloric acid, a reaction occurs; but when a copper penny is placed in hydrochloric acid, no reaction occurs.

   (c) $Ag^+ + Sn(s) \rightarrow Ag(s) + Sn^{2+}$

      (i)   Give the standard cell potential for the reaction above.

      (ii)   What happens to the cell potential in (i) when $[Ag^+]$ is increased?

      (iii) What happens to the cell potential when the amount of $Sn(s)$ in the cell is increased?

4. $M(s) + Cd^{2+} \rightarrow M^+ + Cd(s)$

The reaction above proceeds spontaneously at 25° C in an electrochemical cell.

(a) The oxidation potential for $M(s)$ must be greater than a certain value. What is that value?

(b) Write the two half reactions and tell which takes place at the anode and which takes place at the cathode.

(c) Describe the changes that occur in the following quantities as the reaction proceeds in the forward direction.

   (i) $[M^+]$

   (ii) E_{cell}

   (iii) G

ANSWERS

Multiple choice

1. **(D)** is correct. Na likes to give up an electron (oxidation) in the reaction:

$$Na \rightarrow Na^+ + e^-$$

When a substance likes to be oxidized, it is a strong reducing agent.

2. **(B)** is correct. H^+ is reduced in the reaction:

$$2\,H^+ + 2e^- \rightarrow H_2$$

By definition, the potential for this reaction is zero, so accordingly, the oxidation potential for H_2 is also zero.

3. **(A)** is correct. MnO_4^- likes to gain electrons (reduction) in either of the following reactions:

$$MnO_4^- + 8\,H^+ + 5e^- \rightarrow Mn_2^+ + 2\,H_2O$$

$$MnO_4^- + 2\,H_2O + 3e^- \rightarrow MnO_2 + 4\,OH^-$$

When a substance likes to be reduced, it is a strong oxidizing agent.

4. **(C)** is correct. The two half reactions are:

$$2\,Fe^{3+} + 2e^- \rightarrow 2\,Fe^{2+}$$

$$Mg \rightarrow Mg^{2+} + 2e^-$$

5. **(C)** is correct. The two half reactions are:

$$F_2 + 2e^- \rightarrow 2\,F^-$$

$$2\,Br^- \rightarrow 2e^- + Br_2$$

6. **(E)** is correct. None of the elements involved in this acid-base reaction changes its oxidation state, so no electrons are transferred.

7. **(B)** is correct. The two half reactions are:

$$Mn^{7+} + 3e^- \rightarrow Mn^{4+}$$

$$Cr \rightarrow Cr^{3+} + 3e^-$$

8. **(C)** is correct. The oxidation numbers of the reactants are: Cr^{6+}, O^{2-}, I^-, and H^+, and the oxidation numbers of the products are: Cr^{3+}, O^{2-}, I^0, and H^+.

Chromium gains electrons and is reduced, iodine loses electrons and is oxidized; the oxidation states of oxygen and hydrogen are not changed.

9. **(B)** is correct. $E°$ for a redox reaction is given by the expression:

$E° = E°_{ox} + E°_{red}$

Al(s) loses 3 electrons in the reaction, so it is oxidized (LEO), and we use the voltage given for the reduction half reaction, but we change the sign. So $E°_{ox} = 1.66$ V.

Cr^{3+} gains 3 electrons in the reaction, so it is reduced (GER), and we use the voltage given for the reduction half reaction. So $E°_{red} = -0.74$ V.

So, $E° = 1.66$ V + (-0.74 V) = 0.92 V.

From the relationship, $\Delta G° = -nFE°$, we know that if $E°$ is positive, then $\Delta G°$ is negative, and if $\Delta G°$ is negative, then the reaction is spontaneous under standard conditions.

10. **(C)** is correct. In a molecule, the more electronegative element takes the negative oxidation state. Hydrogen is more electronegative than calcium, so the oxidation state for Ca is +2 and the oxidation state for H is –1.

In choices (A), (B), and (D), hydrogen is the less electronegative element and it takes the oxidation state of +1, and in choice (E), the oxidation state for hydrogen is 0.

11. **(C)** is correct. The oxidation state of hydrogen remains +1 throughout the reaction.

We have O^- at the start.

When water forms, oxygen has gained an electron and been reduced to O^{2-} (GER). When O_2 forms, oxygen has been oxidized to O^0 through the loss of an electron (LEO). As you can see, in this process, oxygen is both oxidized and reduced.

12. **(B)** is correct. The half-reaction given above is for the oxidation of Fe (LEO). If the presence of Zn impedes this process it is because Zn is oxidized instead of Fe. Iron nails are often coated with zinc to help keep them from rusting.

13. **(E)** is correct. A voltage of 2.0 V is not enough to cause the reduction of Na^+ (more than 2.7 V is needed), so no solid sodium will form. A voltage of 2.0 V will cause the reduction of H_2O, which forms hydrogen gas, and the oxidation of Cl^-, which forms chlorine gas.

From ANOX and REDCAT, we know that hydrogen gas is formed at the cathode and that chlorine gas is formed at the anode.

14. **(A)** is correct. We add the reduction potential for Fe^{2+} (–0.4 V) to the oxidation potential for Cu (–0.3 V, the reverse of the reduction potential) to get –0.7 V.

15. **(D)** is correct. To get the reaction potential, we add the reduction potential for the reduction half-reaction to the oxidation potential for the oxidation half–reaction.

Here are the reaction potentials for choices (A)–(D):

(A) (–1.2 V) + (–0.3 V) = –1.5 V

(B) (–1.2 V) + (+0.8 V) = –0.4 V

(C) (–0.8 V) + (–0.3 V) = –1.1 V

(D) (–0.8 V) + (+1.2 V) = +0.4 V

(E) $Cu^{2+} + Zn^{2+} \rightarrow Cu + Zn$

Choice (E) is a combination of two reduction half-reactions, which can't happen.

Choice (D) is the only reaction with a positive voltage, which means that it is the only reaction listed that occurs spontaneously.

16. **(B)** is correct. The oxidation-reduction reaction in a galvanic cell occurs spontaneously and provides a voltage which causes a flow of electrons, so $\Delta G°$ is negative and $E°$ is positive. Also, from the equation $\Delta G° = nFE°$, we know that $\Delta G°$ and $E°$ always have opposite signs.

We know that Keq must be greater than 1 from either of the following equations:

$\Delta G° = -2.303RT\log K$, which tells us that if $\Delta G°$ is to be negative, then $\log K$ must be positive, which means that K must be greater than 1.

Or:

$\log K = \dfrac{nE°}{0.0592}$, which tells us that if $E°$ is to be positive, then $\log K$ must be positive, which means that K must be greater than 1.

17. **(C)** is correct. Let's look at the Nernst equation, which relates cell potential to concentration.

$E = E° - \dfrac{0.059}{2} \log Q$ at 25 °C.

The smaller Q becomes, the larger E will become.

Remember, Q is the reaction quotient, which takes the form of K_{eq}, except with initial conditions instead of equilibrium conditions.

In this case $Q = \dfrac{\left[Ni^{2+}\right]}{\left[Cu^{2+}\right]}$, so increasing $[Ni^{2+}]$ increases Q, which decreases E.

18. **(B)** is correct. The net ionic equation is as follows:

$Cu + H^+ + NO_3^- \rightarrow Cu^{2+} + NO + H_2O$

Cu is oxidized: $Cu \rightarrow Cu^{2+} + 2e^-$

NO_3^- is reduced: $N^{5+} + 3e^- \rightarrow N^{2+}$

So Cu is oxidized and NO_3^- is the oxidizing agent.

H^+ does not change its oxidation state.

19. **(C)** is correct. First let's find out how many electrons are provided by the current.

Coulombs = (seconds) (amperes) = (600)(5.00)

Moles of electrons = $\dfrac{(\text{coulombs})}{(96,500)} = \dfrac{(600)(5.00)}{(96,500)}$ moles

In $AlCl_3$, we have Al^{3+}, so the half-reaction for the plating of aluminum is:

$Al^{3+} + 3e^- \rightarrow Al(s)$

So we get $\dfrac{1}{3}$ as many moles of $Al(s)$ as we have moles of electrons.

Moles of Al(s) = (moles of electrons)$\left(\dfrac{1}{3}\right)$ = $\dfrac{(600)(5.00)}{(96,500)(3)}$ moles

Now, grams = (moles)(MW)

Grams of Al(s) = $\dfrac{(600)(5.00)}{(96,500)(3)}$ (27.0) = $\dfrac{(600)(5.00)(27.0)}{(96,500)(3)}$ grams

20. **(C)** is correct. First let's find out how many moles of zinc we have.

$$\text{Moles} = \frac{\text{grams}}{\text{MW}}$$

$$\text{Moles of Zn} = \frac{(6.54 \text{ g})}{(65.4 \text{ g/mol})} = 0.100 \text{ mole}$$

Based on the half-reaction, we can see that for every mole of Zn consumed, we get 2 moles of electrons. So we have $(2)(0.100) = 0.20$ moles of electrons.

$$\text{Moles of electrons} = \frac{\text{coulombs}}{96,500}$$

So, coulombs = (moles of electrons)(96,500)

= $(0.200)(96,500)$ = a little less than 20,000 = exactly 19,300

Problems

1. (a) Use the reduction potentials from the chart given with the test.

$Zn(s) \rightarrow Zn^{2+} + 2e^-$	$E° =$	$+0.76$ V
$Cu^{2+} + 2e^- \rightarrow Cu(s)$	$E° =$	$+0.34$ V
		$+1.10$ V

(b) Use the following expression:

$\Delta G = -nFE$

$n = 2$, because two moles of electrons are exchanged in the redox reaction.

$E = 1.10$ V, from part (a)

$F = 96,500$ C/mol

$\Delta G = -(2)(96,500 \text{ C/mol})(1.10 \text{ V}) = -212,300 \text{ C-V/mol} = -212,300 \text{ J/mol} = -212 \text{ kJ/mol}$

(c) You have two options:

$$\log K = \frac{nE°}{0.0592} = \frac{(2)(1.10)}{(0.0592)} = 37.1$$

$K = 1.45 \times 10^{37}$

Or:

$$\log K = \frac{\Delta G°}{-2.303 \, RT} = \frac{(-212,000 \text{ J/mol})}{(-2.303)(8.31 \text{ J/mol} - \text{K})(298 \text{ K})} = 37.2$$

$K = 1.49 \times 10^{37}$

(d) Use the Nernst equation for 25 °C:

$$E_{cell} = E° - \frac{0.0592}{n} \log Q$$

$$E_{cell} = E° - \frac{0.0592}{n} \log \frac{\left[Zn^{2+}\right]}{\left[Cu^{2+}\right]}$$

$$E_{cell} = 1.10 \text{ V} - \frac{0.0592}{2} \log \frac{(1.90)}{(0.10)} \text{ V}$$

$$E_{cell} = 1.10 \text{ V} - 0.04 \text{ V} = 1.06 \text{ V}$$

2. (a) Silver half-reaction: $Ag^+ + e^- \rightarrow Ag(s)$

Silver gains an electron, so it is reduced (GER). Reduction takes place at the cathode (REDCAT).

Water half-reaction: $2 H_2O \rightarrow O_2 + 4 H^+ + 4e^-$

Water gives up electrons, so it is oxidized (LEO). Oxidation takes place at the anode (ANOX)

(b) First let's find out how many electrons were supplied by the current.

Coulombs = (amperes)(seconds)

Coulombs = (2.00 A)(10.0 min)(60 sec/min) = 1,200 C

$$\text{Moles of electrons} = \frac{\text{coulombs}}{96,500} = \frac{1,200}{96,500} = 0.0124 \text{ moles}$$

From the water half-reaction we know that one mole of oxygen gas is produced for every 4 electrons given up, so there will be $\frac{1}{4}$ as many moles of O_2 as there are electrons.

Moles of $O_2 = (\frac{1}{4})$(moles of electrons) $= (\frac{1}{4})(0.0124 \text{ mol}) = 3.10 \times 10^{-3}$ moles

At STP, Volume of gas = (moles)(22.4 L/mol)

Volume of O_2 = $(3.10 \times 10^{-3} \text{ mol})(22.4 \text{ L/mol}) = 0.0694$ L

(c) From (b), we know that the current provided 0.0124 moles of electrons.

From the silver half-reaction, we know that for every mole of electrons consumed, one mole of Ag(s) is produced. So we have 0.0124 moles of Ag(s).

Grams = (moles)(MW)

Grams of Ag(s) = (0.0124 mol)(107.87 g/mol) = 1.34 grams

(d) From (b), we know that the current provided 0.0124 moles of electrons. From the water half-reaction we know that 4 moles of H^+ were produced for every 4 electrons given up, so the number of moles of H^+ will be the same as the number of electrons.

Moles of H^+ = 0.0124

We can assume that the volume of solution doesn't change during the electrolysis.

$$\text{Molarity} = \frac{\text{moles}}{\text{volume}}$$

$$[H^+] = \frac{(0.0124 \text{ mol})}{(0.800 \text{ L})} = 0.0155 \text{ } M$$

$$pH = -\log[H^+] = -\log(0.0155) = 1.81$$

Essays

3. (a) The salt bridge is necessary to maintain electrical neutrality in the two compartments where the half-reactions are taking place. It does this by allowing anions (–) to move into the anode compartment and cations (+) to move into the cathode compartment.

    (b) From the table of reduction potentials, we can see that Fe wants to be oxidized (reading the table from right to left gives a positive oxidation potential), so it can act as the reducing agent for H^+ ions.

    Cu, on the other hand, does not want to be oxidized (reading the table from right to left gives a negative oxidation potential), so it will not reduce the H^+ ions.

    (c) (i) Use the table of standard potentials.

    $Ag^+ + e^- \rightarrow Ag(s)$ $E°$ =   +0.80 V

    $Sn(s) \rightarrow Sn^{2+} + e^-$ $E°$ =   <u>+0.14 V</u>

                                            +0.94 V

    (ii) Use the Nernst equation:

    $$E_{cell} = E° - \frac{0.0592}{n} \log Q$$

    $$E_{cell} = E° - \frac{0.0592}{n} \log \frac{[Sn^{2+}]}{[Ag^+]}$$

    When $[Ag^+]$ is increased, $\log \dfrac{[Sn^{2+}]}{[Ag^+]}$ decreases, which means that a smaller number is subtracted from $E°$, which means that E_{cell} increases.

    (iii) The cell potential changes with changing concentrations. The concentration of a solid is constant, so changing the amount of solid Sn present in the cell will have no effect on the cell potential.

4. (a) The reduction potential for Cd^{2+} is equal to –0.40 V. In order for the reaction to proceed spontaneously, the cell potential must be greater than zero, so the oxidation potential for M(s) must be greater than +0.40 V.

    (b) $M(s) \rightarrow M^+ + e^-$

    M(s) loses an electron and is oxidized (LEO), so this half-reaction takes place at the anode (ANOX).

    $Cd^{2+} + 2e^- \rightarrow Cd(s)$

    Cd^{2+} gains electrons and is reduced (GER), so this half-reaction takes place at the cathode (REDCAT).

    (c) (i) As the reaction proceeds in the forward direction, more M^+ will be generated, so $[M^+]$ will increase.

    (ii) Use the Nernst equation:

    $$E_{cell} = E° - \frac{0.0592}{n} \log Q$$

$$E_{cell} = E° - \frac{0.0592}{n} \log \frac{[M^+]}{[Cd^{2+}]}$$

As the reaction proceeds, $[M^+]$ increases and $[Cd^{2+}]$ decreases, thereby increasing log , which means that progressively larger numbers are subtracted from $E°$, which means that E_{cell} decreases.

(iii) Use the equation:

$\Delta G = -nFE$

From (ii), we know that E is decreasing. As E decreases, G becomes less negative, so it increases. That means that as the reaction proceeds, it becomes less spontaneous.

NUCLEAR DECAY

How often does this topic appear on the test?
In the multiple-choice section, this topic appears in about 3 out of 75 questions.
In the free-response section, you'll see this topic occasionally.

A nucleus is held together by a nonelectrical, non-gravitational force called the **nuclear force**.

Some nuclei are more stable than others. When a nucleus is unstable, it can attempt to increase its stability by altering its number of neutrons and protons. This is the process of radioactive decay.

TYPES OF NUCLEAR DECAY

Alpha emission ($_{2}^{4}\alpha$)
In **alpha decay**, the nucleus emits a particle that has the same constitution as a helium nucleus, with 2 protons and 2 neutrons.

$$_{2}^{4}\alpha = _{2}^{4}\text{He}$$

When a nucleus undergoes alpha decay:

- Subtract 4 from the mass number.
- Subtract 2 from the atomic number.

$$_{92}^{238}\text{U} \rightarrow _{2}^{4}\alpha + _{90}^{234}\text{Th}$$

Beta emission ($_{-1}^{0}\beta$)

A beta particle is identical to an electron. In beta decay, the nucleus changes a neutron into a proton and an electron and emits the electron.

$$_{0}^{1}n \rightarrow _{-1}^{0}\beta + _{1}^{1}p$$

When a nucleus undergoes beta decay:

- The mass number remains the same.
- Add 1 to the atomic number.

$$_{6}^{14}C \rightarrow _{-1}^{0}\beta + _{7}^{14}N$$

Positron emission ($_{+1}^{0}\beta$)

A positron is like an electron with a positive charge. In positron emission, the nucleus changes a proton into a neutron and a positron, and emits the positron.

$$_{1}^{1}p \rightarrow _{+1}^{0}\beta + _{0}^{1}n$$

When a nucleus undergoes positron emission:

- The mass number remains the same.
- Subtract 1 from the atomic number.

$$_{5}^{8}B \rightarrow _{+1}^{0}\beta + _{4}^{8}Be$$

Electron capture ($_{-1}^{0}e$)

In electron capture, the nucleus captures a low energy electron and combines it with a proton to form a neutron.

$$_{-1}^{0}e + _{1}^{1}p \rightarrow _{0}^{1}n$$

When a nucleus undergoes electron capture:

- The mass number remains the same.
- Subtract 1 from the atomic number.

$$_{9}^{18}F + _{-1}^{0}e \rightarrow _{8}^{18}O$$

Gamma rays ($_{0}^{0}\gamma$)

Gamma rays are electromagnetic radiation and have no mass and no charge. Gamma rays usually accompany other forms of nuclear decay.

NUCLEAR STABILITY

Nuclei undergo decay to achieve greater stability. You can use the periodic table to predict the kind of decay that an isotope will undergo.

- If an isotope's *mass number is greater than its atomic weight* ($^{16}_{6}C$, for instance), the nucleus will try to gain protons and lose neutrons, so if its mass number is greater than its atomic weight, you can *expect beta decay*.

- If an isotope's *mass number is less than its atomic weight* ($^{11}_{6}C$, for instance), the nucleus will try to lose protons and gain neutrons, so if its mass number is less than its atomic weight, you can *expect positron emission* or *electron capture*.

- Alpha emission is seen mainly in very large nuclei, usually with atomic numbers of 60 or greater.

Half-life

The half-life of a radioactive substance is the time it takes for half of the substance to decay. Most half-life problems can be solved by using a simple chart.

Time	Sample
0	100%
1 Half-life	50%
2 Half-lives	25%
3 Half-lives	12.5%

So a sample with a mass of 120 grams and a half-life of 3 years will decay as follows. Don't forget that the chart should start with the time at zero.

Time	Sample
0	120g
3	60g
6	30g
9	15g

The fact that you're not allowed to use a calculator for Section I and you are not given any half-life formulas for Section II means that you should be able to solve any half-life problem that comes up by using the chart and process of elimination.

MASS DEFECT AND BINDING ENERGY

When protons and neutrons come together to form a nucleus, the mass of the nucleus is less than the sum of the masses of its constituent protons and neutrons. This difference in mass is called the **mass defect**. The mass lost in this process is released in the form of energy. If we reverse the process this is the same amount of energy, called the **binding energy**, required to decompose the nucleus back into protons and neutrons. The relationship between mass and energy is given by Einstein's famous equation.

$$E = mc^2$$

E = energy (J)

m = mass (kg)

c = the speed of light, 3×10^8 m/sec

You can see that because c^2 is such a large number, a very small change in mass results in a very large change in energy.

NUCLEAR DECAY

QUESTION

Multiple choice

Questions 1–4

(A) Alpha decay
(B) Beta (β^-) decay
(C) Electron capture
(D) Gamma radiation
(E) Mass defect

1. In this process the number of protons in a nuclide is increased while the mass number remains constant.

2. In this process a nuclide releases a particle that is the equivalent of a helium nucleus.

3. This is the difference between the mass of a nucleus and the sum of its component nucleons.

4. In this process the number of protons in a nuclide is decreased while the mass number remains constant.

Questions 5–8

(A) $^{26}_{13}\text{Al}$, $^{26}_{12}\text{Mg}$
(B) $^{58}_{28}\text{Ni}$, $^{64}_{28}\text{Ni}$
(C) $^{12}_{5}\text{B}$, $^{8}_{3}\text{Li}$
(D) $^{19}_{9}\text{F}$, $^{20}_{10}\text{Ne}$
(E) $^{39}_{18}\text{Ar}$, $^{39}_{20}\text{Ca}$

5. This pair could be the only two elements present in a sample undergoing alpha decay.

6. This pair could be the only two elements present in a sample undergoing β^+ decay.

7. This pair are isotopes of each other.

8. This pair could be the only two elements present in a sample undergoing electron capture.

9. The nuclide $^{128}_{50}\text{Sn}$ is unstable. Which of the following decay types would $^{128}_{50}\text{Sn}$ be expected to undergo?

    I. Beta decay (β^-) to increase the ratio of protons to neutrons.
    II. Positron emission (β^+) to decrease the ratio of protons to neutrons.
    III. Electron capture to decrease the ratio of protons to neutrons.

    (A) I only
    (B) II only
    (C) I and III only
    (D) II and III only
    (E) I, II, and III

10. Which of the following statements is true regarding the mass and magnitude of charge of alpha particles and beta particles?

    (A) Alpha particles are more highly charged and have greater mass than beta particles.
    (B) Beta particles are more highly charged and have greater mass than alpha particles.
    (C) Alpha particles are more highly charged than beta particles, but beta particles have greater mass.
    (D) Beta particles are more highly charged than alpha particles, but alpha particles have greater mass.
    (E) Alpha particles are more highly charged than beta particles, but the masses of the two types of particles are the same.

11. Strontium-90 decays through the emission of beta particles. It has a half-life of 29 years. How long does it take for 80% of a sample of strontium-90 to decay?

    (A) 9.3 years
    (B) 21 years
    (C) 38 years
    (D) 67 years
    (E) 96 years

12. A sample of radioactive material undergoing nuclear decay is found to contain only potassium and calcium. The sample could be undergoing which of the following decay processes?

    I. Beta (β^-) decay
    II. Alpha decay
    III. Electron capture

    (A) I only
    (B) II only
    (C) I and III only
    (D) II and III only
    (E) I, II, and III

13. A sample of radioactive material undergoing nuclear decay is found to contain only $_{84}$Po and $_{82}$Pb. The sample could be undergoing which of the following decay processes?

    I. Beta (β^-)decay
   II. Alpha decay
  III. Electron capture

(A) I only
(B) II only
(C) I and III only
(D) II and III only
(E) I, II, and III

14. A $_{84}^{214}$Po nuclide emits two alpha particles and two beta (β^-) particles. The resulting nuclide is

(A) $_{82}^{210}$Pb

(B) $_{83}^{210}$Bi

(C) $_{84}^{210}$Po

(D) $_{82}^{206}$Pb

(E) $_{84}^{206}$Po

15. After 44 minutes, a sample of $_{19}^{44}$K is found to have decayed to 25% of the original amount present. What is the half life of $_{19}^{44}$K ?

(A) 11 minutes
(B) 22 minutes
(C) 44 minutes
(D) 66 minutes
(E) 88 minutes

Essays

1. Use the principles of nuclear chemistry to explain each of the following.

    (a) Gamma radiation penetrates farther into the human body than either alpha or beta radiation.

    (b) A nucleus weighs less than the sum of the weights of its neutrons and protons.

    (c) Arsenic-81 is unstable. What form of radioactive decay would it be expected to undergo?

    (d) Potassium-38 decays by electron capture. Write the balanced nuclear reaction for this process.

    (e) In a nuclear explosion, a small mass has enormous destructive power.

2.

Isotope	Half-life	Mode of Decay
$^{21}_{11}$Na	23 sec	β^+
$^{23}_{11}$Na	—	—
$^{25}_{11}$Na	60 sec	β^-
$^{26}_{11}$Na	1.0 sec	β^-

    (a) Write the balanced nuclear reaction for sodium-21.

    (b) Write the balanced nuclear reaction for sodium-26.

    (c) A sample of sodium-25 is observed to decay for 5 minutes. After this time, no change in the mass of the sample is detected. Explain.

    (d) Describe alpha, beta (β^-), and gamma radiation in terms of mass and charge.

ANSWERS

Multiple choice

1. **(B)** is correct. In beta decay, a nuclide releases a β^- particle (which is the same as an electron) and converts a neutron to a proton.

    $$^{1}_{0}n \rightarrow \, ^{1}_{1}p + \, ^{0}_{-1}\beta$$

2. **(A)** is correct. An alpha particle ($^{4}_{2}\alpha$) has two protons and two neutrons, the same as a helium nucleus.

3. **(E)** is correct. Mass defect is the mass that seems to disappear from neutrons and protons when they are brought together to form a nucleus.

    Mass defect is the m in Einstein's famous equation for the equivalence of mass and energy, $E = mc^2$.

4. **(C)** is correct. In electron capture, a nuclide absorbs one of its low energy electrons and combines it with a proton to form a neutron.

    $$^{1}_{1}p + \, ^{0}_{-1}e \rightarrow \, ^{1}_{0}n$$

5. **(C)** is correct. In alpha decay, a particle with the mass (4) and charge (+2) of a helium nucleus is given off, so the two nuclides must differ by a mass of 4 and by a charge of 2.

$$^{12}_{5}B \rightarrow {}^{8}_{3}Li + {}^{4}_{2}\alpha$$

6. **(A)** is correct. In β^+ decay, the mass number remains constant and the proton number decreases by one, so the two nuclides must have the same mass number and differ by one in their proton numbers.

$$^{26}_{13}Al \rightarrow {}^{26}_{12}Mg + {}_{+1}\beta$$

7. Isotopes are atoms of the same element (same number of protons) with differing mass numbers.

8. **(A)** is correct. In electron capture, the mass number remains constant and the proton number decreases by one, so the two nuclides must have the same mass number and differ by one in their proton numbers.

$$^{26}_{13}Al + e^- \rightarrow {}^{26}_{12}Mg$$

9. **(A)** is correct. From the periodic table, we can see that Sn has an atomic mass of 118.71, so 128 is a very large mass number for Sn. The nuclide will decay to increase its proton to neutron ratio, thereby making itself more stable.

10. **(A)** is correct.

An alpha particle is a helium nucleus, so it has a mass of 4 g/mol and a charge of +2.

A beta particle is an electron, so its mass is very small compared to the masses of the protons and neutrons in the alpha particle. The charge on a beta particle is the same as the charge on an electron, –1.

11. **(D)** is correct. Make a chart. Always start at time = 0. We're looking for the time it takes for 80% of the stuff to decay. That's the time when 20% of the stuff remains.

Half-lives	Time	Stuff
0	0	100%
1	29 years	50%
2	58 years	25%
3	87 years	12.5%

It takes between 2 and 3 half-lives to get to the point when 20% remains. The correct answer is the only choice between 58 years and 87 years.

12. **(C)** is correct. Since decay is occurring and only potassium and calcium are present, one must be decaying to produce the other. Potassium and calcium differ by one proton, so the decay process must either add or subtract a proton.

Beta decay (I) is possible:

$$_{19}K \rightarrow {}_{20}Ca + {}_{-1}\beta$$

Electron capture (III) is possible:

$$_{20}Ca + {}_{-1}e \rightarrow {}_{19}K$$

Alpha decay (II) causes the loss of two protons, so it can't be occurring if only K and Ca are present.

13. **(B) is correct.** Since decay is occurring and only Po and Pb are present, one must be decaying to produce the other. Po has 84 protons and Pb has 82. The only way that a decay process can involve only these two elements is if Po undergoes alpha decay to produce Pb.

Alpha decay (II):

$$_{84}Po \rightarrow {}_{82}Pb + {}_2^4\alpha$$

If beta decay (I) or electron capture (III) were occurring, the proton count would be changing one at a time and $_{83}Bi$ would also be present in the sample.

14. **(D) is correct.** Let's do the math, you set it up like this:

$$_{84}^{214}Po - {}_2^4\alpha - {}_2^4\alpha - {}_{-1}\beta - {}_{-1}\beta =$$

For the mass number we have:

$$214 - 4 - 4 = 206$$

For the proton number we have:

$$84 - 2 - 2 - (-1) - (-1) = 84 - 4 + 2 = 82$$

So the answer is $_{82}^{206}Pb$.

15. **(B) is correct.** Make a chart. Always start at time = 0.

Half-lives	Time	Stuff
0	0	100%
1	X	50%
2	44 min.	25%

It takes two half-lives for the amount of $_{19}^{44}K$ to decrease to 25%. If two half-lives takes 44 minutes, one half-life must be 22 minutes.

Essays

1. (a) Alpha and beta particles have mass and volume, and so the surface of the body can often stop or slow them down. Gamma rays are electromagnetic radiation, which doesn't undergo collisions and can travel farther into the body.

    (b) Some of the mass of the neutrons and protons is lost to nuclear binding energy, which is released by the stable nucleus.

    (c) Stable arsenic has an atomic weight of 75, so arsenic 81 has too many neutrons. It will undergo β^- decay, which converts a neutron into a proton.

    $$_{33}^{75}As \rightarrow {}_{34}^{75}Se + {}_{-1}\beta$$

    (d) In electron capture, the nucleus captures an electron from a lower energy level and combines it with a proton to form a neutron.

    $$_{19}^{38}K + {}_{-1}e \rightarrow {}_{18}^{38}Ar$$

    (e) Remember Einstein's equation: $E = mc^2$.

    This means that the energy released by a nuclear process is 9×10^{16} times as large as the mass consumed.

2.   (a) In β^+ decay, a proton is converted into a neutron and a positron is emitted.

$$^{22}_{11}\text{Na} \rightarrow {}^{21}_{10}\text{Ne} + {}_{+1}\beta$$

(b) In β^- decay, a neutron is converted into a proton and a β^- particle (electron) is emitted.

$$^{26}_{11}\text{Na} \rightarrow {}^{26}_{12}\text{Mg} + {}_{-1}\beta$$

(c) Over the course of the decay process, only β^- particles are emitted. Neutrons are converted into protons, but there is no change in the mass numbers of the nuclides undergoing decay. Beta particles are virtually massless, so the loss of beta particles may not be detected.

(d) Alpha particles have the mass (4) and charge (+2) of a helium nucleus.

Beta (β^-) particles have the mass (insignificant) and charge (–1) of an electron.

Gamma radiation has neither mass nor charge. Gamma radiation is electromagnetic radiation.

15

LABORATORY

How often does this topic appear on the test?
In the multiple-choice section, this topic appears in about 5 out of 75 questions.
In the free-response section, you'll see this topic almost every year.

There will be some questions on the test that are specifically about lab technique, but most "lab" questions will be about specific chemistry topics, placed in a lab setting to make them seem more intimidating. You just need to remember some basic rules and combine them with science and common sense.

SAFETY

Here are some basic safety rules that might turn up in test questions.

- Don't put chemicals in your mouth. Your mother told you this when you were four years old and it still holds true for the AP test.

- When diluting an acid, always add the acid to the water. This is to avoid the spattering of hot solution.

- Always work with good ventilation; many common chemicals are toxic.

- When heating substances, do it slowly. When you heat things too quickly, they can spatter, burn, or explode.

ACCURACY

Here are some rules for ensuring the accuracy of experimental results.

- When titrating, rinse the buret with the solution to be used in the titration instead of with water. If you rinse the buret with water, you might dilute the solution, which will cause the volume added from the buret to be too large.

- Allow hot objects to return to room temperature before weighing. Hot objects on a scale create convection currents that may make the object seem lighter than it is.

- Don't weigh reagents directly on a scale. Use a glass or porcelain container to prevent corrosion of the balance pan.

- When collecting a gas over water, remember to take into account the pressure and volume of the water vapor.

- Don't contaminate your chemicals. Never insert another piece of equipment into a bottle containing a chemical. Instead you should always pour the chemical into another clean container. Also, don't let the inside of the stopper for a bottle containing a chemical touch another surface.

- When mixing chemicals, stir slowly to ensure even distribution.

- Be conscious of significant figures when you record your results. The number of significant figures that you use should indicate the accuracy of your results.

IDENTIFYING CHEMICALS IN SOLUTION

PRECIPITATION

One of the most useful ways of identifying unknown ions in solution is precipitation. You can use the solubility rules given in the solubility chapter to see how the addition of certain ions to solution will cause the specific precipitation of other ions. For instance:

The fact that $BaSO_4$ is insoluble can be used to identify either Ba^{2+} or SO_4^{2-} in solution; if the solution contains Ba^{2+} ions, then the addition of SO_4^{2-} will cause a precipitation reaction. The inverse is true for a solution that contains SO_4^{2-} ions.

In the same way, the insolubility of AgCl can be used to identify either Ag^+ or Cl^- in solution.

CONDUCTION

You can tell whether a solution contains ions or not by checking to see if the solution conducts electricity. Ionic solutes conduct electricity in solution, nonionic solutes do not.

FLAME TESTS

Flame tests can be used to identify Li^+, Na^+, and K^+, as well as the other alkali metals.

The alkaline earths, including Ba^{2+}, Sr^{2+}, and Ca^{2+} also burn with distinctively colored flames.

ACID-BASE REACTION

- When a base is added to an NH_4^+ solution, the distinctive odor of ammonia can be detected.

- When an acid is added to a solution containing S^{2-}, the rotten-egg odor of H_2S can be detected.

- When acid is added to a solution containing CO_3^{2-}, CO_2 gas is produced.

COLORED SOLUTIONS

- Many of the transition metals form ions with distinctive colors.

- Bromine and iodine will show a dark brown color when placed in an nonpolar solvent.

- Permanganate ion (MnO_4^-), a strong oxidizing agent, turns a solution purple.

- Dichromate ion ($C_2O_7^{2-}$), also a strong oxidizing agent, turns a solution orange.

LABORATORY

QUESTIONS

Multiple choice

Questions 1–4

    (A) Oxidation-reduction
    (B) Neutralization
    (C) Fusion
    (D) Combination
    (E) Decomposition

Which of the reaction types listed above best describes each of these processes?

1. $CO_2(g) + CaO(s) \rightarrow CaCO_3(s)$

2. $2\,Fe^{3+}(aq) + 2\,I^-(aq) \rightarrow 2\,Fe^{2+}(aq) + I_2(aq)$

3. $CH_3COOH(aq) + NaOH(aq) \rightarrow$
               $CH_3COONa(aq) + H_2O(l)$

4. $CH_4(g) + 2\,O_2(g) \rightarrow CO_2(g) + 2\,H_2O(g)$

Questions 5–8

    (A) Na^+
    (B) Cu^{2+}
    (C) Ag^+
    (D) Al^{3+}
    (E) NH_4^+

5. This ion turns an aqueous solution deep blue.

6. This ion forms a white precipitate when added to a solution containing chloride ions.

7. This ion produces a yellow flame when burned.

8. This ion produces a strong odor when added to a basic solution.

9. Which of the following indicators would be most useful in identifying the equivalence point of a titration for a solution that has a hydrogen ion concentration of $7 \times 10^{-4} M$ at the equivalence point?

(A) Methyl violet (pH range for color change is 0.1 – 2.0)
(B) Methyl yellow (pH range for color change is 1.2 – 2.3)
(C) Methyl orange (pH range for color change is 2.9 – 4.0)
(D) Methyl red (pH range for color change is 4.3 – 6.2)
(E) Bromthymol blue (pH range for color change is 6.1 – 7.6)

10. The volume of a liquid is to be measured. Which of the following cylindrical flasks would take the most accurate measurement?

(A) A flask with 1 ml gradations and a diameter of 1 cm.
(B) A flask with 1 ml gradations and a diameter of 3 cm.
(C) A flask with 5 ml gradations and a diameter of 1 cm.
(D) A flask with 5 ml gradations and a diameter of 3 cm.
(E) A flask with 10 ml gradations and a diameter of 1 cm.

11. Which of the following is (are) considered to be proper laboratory procedure?

I. Reading the height of a fluid in a buret from a point level with the fluid's meniscus.
II. Placing a sample to be weighed directly on the pan of the balance.
III. Stirring a solution constantly during a titration.

(A) I only
(B) III only
(C) I and III only
(D) II and III only
(E) I, II, and III

12. A 0.1-molar NaOH solution is to be released from a buret in a titration experiment to measure the hydrogen ion concentration of an unknown acid. Which of the following laboratory procedures would cause an error in the measure of the concentration of the acid?

I. The buret was rinsed with the NaOH solution immediately before the titration.
II. The buret was rinsed with distilled water immediately before the titration.
III. The buret was rinsed with the unknown acid immediately before the titration.

(A) I only
(B) III only
(C) I and II only
(D) I and III only
(E) II and III only

13. Which of the following is NOT proper procedure for transferring a solution with a pipet?

(A) Rinsing the pipet with the solution to be transferred.
(B) Using your mouth to draw the solution into the pipet.
(C) Covering the top of the pipet with your index finger to keep the solution from escaping.
(D) Draining the solution into a waste beaker until the meniscus drops to the calibration mark.
(E) Touching the pipet to the side of the destination beaker at the end of the transfer.

14. An object that was weighed on a balance was later found to be slightly heavier than the weight that was recorded by the balance. Which of the following could have caused the discrepancy?

    I. There was some foreign matter on the weighing paper along with the object.
    II. The object was hot when it was weighed.
    III. The experimenter neglected to account for the weight of the weighing paper.

    (A) I only
    (B) II only
    (C) I and II only
    (D) I and III only
    (E) I, II, and III

15. An experimenter wishes to use test paper to find the pH of a solution. Which of the following is part of the proper procedure for this process?

    (A) Dipping the test paper in the solution while stirring.
    (B) Dipping the test paper in the solution without stirring.
    (C) Pouring some of the solution onto the dry test paper.
    (D) Dipping the test paper in distilled water and slowly adding the solution to the water while stirring.
    (E) Dipping the test paper in distilled water and slowly adding the solution to the water without stirring.

Essays

1. A titration experiment was conducted to determine the pH of a known volume of a strong monoprotic acid solution. A hydroxide solution of known concentration was poured into a buret and then titrated into the acid solution. The volume of hydroxide solution titrated into the acid solution was measured at the equivalence point and used to calculate the concentration of the acid solution. Which of the following situations would cause an error in the calculated value of the pH of the acid solution? Explain.

    (a) The buret was rinsed with the hydroxide solution before the solution was poured into the buret.

    (b) The experimenter did not notice that a few drops of hydroxide solution spattered outside the acid solution container during the titration.

    (c) The buret was rinsed with distilled water before the hydroxide solution was added.

    (d) The experimenter read the hydroxide solution level from the top of the fluid instead of the bottom of the meniscus both before the titration and at the equivalence point.

    (e) Some hydroxide solution was spilled while the experimenter was pouring it into the buret.

2. An experiment was conducted to determine the molecular weight of a pure salt sample. The mass of the salt sample was known. The salt was dissolved in a container of water of known mass and the freezing point of the solution was measured. The molecular weight was calculated by the freezing point depression method. How would the calculated value of the molecular weight be affected by each of the following?

    (a) The experimenter failed to take the dissociation of the salt into account.

    (b) The experimenter mistook molarity for molality, and use liters of solution instead of kilograms of solvent in the calculation to find the number of moles of solute.

    (c) The container used for the experiment was not rinsed and contained dust particles.

    (d) The experimenter misread the thermometer and recorded a freezing point that was higher than the true value.

    (e) The experimenter did not notice that some solid salt did not completely dissolve.

3. Use your knowledge of chemical principles to answer or explain each of the following.

    (a) When helium gas is to be collected in a jar by the displacement of air, the opening of the jar must be directed downward. When carbon dioxide gas is to be collected in a jar by the displacement of air, the opening of the jar must be directed upward.

    (b) Will the molar quantity calculated for a gas collected over water be too large or too small if the experimenter fails to take into account the vapor pressure of water?

    (c) Why is it easier to separate oxygen gas from hydrogen gas by the method of successive effusion than it is to separate oxygen gas from nitrogen gas by the same method?

    (d) Give an explanation for why an attempt to separate two liquids by distillation would fail?

ANSWERS

Multiple choice

1. **(D)** is correct. In a combination (or composition, or synthesis) reaction, two substances combine to form a more complex substance.

    A combination reaction is the opposite of a decomposition reaction, so if this reaction occurred in reverse, it would be a decomposition reaction.

2. **(A)** is correct. In an oxidation-reduction reaction, electrons are transferred between the reactants, causing the oxidation state of the element that is oxidized to increase and the oxidation state of the element that is reduced to decrease. In this reaction, Fe^{3+} is reduced to Fe^{2+} and I^- is oxidized to I^0.

3. **(B)** is correct. In a neutralization reaction, an acid (in this case, CH_3COOH) and a base (NaOH) react to form water and a salt (CH_3COONa).

4. **(A)** is correct. This reaction, the combustion of an organic compound, is also an oxidation-reduction reaction. As we said above, in a redox reaction, electrons are transferred between the reactants, causing the oxidation state of the element that is oxidized to increase and the oxidation state of the element that is reduced to decrease. In this reaction, H^- is oxidized to H^+ and O^0 is reduced to O^{2-}.

5. **(B)** is correct. Copper, along with most of the transition metals, forms colored solutions with water. This is true because the d electrons of the transition metals are constantly changing energy levels and emitting radiation in the visible spectrum.

6. **(C)** is correct. Silver is the only ion listed that forms an insoluble chloride.

7. **(A)** is correct. Sodium, along with the other Group IA elements, produces a colored flame in the flame test.

8. **(E)** is correct. Ammonium ion reacts with hydroxide ion to form ammonia, which has a strong, distinct odor. This reaction is shown below.

    $$NH_4^+ + OH^- \rightarrow NH_3 + H_2O$$

9. **(C)** is correct. If $[H^+]$ is $7 \times 10^{-4}M$, then the pH must be between 3 and 4. Only methyl orange changes color between 3 and 4.

10. **(A)** is correct. Volume = (height)(cross-sectional area).

    The smaller the gradations, the more accurately the height can be measured. The smaller the area, the farther apart the 1 ml gradations will be and the more accurately the height of the fluid can be measured.

11. **(C)** is correct. Choices (I) and (III) are proper experimental procedure.

    (II) is not; a sample should always be weighed in a glass or porcelain container to prevent a reaction with the balance pan.

12. **(E) is correct.** Rinsing the buret with the NaOH solution (I) is proper procedure and will not change the concentration of the NaOH solution and will not cause an error. Rinsing the buret with distilled water (II) will dilute the NaOH solution, lowering the concentration and causing an error, and rinsing the buret with the unknown acid (III) will cause some of the NaOH solution to be neutralized in the buret, lowering its concentration and causing an error.

13. **(B) is correct.** You should never use your mouth to draw solution into a pipet. Instead, you should use a rubber suction bulb.

    All of the other choices are part of the proper procedure.

14. **(B) is correct.** When a hot object is weighed (II), convection currents around the object can reduced the apparent mass measured by the balance.

    Choices (I) and (III) would both cause the weight measured by the balance to be greater than the actual weight of the object. We're looking for the opposite effect.

15. **(C) is correct.**

    (A) and (B) are wrong because there is a danger of contaminating the solution by adding the paper.

    (D) and (E) are wrong because adding the solution to distilled water completely changes the solution and defeats the purpose of testing it.

    So pouring the solution onto the dry test paper (C) is the proper procedure.

Essays

1. A note for the answers:

    In this experiment, the volume of OH^- added is directly measured.

    Moles = (molarity)(volume) is used to find the moles of OH^- added.

    The moles of OH^- added to reach the equivalence point is equal to the number of moles of H^+ originally present in the acid solution.

    Molarity = $\dfrac{\text{moles}}{\text{volume}}$ is used to find $[H^+]$ of the acid solution.

    pH = $-\log[H^+]$ is used to calculate the pH.

    (a) This is proper experimental procedure and will have no adverse effect on the calculated value of the acid solution.

    (b) This will make the measured volume of the hydroxide solution larger than the actual amount added. It will also make the calculated value for the moles of OH^- and H^+ too large, the calculated value of $[H^+]$ will be too large, and the calculated pH will be too small.

    (c) This will dilute the hydroxide solution, which means that too large a volume of hydroxide solution will be added, the calculated value for the moles of OH^- and H^+ will be too large, the calculated $[H^+]$ will be too large, and the calculated pH will be too small.

    (d) The levels were read consistently even though they were read from the wrong spot. The two errors should cancel and the calculated pH should be correct.

    (e) This will not affect the concentration of the hydroxide solution or the measurement of the volume poured into the acid solution, so the calculated pH should not be affected.

2. A note for the answers:

In this experiment, the freezing point of the solution is measured, and from the freezing point the freezing point depression, ΔT, is calculated.

The equation $m = \dfrac{\Delta T}{kx}$ is used to calculate the molality of the solution.

Moles = (molality)(kg of solvent) is used to calculate the number of moles of salt.

$MW = \dfrac{grams}{moles}$ is used to calculate the molecular weight of the salt.

(a) The experimenter makes $x = 1$, instead of 2 or 3. So the calculated value of m will be too large, the calculated value of moles of salt will be too large, and the calculated MW will be too small.

(b) Moles = (molality)(kg of solvent)   Moles = (molarity)(liters of solution)

Because the solvent is water, the distinction between kilograms and liters is not important (for water, 1kg = 1 L), but the distinction between solvent and solution might make a difference.

Liters of solution will be a little larger than kilograms of solvent, so the calculated value for moles of salt will be too large, and the calculated MW will be too small.

(c) Extra particles in the solution will cause the measured freezing point to be too low. ΔT will be too large, m will be too large, and the calculated MW will be too small.

(d) If the freezing point is too high, the calculated ΔT will be too small, m will be too small, and the calculated MW will be too large.

(e) If some salt does not dissolve, then the grams of salt used in the calculation will be larger than the amount actually in the solution, and the calculated MW will be too large.

3. (a) Helium (MW = 4 g/mol) is less dense than air, so it will rise to the top of the jar, displacing air downward.

Carbon dioxide (MW = 44 g/mol) is more dense than air, so it will sink to the bottom of the jar, displacing air upward.

(b) If the vapor pressure from water is ignored, the pressure of the gas used in the calculation will be too large.

$$n = \frac{PV}{RT}$$

If P is too large, then n, the calculated molar quantity of gas, will be too large.

(c) Separation of gases by successive effusion depends on Graham's law.

$$\frac{v_1}{v_2} = \sqrt{\frac{MW_2}{MW_1}}$$

The greater the difference in molecular weights, the greater the difference in average molecular speeds, and the greater the difference in rates of effusion.

Oxygen gas (32 g/mol) and nitrogen gas (28 g/mol) have similar molecular weights.

Oxygen gas (32 g/mol) and hydrogen gas (2 g/mol) have very different molecular weights.

(d) The most likely reason for the failure of separation by distillation would be that the boiling points of the two liquids are too close together.

16
ORGANIC CHEMISTRY

Organic chemistry is the study of carbon compounds.

There is very little actual organic chemistry on the test. Instead of asking questions that are specifically about organic compounds, the test makers place organic compounds in questions about other parts of chemistry.

Here is a review of some of the basic organic compounds.

HYDROCARBONS

Hydrocarbons are compounds that contain only carbon and hydrogen.

ALKANES

Alkanes are hydrocarbons that contain only single bonds. They are also known as saturated hydrocarbons.

Alkane (C_nH_{2n+2})	Formula
Methane	CH_4
Ethane	C_2H_6
Propane	C_3H_8
Butane	C_4H_{10}
Pentane	C_5H_{12}

ALKENES

Alkenes are hydrocarbons that contain double bonds. They are examples of unsaturated hydrocarbons.

Alkene (C_nH_{2n})	Formula
Ethylene	C_2H_4
Propene	C_3H_6
Butene	C_4H_8
Pentene	C_5H_{10}

ALKYNES

Alkynes are hydrocarbons that contain triple bonds. They are also examples of unsaturated hydrocarbons.

Alkyne (C_nH_{2n-2})	Formula
Ethyne	C_2H_2
Propyne	C_3H_4
Butyne	C_4H_6
Pentyne	C_5H_8

HYDROCARBON RINGS

Many hydrocarbons form rings instead of chains. One of most important classes of these compounds is the aromatic hydrocarbons, the simplest of which is benzene, C_6H_6.

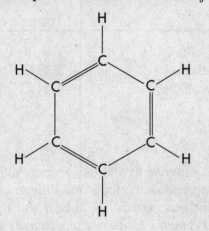

SOME FUNCTIONAL GROUPS

The presence of certain groups of atoms, called functional groups, in organic compounds can give the compounds specific chemical properties.

ALCOHOLS

Alcohols are organic compounds in which a hydrogen has been replaced with a hydroxide group (OH).

Alcohol	Formula
Methanol	CH_3OH
Ethanol	C_2H_5OH
Propanol	C_3H_7OH

ORGANIC ACIDS

Organic acids are organic compounds in which a hydrogen has been replaced with a carboxyl group (COOH).

Organic Acid	Formula
Formic Acid	$HCOOH$
Acetic Acid	CH_3COOH
Butyric Acid	C_3H_7COOH

HALIDES

Halides are organic compounds in which one or more hydrogens have been replaced with a halide (F, Cl, Br, I).

Halide	Formula
Chloromethane	CH_3Cl
Chloroethane	C_2H_5Cl
Chloropropane	C_3H_7Cl

ISOMERS

Among organic compounds, it is common to find two or more molecules with the same molecular formula, but with different arrangements of atoms and different chemical properties. These molecules are called isomers. For instance, ethanol (C_2H_5OH) and dimethyl ether (CH_3-O-CH_3) are isomers because each compound contains 2 carbon atoms, 6 hydrogen atoms, and 1 oxygen atom.

17

DESCRIPTIVE CHEMISTRY

This is the first section you'll see on Section II of the test. You'll be given 10 minutes to write the formulas for 5 out of 8 possible chemical reactions.

This is a tough section. The test makers say that this section is on the test because the knowledge of specific facts is important to the understanding of general concepts. That's all well and good, but you should be aware that this section is basically filled with chemistry trivia.

Rather than wasting your time trying to memorize an infinite number of possible chemical reactions, your best bet is to understand some general rules for approaching this section, which we give you below. And remember, you don't have to do the three hardest ones.

NET IONIC EQUATIONS

If you follow the directions given at the beginning of this section of the test, you'll be writing your answers in net ionic form. That means three things to you.

Don't balance the equations and don't write down the phases (s, aq, etc.) of the reactants and products

You don't get points for balancing or writing down phases, so balancing and writing down phases are a waste of time.

For instance:

If Pb^{2+} and Cl^- ions are placed in solution, $PbCl_2$ will precipitate. You *could* write:

$$Pb^{2+}(aq) + 2\ Cl^-(aq) \rightarrow PbCl_2(s)$$

but you *should* write:

$$Pb^{2+} + Cl^- \rightarrow PbCl_2$$

Substances that dissociate extensively should be written as ions

All the reactions are assumed to take place in water unless otherwise stated, so things that ionize in water should be written as ions.

For instance:

$NaNO_3$ ionizes, so it should be written as Na^+ and NO_3^-.
AgCl does not ionize, so it should be written as AgCl.
$Ca(OH)_2$ ionizes to some extent, so either $Ca(OH)_2$ or Ca^{2+} and OH^- are okay.

Leave out any molecules or ions that are not changed in the reaction

Let's say you're given this situation:

Solutions of sodium chloride and silver nitrate are mixed.
You know from your solubility rules that silver chloride precipitates.

The full reaction is:

$$Na^+ + Cl^- + Ag^+ + NO_3^- \rightarrow Na^+ + NO_3^- + AgCl$$

Leaving out things that are not changed results in:

$$Ag^+ + Cl^- \rightarrow AgCl$$

SCORING

Each of the 5 questions that you answer on this section is worth 3 points, for a total of 15. On each question, you get 1 point for correct reactants and 2 points for correct products. The average score for this section is usually about 5.

- That means if you get only 2 of these right (for 6 points) you've beat the mean, which means you're doing as well on this section as most of the people who get a 3 on the test.

- If you get 3 of these right (for 9 points), that puts you above the 80th percentile for the section, which means you're doing as well as most of the people who get a 4 on the test.

- If you get 4 of these right (for 12 points), that puts you above the 90th percentile for the section, which means you're doing as well as most of the people who get a 5 on the test.

Don't forget partial credit. Even if you don't know what will happen when two reactants react, you can still get a point for writing them down correctly.

CRACKING THE DESCRIPTIVE CHEMISTRY SECTION

The best way to crack this section is to take control of it. That is, you should choose the kind of equations that you are most comfortable writing and look for them among the choices. Approach the section the way a wolf approaches a herd of cattle. There's no point in attacking the biggest bull in the herd if you can grab five stragglers without a fight. The key, of course, is to spot the stragglers. The following methods of approach should give you the tools to answer at least five of the questions in the section.

I. LOOK FOR TWO UNCOMBINED ELEMENTS

There's only one thing you can do with uncombined elements: combine them. Just make sure that you give each element in the product compound a sensible oxidation state.

(a) Hydrogen gas is burned in air.
$H_2 + O_2 \rightarrow H_2O$
Notice that air always means oxygen.

(b) Solid sulfur is burned in oxygen.
$S + O_2 \rightarrow SO_2$

(c) Solid magnesium is heated in nitrogen gas.
$Mg + N_2 \rightarrow Mg_3N_2$

(d) A piece of solid zinc is heated in chlorine gas.
$Zn + Cl_2 \rightarrow ZnCl_2$

(e) A piece of solid barium is placed in oxygen gas.
$Ba + O_2 \rightarrow BaO$

(f) A piece of solid sodium is placed in hydrogen gas.
$Na + H_2 \rightarrow NaH$
Notice that none of the above equations are balanced.

II. LOOK FOR A SINGLE REACTANT

If there is only one reactant, all it can do is break up in a decomposition reaction, so you're guaranteed the reactant partial credit point.

Decomposition reactions usually produce simple salts and oxide gases.

(a) A solution of hydrogen peroxide is placed under a bright light.
$H_2O_2 \rightarrow H_2O + O_2$

(b) Solid calcium carbonate is heated.
$CaCO_3 \rightarrow CaO + CO_2$

(c) Solid potassium chlorate is heated in the presence of a catalyst.
$KClO_3 \rightarrow KCl + O_2$

(d) A sample of solid ammonium carbonate is heated.
$(NH_4)_2CO_3 \rightarrow NH_3 + CO_2 + H_2O$

(e) A piece of solid potassium nitrate is heated.
$KNO_3 \rightarrow KNO_2 + O_2$

III. Look For Water as a Reactant

When metals and nonmetals react with water, they tend to react in predictable ways. In general, metals react with water to form bases and nonmetals react with water to form acids.

Here are three variations.

1. *A pure metal or a metal hydride in water will produce a base and hydrogen gas.*

   (a) Sodium metal is added to distilled water.
   $$Na + H_2O \rightarrow Na^+ + OH^- + H_2$$

   (b) Calcium metal is added to distilled water.
   $$Ca + H_2O \rightarrow Ca(OH)_2 + H_2$$

   (c) Solid calcium hydride is added to water.
   $$CaH_2 + H_2O \rightarrow Ca(OH)_2 + H_2$$

   (d) Solid lithium hydride is added to distilled water.
   $$LiH + H_2O \rightarrow Li^+ + OH^- + H_2$$

2. *A metal oxide in water will produce a base.*
   Metal oxides are called basic anhydrides because they produce bases when added to water.

   (a) Solid potassium oxide is added to water.
   $$K_2O + H_2O \rightarrow K^+ + OH^-$$

   (b) Solid barium oxide is added to water.
   $$BaO + H_2O \rightarrow Ba^{2+} + OH^-$$

   (c) Solid lithium oxide is added to water.
   $$Li_2O + H_2O \rightarrow Li^+ + OH^-$$

   (d) Solid calcium oxide is added to water.
   $$CaO + H_2O \rightarrow Ca(OH)_2$$

3. *A nonmetal oxide in water will produce an acid.*
   Nonmetal oxides are called acid anhydrides because they produce acids in water.

   (a) Solid dinitrogen pentoxide is added to water.
   $$N_2O_5 + H_2O \rightarrow H^+ + NO_3^-$$

   (b) Carbon dioxide gas is bubbled through water.
   $$CO_2 + H_2O \rightarrow H_2CO_3$$

   (c) Solid phosphorous (V) oxide is added to distilled water.
   $$P_2O_5 + H_2O \rightarrow H_3PO_4$$

   (d) Sulfur dioxide gas is bubbled through water.
   $$SO_2 + H_2O \rightarrow H_2SO_3$$

   (e) Sulfur trioxide gas is bubbled through water.
   $$SO_3 + H_2O \rightarrow H^+ + HSO_4^-$$

IV. LOOK FOR AN ACID-BASE NEUTRALIZATION

There are a few variations on this, but you can follow all of them through to get the standard proton donor—proton acceptor equations that you should be used to dealing with.

1. *An acid and a base.*

   (a) Equal molar amounts of potassium hydroxide and hydrochloric acid are mixed.
   $$H^+ + OH^- \rightarrow H_2O$$
   Strong acid and strong base.

   (b) Solutions of nitric acid and sodium hydroxide are mixed.
   $$H^+ + OH^- \rightarrow H_2O$$
   Strong acid and strong base.

   (c) A solution of sodium hydroxide is added to a solution of acetic acid.
   $$HC_2H_3O_2 + OH^- \rightarrow C_2H_3O_2^- + H_2O$$
   Weak acid and strong base.

   (d) Solutions of hydrofluoric acid and potassium hydroxide are mixed.
   $$HF + OH^- \rightarrow F^- + H_2O$$
   Weak acid and strong base.

   (e) Solutions of ammonia and nitric acid are mixed.
   $$NH_3 + H^+ \rightarrow NH_4^+$$
   Strong acid and weak base.

   (f) Solutions of ammonia and sulfuric acid are mixed.
   $$NH_3 + H^+ \rightarrow NH_4^+$$
   Strong acid and weak base.

   (g) Solutions of ammonia and hydrofluoric acid are mixed.
   $$HF + NH_3 \rightarrow F^- + NH_4^+$$
   Weak acid and weak base.

   (h) Solutions of ammonia and carbonic acid are mixed.
   $$H_2CO_3 + NH_3 \rightarrow HCO_3^- + NH_4^+$$
   Weak acid and weak base.

2. *An acid and a basic salt.*
   This is still a straightforward acid-base reaction.

   (a) Solutions of hydrochloric acid and sodium bicarbonate are mixed.
   $$H^+ + HCO_3^- \rightarrow H_2CO_3$$

   (b) Dilute sulfuric acid is added to a solution of potassium fluoride.
   $$H^+ + F^- \rightarrow HF$$

   (c) Excess hydrochloric acid is added to a solution of potassium sulfide.
   $$H^+ + S^{2-} \rightarrow H_2S$$
   The word "excess" is there to indicate that there are enough H^+ ions to form H_2S, instead of just HS^-

3. *A base and an acid salt.*

   (a) Sodium hydroxide solution is added to a solution of ammonium nitrate.
   $$NH_4^+ + OH^- \rightarrow NH_3 + H_2O$$

   (b) Solutions of potassium hydroxide and ammonium chloride are mixed.
   $$NH_4^+ + OH^- \rightarrow NH_3 + H_2O$$

4. *An acid anhydride and a base.*
   If you look at these in two steps, you'll see that they're just like other acid-base neutralizations.

   (a) Carbon dioxide gas is bubbled through a potassium hydroxide solution.
   $$(CO_2 + H_2O \rightarrow H_2CO_3)$$
   $$\underline{+ (H_2CO_3 + OH^- \rightarrow HCO_3^- + H_2O)}$$
   $$CO_2 + OH^- \rightarrow HCO_3^-$$

   (b) Sulfur trioxide gas is bubbled through a sodium hydroxide solution.
   $$(SO_3 + H_2O \rightarrow H^+ + HSO_4^-)$$
   $$\underline{+ (H^+ + OH^- \rightarrow H_2O)}$$
   $$SO_3 + OH^- \rightarrow HSO_4^-$$

   (c) Carbon dioxide gas and ammonia gas are bubbled into distilled water.
   $$(CO_2 + H_2O \rightarrow H_2CO_3)$$
   $$\underline{+ (H_2CO_3 + NH_3 \rightarrow HCO_3^- + NH_4^+)}$$
   $$CO_2 + H_2O + NH_3 \rightarrow HCO_3^- + NH_4^+$$

V. LOOK FOR A MIXTURE OF TWO SALT SOLUTIONS

For these questions, you have to predict which salt precipitates. If you are familiar with the solubility rules, these aren't too bad.

   (a) Solutions of calcium nitrate and sodium sulfate are mixed.
   $$Ca^{2+} + SO_4^{2-} \rightarrow CaSO_4$$

   (b) A solution of silver nitrate is added to a solution of potassium iodide.
   $$Ag^+ + I^- \rightarrow AgI$$

   (c) Solutions of lead (II) nitrate and tri-potassium phosphate are mixed.
   $$Pb^{2+} + PO_4^{3-} \rightarrow Pb_3(PO_4)_2$$

   (d) A solution of ammonium sulfide is added to a solution of magnesium iodide.
   $$Mg^{2+} + S^{2-} \rightarrow MgS$$

   (e) A solution of barium chloride is mixed with a solution of silver (I) sulfate.
   $$Ba^{2+} + Cl^- + Ag^+ + SO_4^{2-} \rightarrow BaSO_4 + AgCl$$

VI. Look For the Combustion of a Carbon Compound

Carbon compounds always burn to form oxide gases. Even if you can't get the reactant formula from the name of a hydrocarbon compound, you can probably get the two product points by knowing that it produces carbon dioxide and water when it burns.

(a) Ethane is burned in air.
$$C_2H_6 + O_2 \rightarrow CO_2 + H_2O$$

(b) Methanol is burned in oxygen.
$$CH_3OH + O_2 \rightarrow CO_2 + H_2O$$

(c) Carbon disulfide is burned in excess oxygen.
$$CS_2 + O_2 \rightarrow CO_2 + SO_2$$
The word "excess" is there to indicate that there is enough oxygen to form CO_2, rather than CO.

(d) Propane is burned in air.
$$C_3H_8 + O_2 \rightarrow CO_2 + H_2O$$

VII. Look For a Solid Transition Metal Placed in Solution

This will be a redox reaction and the solid metal will always be oxidized. Look for two variations.

1. *The solution is a neutral transition metal salt solution.*
The metal ion in solution will be reduced.

(a) Solid manganese flakes are placed in a solution of copper (II) sulfate.
$$Mn + Cu^{2+} \rightarrow Mn^{2+} + Cu$$

(b) A piece of solid nickel is placed in a solution of silver nitrate.
$$Ni + Ag^+ \rightarrow Ni^{2+} + Ag$$

(c) A bar of zinc is immersed in a solution of silver nitrate.
$$Zn + Ag^+ \rightarrow Zn^{2+} + Ag$$

(d) Iron filings are placed in a solution of iron (III) sulfate.
$$Fe + Fe^{3+} \rightarrow Fe^{2+}$$
Here, differing oxidation states of iron are both changed to an intermediate state.

2. *The solution is a strong oxoacid solution.*
The anion of the oxoacid will be reduced to an oxide gas and water will form.

(a) A piece of copper is immersed in dilute nitric acid.
$$Cu + H^+ + NO_3^- \rightarrow Cu^{2+} + NO + H_2O$$

(b) A piece of copper is immersed in concentrated warm sulfuric acid.
$$Cu + H^+ + HSO_4^- \rightarrow Cu^{2+} + SO_2 + H_2O$$

(c) A piece of silver is placed in dilute nitric acid.
$$Ag + H^+ + NO_3^- \rightarrow Ag^+ + NO + H_2O$$

(d) A piece of lead is immersed in concentrated warm sulfuric acid.
$$Pb + H^+ + HSO_4^- \rightarrow Pb^{2+} + SO_2 + H_2O$$

VIII. LOOK FOR TRANSITION METAL IONS IN SOLUTION WITH AMMONIA, HYDROXIDE, CYANIDE, OR THIOCYANATE

Transition metal ions form complex ions with the species above. It doesn't matter how many of them you place on the transition metal, as long as you get the charge on the complex ion correct.

(a) Excess ammonia is added a to solution of silver nitrate.

$$Ag^+ + NH_3 \rightarrow Ag(NH_3)_2^+$$

(b) A solution of sodium cyanide is added to a solution of iron (II) chloride.

$$Fe^{2+} + CN^- \rightarrow Fe(CN)_6^{4-}$$

(c) A solution of potassium thiocyanate is added to a solution of iron (III) chloride.

$$Fe^{3+} + SCN^- \rightarrow Fe(SCN)^{2+}$$

(d) A concentrated solution of ammonia is mixed with a solution of zinc (II) nitrate.

$$Zn^{2+} + NH_3 \rightarrow Zn(NH_3)_4^{2+}$$

(e) Excess ammonia is added to a solution of copper (II) nitrate.

$$Cu^{2+} + NH_3 \rightarrow Cu(NH_3)_4^{2+}$$

THE PRINCETON REVIEW
AP CHEMISTRY
DIAGNOSTIC EXAM

CHEMISTRY

Three hours are allotted for this examination: 1 hour and 30 minutes for Section I, which consists of multiple-choice questions, and 1 hour and 30 minutes for Section II, which consists of problems and essay questions.

SECTION I

Time—1 hour and 30 minutes
Number of questions—75
Percent of total grade—45

This examination contains 75 multiple-choice questions. Therefore for the examination questions please be careful to fill in only the ovals that are preceded by numbers 1 through 75 on your answer sheet.

General Instructions

CALCULATORS MAY NOT BE USED IN THIS PART OF THE EXAMINATION.

INDICATE ALL YOUR ANSWERS TO QUESTIONS IN SECTION I ON THE SEPARATE ANSWER SHEET.
No credit will be given for anything written in this examination booklet, but you may use the booklet for notes or scratchwork. After you have decided which of the suggested answers is best, COMPLETELY fill in the corresponding oval on the answer sheet. Give only one answer to each question. If you change an answer, be sure that the previous mark is erased completely.

Example: Sample Answer

    Chicago is a   Ⓐ ● Ⓒ Ⓓ Ⓔ

    (A) state
    (B) city
    (C) country
    (D) continent
    (E) village

Many candidates wonder whether or not to guess the answer to questions about which they are not certain. In this section of the examination, as a correction for haphazard guessing, one-fourth of the number of questions you answer incorrectly will be subtracted from the number of questions you answer correctly. It is improbable, therefore, that mere guessing will improve your score significantly; it may even lower your score, and it does take time. If, however, you are not sure of the correct answer but have some knowledge of the question and are able to eliminate one or more of the answer choices as wrong, your chance of getting the right answer is improved, and it may be to your advantage to answer such a question.

Use your time effectively, working as rapidly as you can without losing accuracy. Do not spend too much time on questions that are too difficult. Go on to other questions and come back to the difficult ones later if you have time. It is not expected that everyone will be able to answer all the multiple-choice questions.

CHEMISTRY
SECTION I
Time — 1 hour and 30 minutes

Material in the following table may be useful in answering the questions in this section of the examination.

PERIODIC CHART OF THE ELEMENTS

1 H 1.0																	2 He 4.0
3 Li 6.9	4 Be 9.0											5 B 10.8	6 C 12.0	7 N 14.0	8 O 16.0	9 F 19.0	10 Ne 20.2
11 Na 23.0	12 Mg 24.3											13 Al 27.0	14 Si 28.1	15 P 31.0	16 S 32.1	17 Cl 35.5	18 Ar 39.9
19 K 39.1	20 Ca 40.1	21 Sc 45.0	22 Ti 47.9	23 V 50.9	24 Cr 52.0	25 Mn 54.9	26 Fe 55.8	27 Co 58.9	28 Ni 58.7	29 Cu 63.5	30 Zn 65.4	31 Ga 69.7	32 Ge 72.6	33 As 74.9	34 Se 79.0	35 Br 79.9	36 Kr 83.8
37 Rb 85.5	38 Sr 87.6	39 Y 88.9	40 Zr 91.2	41 Nb 92.9	42 Mo 95.9	43 Tc (98)	44 Ru 101.1	45 Rh 102.9	46 Pd 106.4	47 Ag 107.9	48 Cd 112.4	49 In 114.8	50 Sn 118.7	51 Sb 121.8	52 Te 127.6	53 I 126.9	54 Xe 131.3
55 Cs 132.9	56 Ba 137.3	57 *La 138.9	72 Hf 178.5	73 Ta 180.9	74 W 183.9	75 Re 186.2	76 Os 190.2	77 Ir 192.2	78 Pt 195.1	79 Au 197.0	80 Hg 200.6	81 Tl 204.4	82 Pb 207.2	83 Bi 209.0	84 Po (209)	85 At (210)	86 Rn (222)
87 Fr (223)	88 Ra 226.0	89 †Ac 227.0															

*Lanthanum Series														
58 Ce 140.1	59 Pr 140.9	60 Nd 144.2	61 Pm (145)	62 Sm 150.4	63 Eu 152.0	64 Gd 157.3	65 Tb 158.9	66 Dy 162.5	67 Ho 164.9	68 Er 167.3	69 Tm 168.9	70 Yb 173.0	71 Lu 175.0	

†Actinium Series														
90 Th 232.0	91 Pa 231.0	92 U 238.0	93 Np 237.0	94 Pu (244)	95 Am (243)	96 Cm (247)	97 Bk (247)	98 Cf (251)	99 Es (252)	100 Fm (258)	101 Md (258)	102 No (259)	103 Lr (260)	

GO ON TO THE NEXT PAGE

Note: For all questions involving solutions and/or chemical equations, assume that the system is in pure water and at room temperature unless otherwise stated.

Part A

Directions: Each set of lettered choices below refers to the numbered questions or statements immediately following it. Select the one lettered choice that best answers each question or best fits each statement and then fill in the corresponding oval on the answer sheet. A choice may be used once, more than once, or not at all in each set.

Questions 1–3 are based on the following energy diagrams

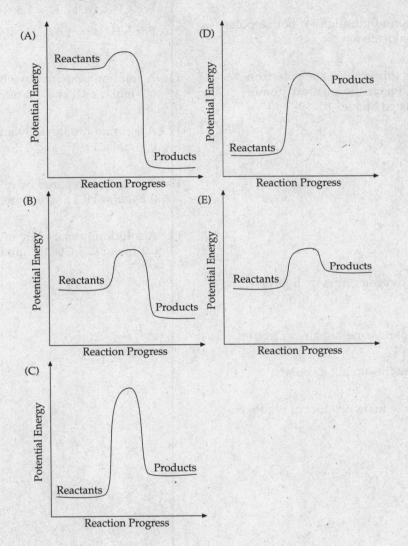

1.   This reaction has the largest activation energy.

2.   This is the most exothermic reaction.

3.   This reaction has the largest positive value for ΔH.

GO ON TO THE NEXT PAGE

Questions 4–6

    (A) $1s^2\,2s^22p^6$
    (B) $1s^2\,2s^22p^6\,3s^2$
    (C) $1s^2\,2s^22p^6\,3s^23p^4$
    (D) $1s^2\,2s^22p^6\,3s^23p^6$
    (E) $1s^2\,2s^22p^6\,3s^23p^6\,4s^2$

4. The ground state configuration of an atom of a paramagnetic element.

5. The ground state configuration for both a potassium ion and a chloride ion.

6. An atom that has this ground-state electron configuration will have the smallest atomic radius of those listed above.

Questions 7–10

    (A) CO_2
    (B) H_2O
    (C) SO_2
    (D) NO_2
    (E) O_2

7. In this molecule, oxygen forms sp^3 hybrid orbitals.

8. This molecule contains one unpaired electron.

9. This molecule contains no pi (π) bonds.

10. This molecule is the main product of photosynthesis.

Questions 11–14

    (A) A solution with a pH of 1
    (B) A solution with a pH of greater than 1 and less than 7
    (C) A solution with a pH of 7
    (D) A solution with a pH of greater than 7 and less than 13
    (E) A solution with a pH of 13

For CH_3COOH, $K_a = 1.8 \times 10^{-5}$

For NH_3, $K_b = 1.8 \times 10^{-5}$

11. A solution prepared by mixing equal volumes of 0.2-molar HCl and 0.2-molar NH_3.

12. A solution prepared by mixing equal volumes of 0.2-molar HNO_3 and 0.2-molar NaOH.

13. A solution prepared by mixing equal volumes of 0.2-molar HCl and 0.2-molar NaCl.

14. A solution prepared by mixing equal volumes of 0.2-molar CH_3COOH and 0.2-molar NaOH.

GO ON TO THE NEXT PAGE

Part B

Directions: Each of the questions or incomplete statements below is followed by five suggested answers or completions. Select the one that is best in each case and then fill in the corresponding oval on the answer sheet.

15. A pure sample of $KClO_3$ is found to contain 71 grams of chlorine atoms. What is the mass of the sample?

   (A) 122 grams
   (B) 170 grams
   (C) 209 grams
   (D) 245 grams
   (E) 293 grams

16. Which of the following experimental procedures is used to separate two substances by taking advantage of their differing boiling points?

   (A) Titration
   (B) Distillation
   (C) Filtration
   (D) Decantation
   (E) Hydration

17. Which of the following sets of quantum numbers (n, l, m_l, m_s) best describes the highest energy valence electron in a ground-state aluminum atom?

   (A) $2, 0, 0, \dfrac{1}{2}$

   (B) $2, 1, 0, \dfrac{1}{2}$

   (C) $3, 0, 0, \dfrac{1}{2}$

   (D) $3, 0, 1, \dfrac{1}{2}$

   (E) $3, 1, 1, \dfrac{1}{2}$

18. Which of the following elements is NOT normally found as a diatomic gas molecule in its uncombined state at room temperature?

   (A) Hydrogen
   (B) Fluorine
   (C) Oxygen
   (D) Nitrogen
   (E) Helium

19. $2\,MnO_4^- + 5\,SO_3^{2-} + 6\,H^+ \rightarrow 2\,Mn^{2+} + 5\,SO_4^{2-} + 3\,H_2O$

   Which of the following statements is true regarding the reaction given above?

   (A) MnO_4^- acts as the reducing agent.
   (B) H^+ acts as the oxidizing agent.
   (C) SO_3^{2-} acts as the reducing agent.
   (D) MnO_4^- is oxidized.
   (E) SO_3^{2-} is reduced.

20. Which of the following can function as both a both a Brønsted-Lowry acid and Brønsted-Lowry base?

   (A) HCl
   (B) H_2SO_4
   (C) HSO_3^-
   (D) SO_4^{2-}
   (E) H^+

21. Which of the following substances experiences the strongest attractive intermolecular forces?

   (A) H_2
   (B) N_2
   (C) CO_2
   (D) NH_3
   (E) CH_4

22. A mixture of gases at equilibrium over water at 43 °C contains 9.0 moles of nitrogen, 2.0 moles of oxygen, and 1.0 mole of water vapor. If the total pressure exerted by the gases is 780 mm Hg, what is the vapor pressure of water at 43 °C?

   (A) 65 mm Hg
   (B) 130 mm Hg
   (C) 260 mm Hg
   (D) 580 mm Hg
   (E) 720 mm Hg

GO ON TO THE NEXT PAGE

23. $...MnO_4^- + ...e^- + ...H^+ \rightarrow ...Mn^{2+} + ...H_2O$

When the half-reaction above is balanced, what is the coefficient for H^+ if all the coefficients are reduced to the lowest whole number?

(A) 3
(B) 4
(C) 5
(D) 8
(E) 10

24. The boiling point of water is known to be lower at high elevations. This is because

(A) hydrogen bonds are weaker at high elevations
(B) the heat of fusion is lower at high elevations
(C) the vapor pressure of water is higher at high elevations
(D) the atmospheric pressure is lower at high elevations
(E) water is more dense at high elevations

25. A hydrocarbon contains 75% carbon by mass. What is the empirical formula for the compound?

(A) CH_2
(B) CH_3
(C) CH_4
(D) C_2H_5
(E) C_3H_8

26. $S(s) + O_2(g) \rightarrow SO_2(g)$ $\Delta H^\circ = x$

$S(s) + \frac{3}{2} O_2(g) \rightarrow SO_3(g)$ $\Delta H^\circ = y$

Based on the information above, what is the standard enthalpy change for the following reaction?

$$2 SO_2(g) + O_2(g) \rightarrow 2 SO_3(g)$$

(A) $x - y$
(B) $y - x$
(C) $2x - y$
(D) $2x - 2y$
(E) $2y - 2x$

27. How much water must be added to a 50.0 ml solution of 0.60 M HNO_3 to produce a 0.40 M solution of HNO_3?

(A) 25 ml
(B) 33 ml
(C) 50 ml
(D) 67 ml
(E) 75 ml

28. In which of the following equilibria would the concentrations of the products be increased if the volume of the system were decreased at constant temperature?

(A) $H_2(g) + Cl_2(g) \rightleftharpoons 2 HCl(g)$
(B) $2 CO(g) + O_2(g) \rightleftharpoons 2 CO_3(g)$
(C) $NO(g) + O_3(g) \rightleftharpoons NO_2(g) + O_2(g)$
(D) $2 HI(g) \rightleftharpoons H_2(g) + I_2(g)$
(E) $N_2O_4(g) \rightleftharpoons 2 NO_2(g)$

29. Which of the following is the strongest acid?

(A) H_2SO_4
(B) HSO_4^-
(C) H_2SO_3
(D) HSO_3^-
(E) H_2S

30. Which of the following can be determined directly from the difference between the boiling point of a pure solvent and the boiling point of a solution of a nonionic solute in the solvent if k_b for the solvent is known?

   I. The mass of solute in the solution
   II. The molality of the solution
  III. The volume of the solution

(A) I only
(B) II only
(C) III only
(D) I and II only
(E) I and III only

GO ON TO THE NEXT PAGE

31. The value of the equilibrium constant K_{eq} is greater than 1 for a certain reaction under standard state conditions. Which of the following statements must be true regarding the reaction?

(A) ΔG° is negative.
(B) ΔG° is positive.
(C) ΔG° is equal to zero.
(D) ΔG° is negative if the reaction is exothermic and positive if the reaction is endothermic.
(E) ΔG° is negative if the reaction is endothermic and positive if the reaction is exothermic.

32. Which of the following aqueous solutions has the highest boiling point?

(A) 0.1 m NaOH
(B) 0.1 m HF
(C) 0.1 m Na_2SO_4
(D) 0.1 m $KC_2H_3O_2$
(E) 0.1 m NH_4NO_3

33. The molecular formula for hydrated ferric oxide, or rust, is generally written as $Fe_2O_3 \bullet x\ H_2O$ because the water content in rust can vary. If a 1-molar sample of hydrated ferric oxide is found to contain 108 g of H_2O, what is the molecular formula for the sample?

(A) $Fe_2O_3 \bullet H_2O$
(B) $Fe_2O_3 \bullet 3\ H_2O$
(C) $Fe_2O_3 \bullet 6\ H_2O$
(D) $Fe_2O_3 \bullet 10\ H_2O$
(E) $Fe_2O_3 \bullet 12\ H_2O$

34. In which of the following reactions is entropy increasing?

(A) $2\ SO_2(g) + O_2(g) \rightarrow 2\ SO_3(g)$
(B) $CO(g) + H_2O(g) \rightarrow H_2(g) + CO_2(g)$
(C) $H_2(g) + Cl_2(g) \rightarrow 2\ HCl(g)$
(D) $2\ NO_2(g) \rightarrow 2\ NO(g) + O_2(g)$
(E) $2\ H_2S(g) + 3\ O_2(g) \rightarrow 2\ H_2O(g) + 2\ SO_2(g)$

35. Which of the following will be true when a pure sample of $CaCl_2$ is dissolved in distilled water?

(A) The concentration of Ca^{2+} ions will be one-fourth the concentration of Cl^- ions.
(B) The concentration of Ca^{2+} ions will be one-half the concentration of Cl^- ions.
(C) The concentration of Ca^{2+} ions will be equal to the concentration of Cl^- ions.
(D) The concentration of Ca^{2+} ions will be twice the concentration of Cl^- ions.
(E) The concentration of Ca^{2+} ions will be four times the concentration of Cl^- ions.

36.
$$... + n \rightarrow {}^{7}_{3}Li + {}^{4}_{2}He$$

For the nuclear reaction shown above, what is the missing reactant?

(A) ${}^{9}_{4}Be$
(B) ${}^{9}_{5}B$
(C) ${}^{10}_{4}Be$
(D) ${}^{10}_{5}B$
(E) ${}^{11}_{5}B$

37. A boiling water bath is sometimes used instead of a flame in heating objects. Which of the following could be an advantage of a boiling water bath over a flame?

(A) The relatively low heat capacity of water will cause the object to become hot more quickly.
(B) The relatively high density of water will cause the object to become hot more quickly.
(C) The volume of boiling water remains constant over time.
(D) The temperature of boiling water remains constant at 100° C.
(E) The vapor pressure of boiling water is equal to zero.

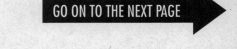

38. The addition of a catalyst to a chemical reaction will bring about a change in which of the following characteristics of the reaction?

    I. The activation energy
    II. The enthalpy change
    III. The value of the equilibrium constant

(A) I only
(B) II only
(C) I and II only
(D) I and III only
(E) II and III only

39. $$2\ NO(g) + O_2(g) \rightarrow 2\ NO_2(g)$$

The reaction above occurs by the following two-step process:

Step I: $NO(g) + O_2(g) \rightarrow NO_3(g)$

Step II: $NO_3(g) + NO(g) \rightarrow 2\ NO_2(g)$

Which of the following is true of Step II if it is the rate-limiting step?

(A) Step II has a lower activation energy and occurs more slowly than Step I.
(B) Step II has a higher activation energy and occurs more slowly than Step I.
(C) Step II has a lower activation energy and occurs more quickly than Step I.
(D) Step II has a higher activation energy and occurs more quickly than Step I.
(E) Step II has the same activation energy and occurs at the same speed as Step I.

40. $$...C_3H_7OH + ...O_2 \rightarrow ...CO_2 + ...H_2O$$

One mole of C_3H_7OH underwent combustion as shown in the reaction above. How many moles of oxygen were required for the reaction?

(A) 2 moles

(B) 3 moles

(C) $\dfrac{7}{2}$ moles

(D) $\dfrac{9}{2}$ moles

(E) 5 moles

Questions 41–44 refer to the phase diagram below.

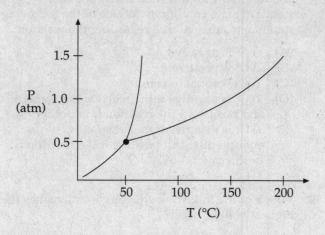

41. If the pressure of the substance shown in the diagram is decreased from 1.0 atmosphere to 0.5 atmosphere at a constant temperature of 100 °C, which phase change will occur?

(A) Freezing
(B) Vaporization
(C) Condensation
(D) Sublimation
(E) Deposition

42. Under what conditions can all three phases of the substance shown in the diagram exist simultaneously in equilibrium?

(A) Pressure = 1.0 atm, Temperature = 150 °C
(B) Pressure = 1.0 atm, Temperature = 100 °C
(C) Pressure = 1.0 atm, Temperature = 50 °C
(D) Pressure = 0.5 atm, Temperature = 100 °C
(E) Pressure = 0.5 atm, Temperature = 50 °C

43. If the temperature of the substance shown in the diagram is increased from 10 °C to 60 °C at a constant pressure of 0.3 atmospheres, which phase change will occur?

(A) Melting
(B) Vaporization
(C) Sublimation
(D) Condensation
(E) Deposition

GO ON TO THE NEXT PAGE

44. Which of the following lists the three phases of the substance shown in the diagram in order of increasing density at 60 °C ?

(A) solid, gas, liquid
(B) solid, liquid, gas
(C) gas, liquid, solid
(D) gas, solid, liquid
(E) liquid, solid, gas

45. A solution to be used as a reagent for a reaction is to be removed from a bottle marked with its concentration. Which of the following is NOT part of the proper procedure for this process.

(A) Pouring the solution down a stirring rod into a beaker.
(B) Inserting a pipet directly into the bottle and drawing out the solution.
(C) Placing the stopper of the bottle upside down on the table top.
(D) Pouring the solution down the side of a tilted beaker.
(E) Touching the stopper of the bottle only on the handle.

46. $$N_2(g) + 3 H_2(g) \rightleftharpoons 2 NH_3(g) + energy$$

Which of the following changes to the equilibrium situation shown above will bring about an increase in the number of moles of NH_3 present at equilibrium?

  I. Adding N_2 gas to the reaction chamber
 II. Increasing the volume of the reaction chamber at constant temperature
III. Increasing the temperature of the reaction chamber at constant volume

(A) I only
(B) II only
(C) I and II only
(D) I and III only
(E) II and III only

47. $$CH_4 + 2 O_2 \rightarrow CO_2 + 2 H_2O$$

If 16 grams of CH_4 reacts with 16 grams of O_2 in the reaction shown above, which of the following will be true?

(A) The mass of H_2O formed will be twice the mass of CO_2 formed.
(B) Equal masses of H_2O and CO_2 will be formed.
(C) Equal numbers of moles of H_2O and CO_2 will be formed.
(D) The limiting reagant will be CH_4.
(E) The limiting reagant will be O_2.

48. Which of the following sets of gases would be most difficult to separate if the method of gaseous effusion is used?

(A) O_2 and CO_2
(B) N_2 and C_2H_4
(C) H_2 and CH_4
(D) He and Ne
(E) O_2 and He

49. Which of the following equilibrium expressions represents the hydrolysis of the CN^- ion?

(A) $K = \dfrac{[HCN][OH^-]}{[CN^-]}$

(B) $K = \dfrac{[CN^-][OH^-]}{[HCN]}$

(C) $K = \dfrac{[CN^-][H_3O^+]}{[HCN]}$

(D) $K = \dfrac{[HCN][H_3O^+]}{[CN^-]}$

(E) $K = \dfrac{[HCN]}{[CN^-][OH^-]}$

GO ON TO THE NEXT PAGE

50. Which of the following is true under any conditions for a reaction that is spontaneous at any temperature?

(A) ΔG, ΔS, and ΔH are all positive.
(B) ΔG, ΔS, and ΔH are all negative.
(C) ΔG and ΔS are negative, and ΔH is positive.
(D) ΔG and ΔS are positive, and ΔH is negative.
(E) ΔG and ΔH are negative, and ΔS is positive.

51. Which of the following pairs of compounds are isomers?

(A) HCOOH and CH_3COOH
(B) CH_3CH_3CHO and C_3H_7OH
(C) C_2H_5OH and CH_3OCH_3
(D) C_2H_4 and C_2H_6
(E) C_3H_8 and C_4H_{10}

52. A sample of an ideal gas confined in a rigid 5.00 liter container has a pressure of 363 mmHg at a temperature of 25 °C. Which of the following expressions will be equal to the pressure of the gas if the temperature of the container is increased to 35 °C?

(A) $\dfrac{(363)(35)}{(25)}$ mmHg

(B) $\dfrac{(363)(25)}{(35)}$ mmHg

(C) $\dfrac{(363)(308)}{(298)}$ mmHg

(D) $\dfrac{(363)(298)}{(308)}$ mmHg

(E) $\dfrac{(363)(273)}{(308)}$ mmHg

53. If the temperature at which a reaction takes place is increased, the rate of the reaction will

(A) increase if the reaction is endothermic and decrease if the reaction is exothermic
(B) decrease if the reaction is endothermic and increase if the reaction is exothermic
(C) increase if the reaction is endothermic and increase if the reaction is exothermic
(D) decrease if the reaction is endothermic and decrease if the reaction is exothermic
(E) remain the same for both an endothermic and an exothermic reaction

54. Which of the following expressions is equal to the hydrogen ion concentration of a 1-molar solution of a very weak monoprotic acid, HA, with an ionization constant K_a?

(A) K_a

(B) K_a^2

(C) $2K_a$

(D) $2K_a^2$

(E) $\sqrt{K_a}$

55. $$2\,NO(g) + 2\,H_2(g) \rightarrow N_2(g) + 2\,H_2O(g)$$

Which of the following is true regarding the relative molar rates of disappearance of the reactants and appearance of the products?

I. N_2 appears at the same rate that H_2 disappears.
II. H_2O appears at the same rate that NO disappears.
III. NO disappears at the same rate that H_2 disappears.

(A) I only
(B) I and II only
(C) I and III only
(D) II and III only
(E) I, II, and III

56. $$SO_4^{2-}, PO_4^{3-}, ClO_4^{-}$$

The geometries of the polyatomic ions listed above can all be described as

(A) square planar
(B) square pyramidal
(C) seesaw-shaped
(D) tetrahedral
(E) trigonal bipyramidal

GO ON TO THE NEXT PAGE

57. $2 \text{ZnS}(s) + 3 \text{O}_2(g) \rightarrow 2 \text{ZnO}(s) + 2 \text{SO}_2(g)$

If the reaction above took place at standard temperature and pressure, what was the volume of $\text{O}_2(g)$ required to produce 40.0 grams of $\text{ZnO}(s)$?

(A) $\dfrac{(40.0)(2)}{(81.4)(3)(22.4)}$ L

(B) $\dfrac{(40.0)(3)}{(81.4)(2)(22.4)}$ L

(C) $\dfrac{(40.0)(2)(22.4)}{(81.4)(3)}$ L

(D) $\dfrac{(40.0)(3)(22.4)}{(81.4)(2)}$ L

(E) $\dfrac{(81.4)(2)(22.4)}{(40.0)(3)}$ L

58. Which of the following salts will produce a colorless solution when added to water?

(A) $\text{Cu(NO}_3\text{)}_2$
(B) NiCl_2
(C) KMnO_4
(D) ZnSO_4
(E) FeCl_3

59. Copper (I) chloride will be LEAST soluble in a 0.02-molar solution of which of the following compounds?

(A) NaCl
(B) CuNO_3
(C) CaCl_2
(D) Na_2CO_3
(E) KI

60. Which of the following procedures will produce a buffered solution?

I. Equal volumes of 1 M NH_3 and 1 M NH_4Cl solutions are mixed.
II. Equal volumes of 1 M H_2CO_3 and 1 M NaHCO_3 solutions are mixed.
III. Equal volumes of 1 M NH_3 and 1 M H_2CO_3 solutions are mixed.

(A) I only
(B) III only
(C) I and II only
(D) II and III only
(E) I, II, and III

61. $$\text{H}_2(g) + \text{I}_2(g) \rightleftharpoons 2 \text{HI}(g)$$

At 450 °C the equilibrium constant, K_c, for the reaction shown above has a value of 50. Which of the following sets of initial conditions at 450 °C will cause the reaction above to produce more H_2?

I. [HI] = 5-molar, [H_2] = 1-molar, [I_2] = 1-molar
II. [HI] = 10-molar, [H_2] = 1-molar, [I_2] = 1-molar
III. [HI] = 10-molar, [H_2] = 2-molar, [I_2] = 2-molar

(A) I only
(B) II only
(C) I and II only
(D) II and III only
(E) I, II, and III

62. $$\text{Cu}^{2+}(aq) + \text{Zn}(s) \rightarrow \text{Cu}(s) + \text{Zn}^{2+}(aq)$$

A galvanic cell that uses the reaction shown above has a standard state electromotive force of 1.1 volts. Which of the following changes to the cell will increase the voltage?

I. An increase in the mass of $\text{Zn}(s)$ in the cell.
II. An increase in the concentration of $\text{Cu}^{2+}(aq)$ in the cell.
III. An increase in the concentration of $\text{Zn}^{2+}(aq)$ in the cell.

(A) I only
(B) II only
(C) III only
(D) I and II only
(E) I and III only

GO ON TO THE NEXT PAGE

63. The nuclide $^{61}_{26}Fe$ decays through the emission of a single beta (β^-) particle. What is the resulting nuclide?

(A) $^{60}_{26}Fe$

(B) $^{62}_{26}Fe$

(C) $^{61}_{27}Co$

(D) $^{62}_{27}Co$

(E) $^{61}_{25}Mn$

64. Which of the following statements is true regarding sodium and potassium?

(A) Sodium has a larger first ionization energy and a larger atomic radius.
(B) Sodium has a larger first ionization energy and a smaller atomic radius.
(C) Sodium has a smaller first ionization energy and a larger atomic radius.
(D) Sodium has a smaller first ionization energy and a smaller atomic radius.
(E) Sodium and potassium will have identical first ionization energies and atomic radii.

65. $HCl(aq) + AgNO_3(aq) \rightarrow AgCl(s) + HNO_3(aq)$

One-half liter of a 0.20-molar HCl solution is mixed with one-half liter of a 0.40-molar solution of $AgNO_3$. A reaction occurs forming a precipitate as shown above. If the reaction goes to completion, what is the mass of AgCl produced?

(A) 14 grams
(B) 28 grams
(C) 42 grams
(D) 70 grams
(E) 84 grams

66.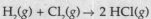

Based on the information given in the table below, what is ΔH° for the above reaction?

Bond	Average Bond Energy (kJ/mol)
H–H	440
Cl–Cl	240
H–Cl	430

(A) −860 kJ
(B) −620 kJ
(C) −440 kJ
(D) −180 kJ
(E) +240 kJ

67. The first ionization energy for magnesium is 730 kJ/mol. The third ionization energy for magnesium is 7700 kJ/mol. What is the most likely value for magnesium's second ionization energy?

(A) 490 kJ/mol
(B) 1400 kJ/mol
(C) 4200 kJ/mol
(D) 7100 kJ/mol
(E) 8400 kJ/mol

68. Molten NaCl is electrolyzed with a constant current of 1.00 ampere. What is the shortest amount of time, in seconds, that it would take to produce 1.00 mole of solid sodium? (1 faraday = 96,500 coulombs)

(A) 19,300 seconds
(B) 32,200 seconds
(C) 48,300 seconds
(D) 64,300 seconds
(E) 96,500 seconds

69. How many moles of KCl must be added to 200 milliliters of a 0.5-molar NaCl solution in order to create a solution where the concentration of Cl^- ion is 1.0-molar? (Assume the volume of the solution remains constant.)

(A) 0.1 moles
(B) 0.2 moles
(C) 0.3 moles
(D) 0.4 moles
(E) 0.5 moles

70. $$HCrO_4^- + Ca^{2+} \rightleftharpoons H^+ + CaCrO_4$$

If the acid dissociation constant for $HCrO_4^-$ is K_a and the solubility product for $CaCrO_4$ is K_{sp}, which of the following gives the equilibrium expression for the reaction above?

(A) $K_a K_{sp}$

(B) $\dfrac{K_a}{K_{sp}}$

(C) $\dfrac{K_{sp}}{K_a}$

(D) $\dfrac{1}{K_{sp}K_a}$

(E) $\dfrac{K_a K_{sp}}{2}$

GO ON TO THE NEXT PAGE

71. A 100 gram sample of pure $^{37}_{18}\text{Ar}$ decays by electron capture with a half-life of 35 days. How long will it take for 90 grams of $^{37}_{17}\text{Cl}$ to accumulate?

    (A) 31 days
    (B) 39 days
    (C) 78 days
    (D) 116 days
    (E) 315 days

72. If the solubility of BaF_2 is equal to x, which of the following expressions is equal to the solubility product, K_{sp}, for BaF_2?

    (A) x^2
    (B) $2x^2$
    (C) x^3
    (D) $2x^3$
    (E) $4x^3$

73. When excess hydroxide ions were added to 1.0 liter of $CaCl_2$ solution, $Ca(OH)_2$ precipitate was formed. If all of the calcium ions in the solution were precipitated in 7.4 grams of $Ca(OH)_2$, what was the initial concentration of the $CaCl_2$ solution?

    (A) 0.05-molar
    (B) 0.10-molar
    (C) 0.15-molar
    (D) 0.20-molar
    (E) 0.30-molar

74. When a solution of $KMnO_4$ was mixed with a solution of HCl, Cl_2 gas bubbles formed and Mn^{2+} ions appeared in the solution. Which of the following has occurred?

    (A) K^+ has been oxidized by Cl^-.
    (B) K^+ has been oxidized by H^+.
    (C) Cl^- has been oxidized by K^+.
    (D) Cl^- has been oxidized by MnO_4^-.
    (E) MnO_4^- has been oxidized by Cl^-.

75. $Ag^+ + e^- \rightarrow Ag$ $\qquad E° = +0.8 \text{ V}$

    $Cd^{2+} + 2\,e^- \rightarrow Cd$ $\qquad E° = -0.4 \text{ V}$

    Based on the reduction potentials given above, what is the reaction potential for the following reaction?

    $$2\,Ag^+ + Cd \rightarrow 2\,Ag + Cd^{2+}$$

    (A) -0.8 V
    (B) -0.4 V
    (C) $+0.4$ V
    (D) $+1.2$ V
    (E) $+2.0$ V

STOP
END OF SECTION I
IF YOU FINISH BEFORE TIME IS CALLED, YOU MAY CHECK YOUR WORK ON THIS SECTION.
DO NOT GO ON TO SECTION II UNTIL YOU ARE TOLD TO DO SO.

CHEMISTRY
SECTION II

Time — 1 hour and 30 minutes

Percent of total grade — 55

Part A: Time—10 minutes

Parts B and C: Suggested time—40 minutes

Part D: Suggested time—40 minutes

<u>General Instructions</u>

CALCULATORS MAY NOT BE USED IN PART A.

Calculators, including those with programming and graphing capabilities, may be used in Parts B, C, and D. However, calculators with typewriter-style (qwerty) keyboards are NOT permitted.

The suggested times will not be announced, and you may proceed freely from one question to the next. Do not spend too long on any one problem.

Pages containing a periodic table, the electrochemical series, and equations commonly used in chemistry will be available for your use.

You may write your answers with either a pen or a pencil. Be sure to write CLEARLY and LEGIBLY. If you make an error, you may save time by crossing it out rather than trying to erase it.

Write all your answers in the essay booklet. Number your answers as the questions are numbered in the examination booklet.

GO ON TO THE NEXT PAGE

MATERIAL IN THE FOLLOWING TABLE MAY BE USEFUL IN ANSWERING THE QUESTIONS IN THIS SECTION OF THE EXAMINATION.

DO NOT DETACH FROM BOOK.

PERIODIC CHART OF THE ELEMENTS

1 H 1.0																		2 He 4.0
3 Li 6.9	4 Be 9.0											5 B 10.8	6 C 12.0	7 N 14.0	8 O 16.0	9 F 19.0	10 Ne 20.2
11 Na 23.0	12 Mg 24.3											13 Al 27.0	14 Si 28.1	15 P 31.0	16 S 32.1	17 Cl 35.5	18 Ar 39.9
19 K 39.1	20 Ca 40.1	21 Sc 45.0	22 Ti 47.9	23 V 50.9	24 Cr 52.0	25 Mn 54.9	26 Fe 55.8	27 Co 58.9	28 Ni 58.7	29 Cu 63.5	30 Zn 65.4	31 Ga 69.7	32 Ge 72.6	33 As 74.9	34 Se 79.0	35 Br 79.9	36 Kr 83.8
37 Rb 85.5	38 Sr 87.6	39 Y 88.9	40 Zr 91.2	41 Nb 92.9	42 Mo 95.9	43 Tc (98)	44 Ru 101.1	45 Rh 102.9	46 Pd 106.4	47 Ag 107.9	48 Cd 112.4	49 In 114.8	50 Sn 118.7	51 Sb 121.8	52 Te 127.6	53 I 126.9	54 Xe 131.3
55 Cs 132.9	56 Ba 137.3	57 *La 138.9	72 Hf 178.5	73 Ta 180.9	74 W 183.9	75 Re 186.2	76 Os 190.2	77 Ir 192.2	78 Pt 195.1	79 Au 197.0	80 Hg 200.6	81 Tl 204.4	82 Pb 207.2	83 Bi 209.0	84 Po (209)	85 At (210)	86 Rn (222)
87 Fr (223)	88 Ra 226.0	89 †Ac 227.0															

*Lanthanum Series

58 Ce 140.1	59 Pr 140.9	60 Nd 144.2	61 Pm (145)	62 Sm 150.4	63 Eu 152.0	64 Gd 157.3	65 Tb 158.9	66 Dy 162.5	67 Ho 164.9	68 Er 167.3	69 Tm 168.9	70 Yb 173.0	71 Lu 175.0

†Actinium Series

90 Th 232.0	91 Pa 231.0	92 U 238.0	93 Np 237.0	94 Pu (244)	95 Am (243)	96 Cm (247)	97 Bk (247)	98 Cf (251)	99 Es (252)	100 Fm (258)	101 Md (258)	102 No (259)	103 Lr (260)

DO NOT DETACH FROM BOOK.

GO ON TO THE NEXT PAGE

INFORMATION IN THE FOLLOWING TABLES MAY BE USEFUL IN ANSWERING THE QUESTIONS IN THIS SECTION OF THE EXAMINATION.

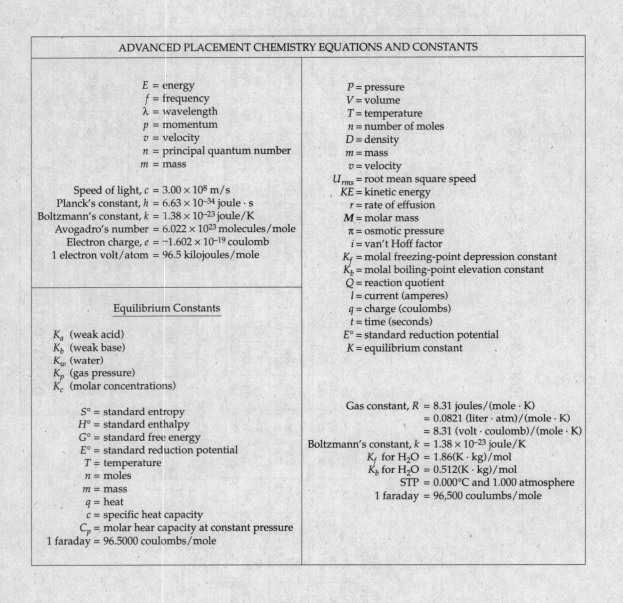

ADVANCED PLACEMENT CHEMISTRY EQUATIONS AND CONSTANTS

E = energy
f = frequency
λ = wavelength
p = momentum
v = velocity
n = principal quantum number
m = mass

Speed of light, $c = 3.00 \times 10^8$ m/s
Planck's constant, $h = 6.63 \times 10^{-34}$ joule · s
Boltzmann's constant, $k = 1.38 \times 10^{-23}$ joule/K
Avogadro's number $= 6.022 \times 10^{23}$ molecules/mole
Electron charge, $e = -1.602 \times 10^{-19}$ coulomb
1 electron volt/atom = 96.5 kilojoules/mole

Equilibrium Constants

K_a (weak acid)
K_b (weak base)
K_w (water)
K_p (gas pressure)
K_c (molar concentrations)

$S°$ = standard entropy
$H°$ = standard enthalpy
$G°$ = standard free energy
$E°$ = standard reduction potential
T = temperature
n = moles
m = mass
q = heat
c = specific heat capacity
C_p = molar hear capacity at constant pressure
1 faraday = 96.5000 coulombs/mole

P = pressure
V = volume
T = temperature
n = number of moles
D = density
m = mass
v = velocity
U_{rms} = root mean square speed
KE = kinetic energy
r = rate of effusion
M = molar mass
π = osmotic pressure
i = van't Hoff factor
K_f = molal freezing-point depression constant
K_b = molal boiling-point elevation constant
Q = reaction quotient
I = current (amperes)
q = charge (coulombs)
t = time (seconds)
$E°$ = standard reduction potential
K = equilibrium constant

Gas constant, R = 8.31 joules/(mole · K)
$= 0.0821$ (liter · atm)/(mole · K)
$= 8.31$ (volt · coulomb)/(mole · K)
Boltzmann's constant, $k = 1.38 \times 10^{-23}$ joule/K
K_f for H_2O = 1.86(K · kg)/mol
K_b for H_2O = 0.512(K · kg)/mol
STP = 0.000°C and 1.000 atmosphere
1 faraday = 96,500 coulombs/mole

GO ON TO THE NEXT PAGE

INFORMATION IN THE FOLLOWING TABLES MAY BE USEFUL IN ANSWERING THE QUESTIONS IN THIS SECTION OF THE EXAMINATION.

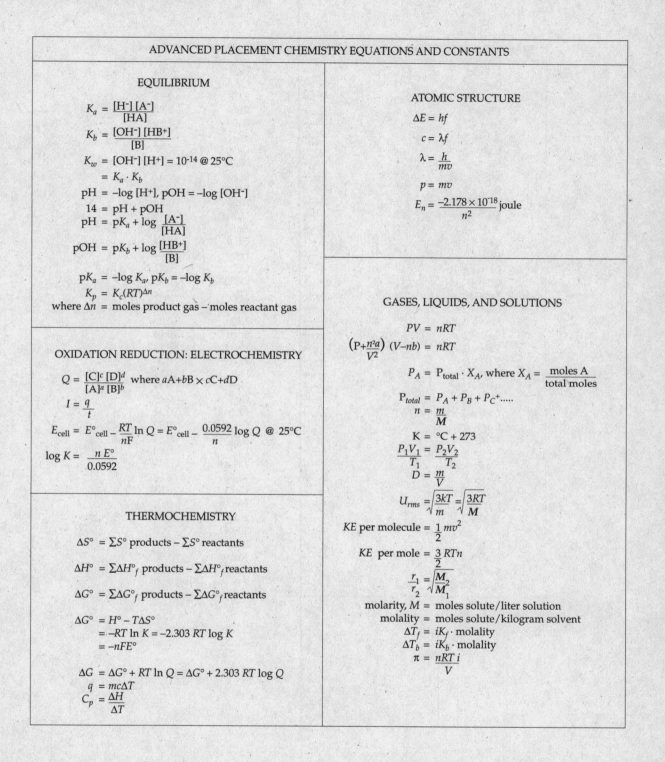

ADVANCED PLACEMENT CHEMISTRY EQUATIONS AND CONSTANTS

EQUILIBRIUM

$$K_a = \frac{[H^+][A^-]}{[HA]}$$

$$K_b = \frac{[OH^-][HB^+]}{[B]}$$

$$K_w = [OH^-][H^+] = 10^{-14} @ 25°C$$
$$= K_a \cdot K_b$$

$$pH = -\log[H^+], \quad pOH = -\log[OH^-]$$

$$14 = pH + pOH$$

$$pH = pK_a + \log\frac{[A^-]}{[HA]}$$

$$pOH = pK_b + \log\frac{[HB^+]}{[B]}$$

$$pK_a = -\log K_a, \quad pK_b = -\log K_b$$

$$K_p = K_c(RT)^{\Delta n}$$

where Δn = moles product gas – moles reactant gas

OXIDATION REDUCTION: ELECTROCHEMISTRY

$$Q = \frac{[C]^c[D]^d}{[A]^a[B]^b} \quad \text{where } aA+bB \times cC+dD$$

$$I = \frac{q}{t}$$

$$E_{cell} = E°_{cell} - \frac{RT}{nF}\ln Q = E°_{cell} - \frac{0.0592}{n}\log Q @ 25°C$$

$$\log K = \frac{nE°}{0.0592}$$

THERMOCHEMISTRY

$$\Delta S° = \Sigma S° \text{ products} - \Sigma S° \text{ reactants}$$

$$\Delta H° = \Sigma \Delta H°_f \text{ products} - \Sigma \Delta H°_f \text{ reactants}$$

$$\Delta G° = \Sigma \Delta G°_f \text{ products} - \Sigma \Delta G°_f \text{ reactants}$$

$$\Delta G° = H° - T\Delta S°$$
$$= -RT \ln K = -2.303\ RT \log K$$
$$= -nFE°$$

$$\Delta G = \Delta G° + RT \ln Q = \Delta G° + 2.303\ RT \log Q$$

$$q = mc\Delta T$$

$$C_p = \frac{\Delta H}{\Delta T}$$

ATOMIC STRUCTURE

$$\Delta E = hf$$

$$c = \lambda f$$

$$\lambda = \frac{h}{mv}$$

$$p = mv$$

$$E_n = \frac{-2.178 \times 10^{-18}}{n^2} \text{ joule}$$

GASES, LIQUIDS, AND SOLUTIONS

$$PV = nRT$$

$$\left(P+\frac{n^2a}{V^2}\right)(V-nb) = nRT$$

$$P_A = P_{total} \cdot X_A, \text{ where } X_A = \frac{\text{moles A}}{\text{total moles}}$$

$$P_{total} = P_A + P_B + P_C + \ldots$$

$$n = \frac{m}{M}$$

$$K = °C + 273$$

$$\frac{P_1 V_1}{T_1} = \frac{P_2 V_2}{T_2}$$

$$D = \frac{m}{V}$$

$$U_{rms} = \sqrt{\frac{3kT}{m}} = \sqrt{\frac{3RT}{M}}$$

$$KE \text{ per molecule} = \frac{1}{2}mv^2$$

$$KE \text{ per mole} = \frac{3}{2}RTn$$

$$\frac{r_1}{r_2} = \sqrt{\frac{M_2}{M_1}}$$

molarity, M = moles solute/liter solution

molality = moles solute/kilogram solvent

$$\Delta T_f = iK_f \cdot \text{molality}$$

$$\Delta T_b = iK_b \cdot \text{molality}$$

$$\pi = \frac{nRT\ i}{V}$$

GO ON TO THE NEXT PAGE

INFORMATION IN THE FOLLOWING TABLES MAY BE USEFUL IN ANSWERING THE QUESTIONS IN THIS SECTION OF THE EXAMINATION.

STANDARD REDUCTION POTENTIALS, E , IN WATER SOLUTION AT 25 °C (in V)		
$Li^+ + e^-$	$\longrightarrow$ $Li(s)$	-3.05
$Cs^+ + e^-$	$\longrightarrow$ $Cs(s)$	-2.92
$K^+ + e^-$	$\longrightarrow$ $K(s)$	-2.92
$Rb^+ + e^-$	$\longrightarrow$ $Rb(s)$	-2.92
$Ba^{2+} + 2\,e^-$	$\longrightarrow$ $Ba(s)$	-2.90
$Sr^{2+} + 2\,e^-$	$\longrightarrow$ $Sr(s)$	-2.89
$Ca^{2+} + 2\,e^-$	$\longrightarrow$ $Ca(s)$	-2.87
$Na^+ + e^-$	$\longrightarrow$ $Na(s)$	-2.71
$Mg^{2+} + 2\,e^-$	$\longrightarrow$ $Mg(s)$	-2.37
$Be^{2+} + 2\,e^-$	$\longrightarrow$ $Be(s)$	-1.70
$Al^{3+} + 3\,e^-$	$\longrightarrow$ $Al(s)$	-1.66
$Mn^{2+} + 2\,e^-$	$\longrightarrow$ $Mn(s)$	-1.18
$Zn^{2+} + 2\,e^-$	$\longrightarrow$ $Zn(s)$	-0.76
$Cr^{3+} + 3\,e^-$	$\longrightarrow$ $Cr(s)$	-0.74
$Fe^{2+} + 2\,e^-$	$\longrightarrow$ $Fe(s)$	-0.44
$Cr^{3+} + e^-$	$\longrightarrow$ Cr^{2+}	-0.41
$Cd^{2+} + 2\,e^-$	$\longrightarrow$ $Cd(s)$	-0.40
$Tl^+ + e^-$	$\longrightarrow$ $Tl(s)$	-0.34
$Co^{2+} + 2\,e^-$	$\longrightarrow$ $Co(s)$	-0.28
$Ni^{2+} + 2\,e^-$	$\longrightarrow$ $Ni(s)$	-0.25
$Sn^{2+} + 2\,e^-$	$\longrightarrow$ $Sn(s)$	-0.14
$Pb^{2+} + 2\,e^-$	$\longrightarrow$ $Pb(s)$	-0.13
$2\,H^+ + 2\,e^-$	$\longrightarrow$ $H_2(g)$	0.00
$S(s) + 2\,H^+ + 2\,e^-$	$\longrightarrow$ H_2S	0.14
$Sn^{4+} + 2\,e^-$	$\longrightarrow$ Sn^{2+}	0.15
$Cu^{2+} + e^-$	$\longrightarrow$ Cu^+	0.15
$Cu^{2+} + 2\,e^-$	$\longrightarrow$ $Cu(s)$	0.34
$Cu^+ + e^-$	$\longrightarrow$ $Cu(s)$	0.52
$I_2(s) + 2\,e^-$	$\longrightarrow$ $2\,I^-$	0.53
$Fe^{3+} + e^-$	$\longrightarrow$ Fe^{2+}	0.77
$Hg_2^{2+} + 2\,e^-$	$\longrightarrow$ $2\,Hg(l)$	0.79
$Ag^+ + e^-$	$\longrightarrow$ $Ag(s)$	0.80
$Hg^{2+} + 2\,e^-$	$\longrightarrow$ $Hg(l)$	0.85
$2\,Hg^{2+} + 2\,e^-$	$\longrightarrow$ Hg_2^{2+}	0.92
$Br_2(l) + 2\,e^-$	$\longrightarrow$ $2\,Br^-$	1.07
$O_2(g) + 4\,H^+ + 4\,e^-$	$\longrightarrow$ $2\,H_2O$	1.23
$Cl_2(g) + 2\,e^-$	$\longrightarrow$ $2\,Cl^-$	1.36
$Au^{3+} + 3\,e^-$	$\longrightarrow$ $Au(s)$	1.50
$Co^{3+} + e^-$	$\longrightarrow$ Co^{2+}	1.82
$F_2(g) + 2\,e^-$	$\longrightarrow$ $2\,F^-$	2.87

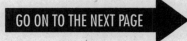
GO ON TO THE NEXT PAGE

CHEMISTRY
SECTION II

The percentages given for the parts represent the score weightings for this section of the examination. You will be given 10 minutes to complete Part A. You should spend about 40 minutes on Parts B and C combined and about 40 minutes on Part D.

THE METHODS USED AND THE STEPS INVOLVED IN ARRIVING AT YOUR ANSWERS MUST BE SHOWN CLEARLY. It is to your advantage to do this since you may obtain partial credit if you do and you will receive little or no credit if you do not. Attention should be paid to significant figures.

Be sure to write your answers in the space provided following each question.

Data necessary for the solution of the problems may be found in the tables on the preceding pages.

Part A
Time — 10 minutes
(15 percent)

YOU MAY NOT USE A CALCULATOR FOR THIS PART.

1. Answer FIVE of the eight options in this part. (Answers to more than five options will not be scored.)

   Give the formulas to show the reactants and the products for FIVE of the following chemical reactions. Each of the reactions occurs in aqueous solution unless otherwise indicated. Represent substances in solution as ions if the substance is extensively ionized. Omit formulas for any ions or molecules that are unchanged by the reaction. In all cases a reaction occurs. You need not balance.

   Example: A strip of magnesium is added to a solution of silver nitrate.

$$Mg + Ag^+ \rightarrow Mg^{2+} + Ag$$

   (a) Sulfur dioxide gas is bubbled through cold water.

   (b) A solution of copper(II) chloride is mixed with a concentrated solution of ammonia.

   (c) A solution of silver nitrate is added to a solution of potassium bromide.

   (d) Ethane is burned in air.

   (e) A piece of solid zinc is placed in a solution of copper(II) nitrate.

   (f) A piece of solid calcium is placed in distilled water.

   (g) Chlorine gas is bubbled through a solution of sodium bromide.

   (h) A solution of sodium iodide and an acidified solution of sodium permanganate are mixed.

Part B

(20 percent)

YOU MAY USE A CALCULATOR FOR THIS PART.

Solve the following problem.

2. A 0.20-molar solution of acetic acid, $HC_2H_3O_2$, at a temperature of 25 °C, has a pH of 2.73.

   (a) Calculate the hydroxide ion concentration, $[OH^-]$.
   (b) What is the value of the acid ionization constant, K_a, for acetic acid at 25 °C?
   (c) How many moles of sodium acetate must be added to 500. ml of a 0.200-molar solution of acetic acid in order to create a buffer with a pH of 4.00? Assume that the volume of the solution is not changed by the addition of sodium acetate.
   (d) In a titration experiment, 100. ml of sodium hydroxide solution was added to 200. ml of a 0.400-molar solution of acetic acid to reach the equivalence point. What was the pH at the equivalence point?

(20 percent)

YOU MAY USE A CALCULATOR FOR THIS PART.

Solve EITHER problem 3 or problem 4 in this part. (A second problem will not be scored.)

3.
$$2\,NO(g) + Cl_2(g) \rightarrow 2\,NOCl(g)$$

The following data were collected for the reaction above. All of the measurements were taken at a temperature of 263 K.

Experiment	Initial [NO] (M)	Initial [Cl$_2$] (M)	Initial rate of disappearance of Cl$_2$ (M/min)
1	0.15	0.15	0.60
2	0.15	0.30	1.2
3	0.30	0.15	2.4
4	0.25	0.25	?

(a) Write the expression for the rate law for the reaction above.

(b) Calculate the value of the rate constant for the above reaction and specify the units.

(c) What is the initial rate of appearance of NOCl in experiment 2?

(d) What is the initial rate of disappearance of Cl$_2$ in experiment 4?

4.

$$CH_4(g) + 2\,O_2(g) \rightarrow CO_2(g) + 2\,H_2O(l)$$

The above reaction for the combustion of methane gas has a standard entropy change, $\Delta S°$, with a value of -242.7 J/mol-K. The following data are also available.

Compound	$\Delta H°_f$ (kJ/mol)
$CH_4\ (g)$	-74.8
$H_2O\ (l)$	-285.9
$CO_2\ (g)$	-393.5

(a) What are the values of $\Delta H°_f$ and $\Delta G°_f$ for $O_2(g)$?

(b) Calculate the standard change in enthalpy, $\Delta H°$, for the combustion of methane.

(c) Calculate the standard free energy change, $\Delta G°$, for the combustion of methane.

(d) How would the value of $\Delta S°$ for the reaction be affected if the water produced in the combustion remained in the gas phase?

GO ON TO THE NEXT PAGE

Part D
(45 percent)

Spend about 40 minutes on this part of the examination. Answering these questions provides an opportunity to demonstrate your ability to present your material in logical, coherent, and convincing English. Your responses will be judged on the basis of accuracy and importance of the detail cited and on the appropriateness of the descriptive material used. Specific answers are preferable to broad, diffuse responses. Illustrative examples and equations may be helpful.

ANSWER THE FOLLOWING ESSAY QUESTION.

5. Oxygen is found in the atmosphere as a diatomic gas, O_2, and as ozone, O_3.

   (a)   Draw the Lewis structures for both molecules.

   (b)   Use the principles of bonding and molecular structure to account for the fact that ozone has a higher boiling point than diatomic oxygen.

   (c)   Use the principles of bonding and molecular structure to account for the fact that ozone is more soluble than diatomic oxygen in water.

   (d)   Explain why the two bonds in O_3 are the same length and are longer than the bond length of the bond in diatomic oxygen.

SELECT <u>TWO</u> OF THE FOUR ESSAY QUESTIONS, NUMBERED 6 THROUGH 9.
(Additional essays will not be scored.)

6. At 25 °C and 1.0 atmosphere pressure, a balloon contains a mixture of four ideal gases: oxygen, nitrogen, carbon dioxide, and helium. The partial pressure due to each gas is 0.25 atmosphere. Use the ideas of kinetic molecular theory to answer each of the following questions.

(a) Rank the gases in increasing order for each of the following and explain.

   (i) Density
   (ii) Average kinetic energy
   (iii) Average molecular velocity

(b) How would the volume of the balloon be affected by each of the following changes to the system?

   (i) The temperature of the gases in the balloon were increased at constant pressure.
   (ii) The gas mixture were replaced with an equal number of moles of pure oxygen.

(c) What changes to the temperature and pressure of the gases would cause deviation from ideal behavior and which gas would be most affected?

GO ON TO THE NEXT PAGE ➤

7. Molten sodium chloride can be electrolyzed to form pure sodium and chlorine.

   (a) Write the balanced equations for the half-reactions that take place at the electrodes during the electrolysis. Indicate which half-reaction takes place at which electrode.

   (b) Describe how the pure sodium and chlorine are separated.

   (c) For the electrolyzation of molten sodium chloride, will the value of each of the following be positive or negative?

      (i) $E_{reaction}$
     (ii) ΔG
    (iii) ΔS

   (d) Explain why, when the molten sodium chloride is replaced with an aqueous solution of sodium chloride, pure sodium is not produced.

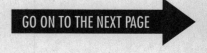

8. $NaC_2H_3O_2$, $Ba(NO_3)_2$, KCl

Aqueous solutions of equal concentration of the three compounds listed above are prepared. What would an experimenter expect to observe when each of the following procedures is performed on each of the solutions?

(a)   The pH of each solution is measured.

(b) Pb^{2+} ions are introduced into each solution.

(c) SO_4^{2-} ions are introduced into each solution.

(d)   The freezing point of each solution is measured and the three temperatures are compared.

GO ON TO THE NEXT PAGE

9. Use chemical principles to explain each of the following.

(a) A pressure cooker is used to cook food at higher temperatures than can be achieved using a regular pot.

(b) Iron nails that are to be used outdoors are coated with zinc.

(c) Food kept in a refrigerator takes longer to spoil than food left out on a kitchen table.

(d) When water is left standing in plumbing during extremely cold weather, there is a danger that the pipes will burst.

END OF EXAMINATION

The Princeton Review

Completely darken bubbles with a No. 2 pencil. If you make a mistake, be sure to erase mark completely. Erase all stray marks.

1.
YOUR NAME: _____
(Print)   Last   First   M.I.

SIGNATURE: _____   DATE: __ / __ / __

HOME ADDRESS: _____
(Print)   Number and Street

_____
City   State   Zip Code

PHONE NO.: _____
(Print)

IMPORTANT: Please fill in these boxes exactly as shown on the back cover of your test book.

2. TEST FORM
_____

3. TEST CODE

4. REGISTRATION NUMBER

5. YOUR NAME

First 4 letters of last name				FIRST INIT	MID INIT

6. DATE OF BIRTH

Month		Day		Year

7. SEX
- MALE
- FEMALE

THE PRINCETON REVIEW
© 1995 The Princeton Review
FORM NO. 00001-PR

For "Type B" questions (numbered 101 to 116), use the special grid-in box at left. When you have finished with these questions, proceed to the column at right to continue your exam.

The Princeton Review

1.

YOUR NAME: _____
(Print)
               Last   First   M.I.

SIGNATURE: _____ DATE: ___ / ___ / ___

HOME ADDRESS: _____
(Print)
          Number and Street

_____
    City   State   Zip Code

PHONE NO.: _____
(Print)

IMPORTANT: Please fill in these boxes exactly as shown on the back cover of your test book.

5. YOUR NAME

First 4 letters of last name				FIRST INIT	MID INIT
A	A	A	A	A	A
B	B	B	B	B	B
C	C	C	C	C	C
D	D	D	D	D	D
E	E	E	E	E	E
F	F	F	F	F	F
G	G	G	G	G	G
H	H	H	H	H	H
I	I	I	I	I	I
J	J	J	J	J	J
K	K	K	K	K	K
L	L	L	L	L	L
M	M	M	M	M	M
N	N	N	N	N	N
O	O	O	O	O	O
P	P	P	P	P	P
Q	Q	Q	Q	Q	Q
R	R	R	R	R	R
S	S	S	S	S	S
T	T	T	T	T	T
U	U	U	U	U	U
V	V	V	V	V	V
W	W	W	W	W	W
X	X	X	X	X	X
Y	Y	Y	Y	Y	Y
Z	Z	Z	Z	Z	Z

2. TEST FORM

_____

3. TEST CODE

0	A	0	0	0	
1	B	1	1	1	
2	C	2	2	2	
3	D	3	3	3	
4	E	4	4	4	
5	F	5	5	5	
6	G	6	6	6	
7		7	7	7	
8		8	8	8	
9		9	9	9	

4. REGISTRATION NUMBER

0	0	0	0	0	0	0
1	1	1	1	1	1	1
2	2	2	2	2	2	2
3	3	3	3	3	3	3
4	4	4	4	4	4	4
5	5	5	5	5	5	5
6	6	6	6	6	6	6
7	7	7	7	7	7	7
8	8	8	8	8	8	8
9	9	9	9	9	9	9

6. DATE OF BIRTH

Month	Day		Year	
JAN				
FEB				
MAR	0	0	0	0
APR	1	1	1	1
MAY	2	2	2	2
JUN	3	3	3	3
JUL		4	4	4
AUG		5	5	5
SEP		6	6	6
OCT		7	7	7
NOV		8	8	8
DEC		9	9	9

7. SEX

MALE

FEMALE

THE PRINCETON REVIEW
© 1995 The Princeton Review
FORM NO. 00001-PR

---

1 A B C D E
2 A B C D E
3 A B C D E
4 A B C D E
5 A B C D E
6 A B C D E
7 A B C D E

8 A B C D E
9 A B C D E
10 A B C D E
11 A B C D E
12 A B C D E
13 A B C D E
14 A B C D E
15 A B C D E
16 A B C D E
17 A B C D E
18 A B C D E
19 A B C D E
20 A B C D E
21 A B C D E
22 A B C D E
23 A B C D E

24 A B C D E
25 A B C D E
26 A B C D E
27 A B C D E
28 A B C D E
29 A B C D E
30 A B C D E
31 A B C D E
32 A B C D E
33 A B C D E
34 A B C D E
35 A B C D E
36 A B C D E
37 A B C D E
38 A B C D E
39 A B C D E
40 A B C D E
41 A B C D E
42 A B C D E
43 A B C D E
44 A B C D E
45 A B C D E
46 A B C D E

47 A B C D E
48 A B C D E
49 A B C D E
50 A B C D E
51 A B C D E
52 A B C D E
53 A B C D E
54 A B C D E
55 A B C D E
56 A B C D E
57 A B C D E
58 A B C D E
59 A B C D E
60 A B C D E
61 A B C D E
62 A B C D E
63 A B C D E
64 A B C D E
65 A B C D E
66 A B C D E
67 A B C D E
68 A B C D E
69 A B C D E

	I		II		CE
101	T	F	T	F	
102	T	F	T	F	
103	T	F	T	F	
104	T	F	T	F	
105	T	F	T	F	
106	T	F	T	F	
107	T	F	T	F	
108	T	F	T	F	
109	T	F	T	F	
110	T	F	T	F	
111	T	F	T	F	
112	T	F	T	F	
113	T	F	T	F	
114	T	F	T	F	
115	T	F	T	F	
116	T	F	T	F	

For "Type B" questions (numbered 101 to 116), use the special grid-in box at left. When you have finished with these questions, proceed to the column at right to continue your exam.

ANSWERS AND
EXPLANATIONS

SECTION I-MULTIPLE CHOICE

Questions 1–3 are based on the following energy diagrams

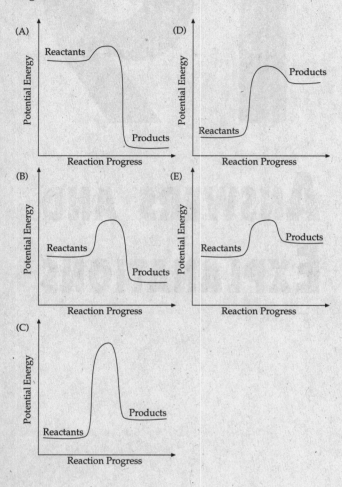

(A)
(B)
(C)
(D)
(E)

1. This reaction has the largest activation energy.

1.

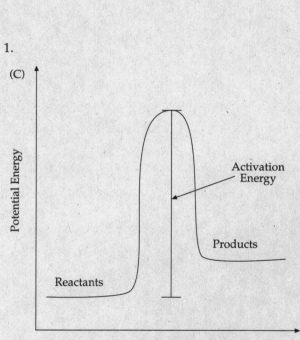

(C) **is correct.** This reaction has the largest rise from the energy level of the reactants to the peak energy that must be overcome in order for the reaction to proceed.

QUESTIONS	EXPLANATIONS

EXPLANATIONS

2.

(A)

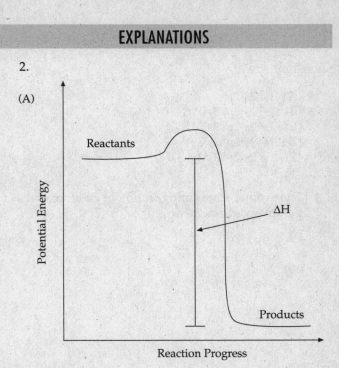

2. This is the most exothermic reaction.

(A) is correct. This reaction has the largest energy drop from the level of the reactants to the level of the products. That makes it the most exothermic.

3.

(D)

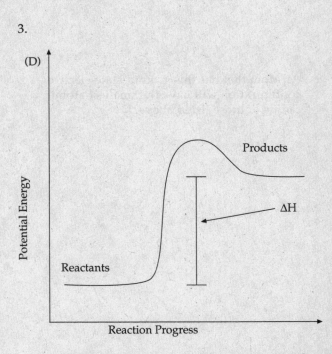

3. This reaction has the largest positive value for ΔH.

(D) is correct. This reaction has the largest rise in energy from the level of the reactants to the level of the products. That makes it the most endothermic and gives it the largest positive value for ΔH.

QUESTIONS	EXPLANATIONS

Questions 4–6

    (A) $1s^2\ 2s^22p^6$
    (B) $1s^2\ 2s^22p^6\ 3s^2$
    (C) $1s^2\ 2s^22p^6\ 3s^23p^4$
    (D) $1s^2\ 2s^22p^6\ 3s^23p^6$
    (E) $1s^2\ 2s^22p^6\ 3s^23p^6\ 4s^2$

4. The ground state configuration of an atom of a paramagnetic element.

4. **(C) is correct.** A paramagnetic element is one whose electrons are not completely spin-paired. For choice (C), sulfur, Hund's rule says that the first three electrons in the $3p$ subshell will each occupy an empty orbital. The fourth electron will pair up, leaving two electrons unpaired. All of the other choices have completed subshells, so all the electrons will be spin-paired.

5. The ground state configuration for both a potassium ion and a chloride ion.

5. **(D) is correct.** A potassium atom loses an electron when it ionizes; a chlorine atom gains an electron. Both end up with the same ground state electron configuration as an argon atom, given in choice (D).

6. An atom that has this ground-state electron configuration will have the smallest atomic radius of those listed above.

6. **(A) is correct.** This atom (neon) has electrons in only two shells. All of the other choices have electrons at higher energy levels, farther away from the nucleus.

QUESTIONS	EXPLANATIONS

Questions 7–10

    (A) CO_2
    (B) H_2O
    (C) SO_2
    (D) NO_2
    (E) O_2

7. In this molecule, oxygen forms sp^3 hybrid orbitals.

7. **(B) is correct.** The Lewis structure for water is shown below:

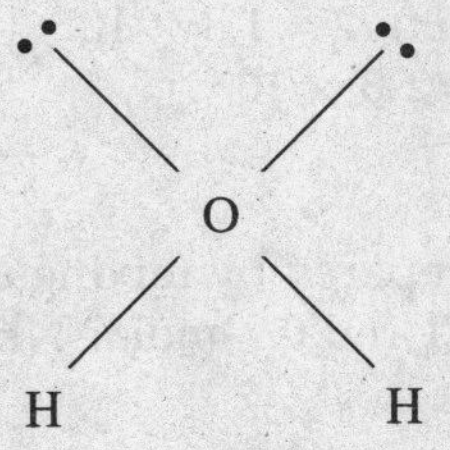

The central oxygen atom forms sp^3 hybrid orbitals, resulting in a tetrahedral structure. The central oxygen atom has two unbonded electron pairs, which gives the molecule a bent shape.

8. This molecule contains one unpaired electron.

8. **(D) is correct.** NO_2 has an odd number (17) of valence electrons, so when we draw the Lewis structure, there must be an unpaired electron:

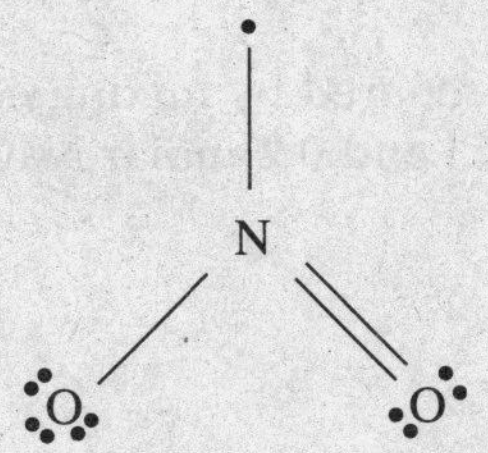

9. This molecule contains no pi (π) bonds.

9. **(B) is correct.** Water has only single bonds, so it has only sigma (σ) bonds. All of the other molecules have at least one double bond. The second bond in a double bond is a pi (π) bond.

10. This molecule is the main product of photosynthesis.

10. **(E) is correct.** In photosynthesis, CO_2 is consumed and O_2 is produced.

QUESTIONS	EXPLANATIONS

Questions 11–14

(A) A solution with a pH of 1
(B) A solution with a pH of greater than 1 and less than 7
(C) A solution with a pH of 7
(D) A solution with a pH of greater than 7 and less than 13
(E) A solution with a pH of 13

For CH_3COOH, $K_a = 1.8 \times 10^{-5}$
For NH_3, $K_b = 1.8 \times 10^{-5}$.

11. A solution prepared by mixing equal volumes of 0.2-molar HCl and 0.2-molar NH_3.

11. **(B) is correct.** This is a mixture of a strong acid and a weak base, so at the equivalence point, the mixture will be acidic, with a pH less than 7.

12. A solution prepared by mixing equal volumes of 0.2-molar HNO_3 and 0.2-molar NaOH.

12. **(C) is correct.** This is a mixture of a strong acid and a strong base, so at the equivalence point, they will have completely neutralized each other and only salt water will be left. So the solution will be neutral and the pH will be 7.

13. A solution prepared by mixing equal volumes of 0.2-molar HCl and 0.2-molar NaCl.

13. **(A) is correct.** Both HCl and NaCl dissociate completely, but NaCl will have no effect on the pH of the solution.

Since we are doubling the volume of the HCl solution by adding the salt water, the concentration of HCl will be cut in half, to 0.1-molar. HCl is a strong acid, so $[H^+] = 0.1$-molar and pH = $-\log[H^+] = 1$.

14. A solution prepared by mixing equal volumes of 0.2-molar CH_3COOH and 0.2-molar NaOH.

14. **(D) is correct.** This is a mixture of a weak acid and a strong base, so at the equivalence point, the mixture will be basic, with a pH greater than 7.

QUESTIONS	EXPLANATIONS

15. A pure sample of $KClO_3$ is found to contain 71 grams of chlorine atoms. What is the mass of the sample?

    (A) 122 grams
    (B) 170 grams
    (C) 209 grams
    (D) 245 grams
    (E) 293 grams

15. **(D) is correct.** Remember: moles = $\dfrac{\text{grams}}{\text{MW}}$

So, moles of chlorine $\dfrac{(71g)}{(35.5g/mol)} = 2$ moles

If there are 2 moles of chlorine, there must be 2 moles of $KClO_3$.

The molecular weight of $KClO_3$ is 122.5.

So, grams of $KClO_3$ = (moles)(MW)
    = (2 mol)(122.5 g/mol)
    = 245 grams

16. Which of the following experimental procedures is used to separate two substances by taking advantage of their differing boiling points?

    (A) Titration
    (B) Distillation
    (C) Filtration
    (D) Decantation
    (E) Hydration

16. **(B) is correct.** In distillation, two substances are heated until one of them boils. The gaseous substance is separated from the remaining liquid or solid and condensed in a separate container.

The other answers:

(A) Titration is used to determine the volume of one solution required to react with a given volume of another solution.

(C) Filtration is used to separate a solid from a liquid by passing the solution through a membrane.

(D) Decantation is used to separate a solid from a liquid by letting the solid settle to the bottom of a container and then pouring off the liquid.

(E) Hydration occurs when ions enter into solution with water.

17. Which of the following sets of quantum numbers (n, l, m_l, m_s) best describes the highest energy valence electron in a ground-state aluminum atom?

    (A) $2, 0, 0, \dfrac{1}{2}$

    (B) $2, 1, 0, \dfrac{1}{2}$

    (C) $3, 0, 0, \dfrac{1}{2}$

    (D) $3, 0, 1, \dfrac{1}{2}$

    (E) $3, 1, 1, \dfrac{1}{2}$

17. **(E) is correct.** Aluminum's valence electrons are in the $3p$ subshell.

That means that $n = 3$, $l = 1$, $m_l = -1, 0$, or 1, and $m_s = \dfrac{1}{2}$ or $-\dfrac{1}{2}$

18. Which of the following elements is NOT normally found as a diatomic gas molecule in its uncombined state at room temperature?

    (A) Hydrogen
    (B) Fluorine
    (C) Oxygen
    (D) Nitrogen
    (E) Helium

18. **(E) is correct.** All five elements are gases at room temperature, but helium is a noble gas, and does not form diatomic molecules.

19. $2 MnO_4^- + 5 SO_3^{2-} + 6 H^+ \rightarrow 2 Mn^{2+} + 5 SO_4^{2-} + 3 H_2O$

    Which of the following statements is true regarding the reaction given above?

    (A) MnO_4^- acts as the reducing agent.
    (B) H^+ acts as the oxidizing agent.
    (C) SO_3^{2-} acts as the reducing agent.
    (D) MnO_4^- is oxidized.
    (E) SO_3^{2-} is reduced.

19. **(C) is correct.**

    SO_3^{2-} is oxidized ($S^{4+} \rightarrow S^{6+} + 2 e^-$, LEO), so SO_3^{2-} acts as the reducing agent.

    MnO_4^- is reduced ($Mn^{7+} + 5 e^- \rightarrow Mn^{2+}$, GER), so MnO_4^- acts as the oxidizing agent.

20. Which of the following can function as both a Brønsted-Lowry acid and Brønsted-Lowry base?

    (A) HCl
    (B) H_2SO_4
    (C) HSO_3^-
    (D) SO_4^{2-}
    (E) H^+

20. **(C) is correct.** HSO_3^- is amphoteric.

    It can act as a Brønsted-Lowry acid, giving up a proton to become SO_3^{2-}.

    It can act as a Brønsted-Lowry base, gaining a proton to become H_2SO_3.

    HCl (A) and H_2SO_4 (B) can only give up protons.

    SO_4^{2-} (D) can only gain protons.

    H^+ (E) *is* a proton.

21. Which of the following substances experiences the strongest attractive intermolecular forces?

    (A) H_2
    (B) N_2
    (C) CO_2
    (D) NH_3
    (E) CH_4

21. **(D) is correct.** NH_3 is the only molecule listed that undergoes hydrogen bonding. In fact, it is the only polar molecule listed.

QUESTIONS	EXPLANATIONS
22. A mixture of gases at equilibrium over water at 43 °C contains 9.0 moles of nitrogen, 2.0 moles of oxygen, and 1.0 mole of water vapor. If the total pressure exerted by the gases is 780 mm Hg, what is the vapor pressure of water at 43 °C?	22. **(A) is correct.** From Dalton's law, partial pressure of a gas in a sample is directly proportional to its molar quantity, so if $\frac{1}{12}$ of the gas in the sample is water vapor, then $\frac{1}{12}$ of the total pressure will be due to water vapor. So the partial pressure of water vapor is $\left(\frac{1}{12}\right)(780) = 65$ mm Hg.

(A) 65 mm Hg
(B) 130 mm Hg
(C) 260 mm Hg
(D) 580 mm Hg
(E) 720 mm Hg

The gases are at equilibrium, so the partial pressure of the water vapor will be the same as the vapor pressure of the water.

23. $$...MnO_4^- + ...e^- + ...H^+ \rightarrow ...Mn^{2+} + ...H_2O$$

When the half-reaction above is balanced, what is the coefficient for H^+ if all the coefficients are reduced to the lowest whole number?

(A) 3
(B) 4
(C) 5
(D) 8
(E) 10

23. **(D) is correct.** Backsolve. Start with (C). If there are 5 H^+, there can't be a whole number coefficient for H_2O, so (C) is wrong. You should also be able to see that the answer can't be an odd number, so (A) is also wrong.

Try (D).

If there are 8 H^+, then there are 4 H_2O.

If there are 4 H_2O, then there is 1 MnO_4^-.

If there is 1 MnO_4^-, then there is 1 Mn^{2+}.

Mn^{7+} (in MnO_4^-) is reduced to Mn^{2+}, so there are 5 e^-.

These are the lowest whole number coefficients, so **(D) is correct.**

24. The boiling point of water is known to be lower at high elevations. This is because

(A) hydrogen bonds are weaker at high elevations
(B) the heat of fusion is lower at high elevations
(C) the vapor pressure of water is higher at high elevations
(D) the atmospheric pressure is lower at high elevations
(E) water is more dense at high elevations

24. **(D) is correct.** Vapor pressure increases with increasing temperature. Water boils when its vapor pressure is equal to the atmospheric pressure. So if the atmospheric pressure is lowered, then water will boil at a lower temperature.

QUESTIONS	EXPLANATIONS

25. A hydrocarbon contains 75% carbon by mass. What is the empirical formula for the compound?

(A) CH_2
(B) CH_3
(C) CH_4
(D) C_2H_5
(E) C_3H_8

25. **(C) is correct.** Let's say we have 100 grams of the compound.

$$Moles = \frac{grams}{MW}$$

$$Moles\ of\ carbon = \frac{(75g)}{(12g/mol)} = 6\ moles$$

$$Moles\ of\ hydrogen = \frac{(25g)}{(1g/mol)} = 25\ moles$$

According to our rough calculation, there are about four times as many moles of hydrogen in the compound as there are moles of carbon, so the empirical formula is CH_4.

26.
$$S(s) + O_2(g) \rightarrow SO_2(g) \qquad \Delta H° = x$$

$$S(s) + \frac{3}{2} O_2(g) \rightarrow SO_3(g) \qquad \Delta H° = y$$

Based on the information above, what is the standard enthalpy change for the following reaction?

$$2\ SO_2(g) + O_2(g) \rightarrow 2\ SO_3(g)$$

(A) $x - y$
(B) $y - x$
(C) $2x - y$
(D) $2x - 2y$
(E) $2y - 2x$

26. **(E) is correct.** The equations given on top give the heats of formation of all the reactants and products (remember, the heat of formation of O_2, an element in its most stable form, is zero).

$$\Delta H°_{reaction} = \Delta H°_{products} - \Delta H°_{reactants}$$

First the products.

From SO_3, we get $2y$. That's it for the products.

Now the reactants.

From SO_2 we get $2x$. The heat of formation of O_2 is defined to be zero, so that's it for the reactants.

$\Delta H°$ for the reaction $= 2y - 2x$

27. How much water must be added to a 50.0 ml solution of 0.60 M HNO_3 to produce a 0.40 M solution of HNO_3?

(A) 25 ml
(B) 33 ml
(C) 50 ml
(D) 67 ml
(E) 75 ml

27. **(A) is correct.**

Remember: moles = (molarity)(volume)

The number of moles of HNO_3 will remain constant during the dilution.

Moles of HNO_3 = (0.60 M)(50.0 ml)
    = 30 millimoles.

Now we can find how much water it will take to create a 0.40 M solution with 30 millimoles of HNO_3.

$$Volume = \frac{moles}{molarity} = \frac{30\ millimoles}{0.40\ M} = 75\ ml$$

But 75 ml isn't the answer. We started with 50 ml of solution and ended up with 75 ml of solution, so we must have added 25 ml of water.

QUESTIONS	EXPLANATIONS

28. In which of the following equilibria would the concentrations of the products be increased if the volume of the system were decreased at constant temperature?

   (A) $H_2(g) + Cl_2(g) \rightleftharpoons 2\ HCl(g)$
   (B) $2\ CO(g) + O_2(g) \rightleftharpoons 2\ CO_3(g)$
   (C) $NO(g) + O_3(g) \rightleftharpoons NO_2(g) + O_2(g)$
   (D) $2\ HI(g) \rightleftharpoons H_2(g) + I_2(g)$
   (E) $N_2O_4(g) \rightleftharpoons 2\ NO_2(g)$

28. **(B) is correct.** According to Le Chatelier's law, the equilibrium will shift to counteract any stress that is placed on it.

   If the volume is decreased, the equilibrium must shift towards the side with fewer moles of gas. Only choice (B) has fewer moles of gas on the product side (2 moles) than on the reactant side (3 moles).

29. Which of the following is the strongest acid?

   (A) H_2SO_4
   (B) HSO_4^-
   (C) H_2SO_3
   (D) HSO_3^-
   (E) H_2S

29. **(A) is correct.** H_2SO_4 is stronger than HSO_4^- because a diprotic acid is always more willing to give up its first H^+ ion than its second one.

   H_2SO_4 is stronger than all the other choices because the more oxygen atoms that are attached to the central atom (sulfur, in this case), the stronger the acid becomes.

30. Which of the following can be determined directly from the difference between the boiling point of a pure solvent and the boiling point of a solution of a nonionic solute in the solvent if k_b for the solvent is known?

   I.   The mass of solute in the solution
   II. The molality of the solution
   III. The volume of the solution

   (A) I only
   (B) II only
   (C) III only
   (D) I and II only
   (E) I and III only

30. **(B) is correct.** We don't know how much solution we have, so we can't find out (I) the mass of the solute or (III) the volume of the solution.

   We can get (II) the molality from the boiling point elevation with the expression $\Delta T = k_b m x$. Because the substance is nonionic, it will not dissociate and x will be equal to 1, so we can leave it out of the calculation.

   $$m = \frac{\Delta T}{k_b}$$

31. The value of the equilibrium constant K_{eq} is greater than 1 for a certain reaction under standard state conditions. Which of the following statements must be true regarding the reaction?

   (A) $\Delta G°$ is negative.
   (B) $\Delta G°$ is positive.
   (C) $\Delta G°$ is equal to zero.
   (D) $\Delta G°$ is negative if the reaction is exothermic and positive if the reaction is endothermic.
   (E) $\Delta G°$ is negative if the reaction is endothermic and positive if the reaction is exothermic.

31. **(A) is correct.** From the relationship $\Delta G° = -RT \ln K$, we can see that if K is greater than 1, then $\ln K$ must be greater than 1, which means that $\Delta G°$ must be less than zero.

32. Which of the following aqueous solutions has the highest boiling point?

(A) 0.1 m NaOH
(B) 0.1 m HF
(C) 0.1 m Na_2SO_4
(D) 0.1 m $KC_2H_3O_2$
(E) 0.1 m NH_4NO_3

32. **(C) is correct.** The formula for boiling point elevation is $\Delta T = k_b m x$, where x is the number of particles into which the solute dissociates. So, the more particles that the solute dissociates into, the greater the boiling point elevation.

The salts in all the answer choices except (C) dissociate into two particles. For choice (C), each Na_2SO_4 dissociates into three particles, two Na^+ and one SO_4^{2-}.

33. The molecular formula for hydrated ferric oxide, or rust, is generally written as $Fe_2O_3 \bullet x\ H_2O$ because the water content in rust can vary. If a 1-molar sample of hydrated ferric oxide is found to contain 108 g of H_2O, what is the molecular formula for the sample?

(A) $Fe_2O_3 \bullet H_2O$
(B) $Fe_2O_3 \bullet 3\ H_2O$
(C) $Fe_2O_3 \bullet 6\ H_2O$
(D) $Fe_2O_3 \bullet 10\ H_2O$
(E) $Fe_2O_3 \bullet 12\ H_2O$

33. **(C) is correct.** Moles = $\dfrac{\text{grams}}{\text{MW}}$.

Moles of H_2O = $\dfrac{(108\ g)}{(18\ g/mol)}$ = 6 moles

So if 1 mole of hydrate contains 6 moles of H_2O, then its formula must be $Fe_2O_3 \bullet 6\ H_2O$.

34. In which of the following reactions is entropy increasing?

(A) $2\ SO_2(g) + O_2(g) \rightarrow 2\ SO_3(g)$
(B) $CO(g) + H_2O(g) \rightarrow H_2(g) + CO_2(g)$
(C) $H_2(g) + Cl_2(g) \rightarrow 2\ HCl(g)$
(D) $2\ NO_2(g) \rightarrow 2\ NO(g) + O_2(g)$
(E) $2\ H_2S(g) + 3\ O_2(g) \rightarrow 2\ H_2O(g) + 2\ SO_2(g)$

34. **(D) is correct.** Choice (D) is the only reaction where the number of moles of gas is increasing, going from 2 moles of gas on the reactant side to 3 moles of gas on the product side.

In all the other choices, the number of moles of gas either decreases or remains constant.

35. Which of the following will be true when a pure sample of $CaCl_2$ is dissolved in distilled water?

   (A) The concentration of Ca^{2+} ions will be one-fourth the concentration of Cl^- ions.
   (B) The concentration of Ca^{2+} ions will be one-half the concentration of Cl^- ions.
   (C) The concentration of Ca^{2+} ions will be equal to the concentration of Cl^- ions.
   (D) The concentration of Ca^{2+} ions will be twice the concentration of Cl^- ions.
   (E) The concentration of Ca^{2+} ions will be four times the concentration of Cl^- ions.

35. **(B) is correct.** For every $CaCl_2$ that dissolves, we get one Ca^{2+} ion and two Cl^- ions. So the concentration of Ca^{2+} ions will be one-half that of the Cl^- ions.

36.
$$... + n \rightarrow {}_3^7Li + {}_2^4He$$

For the nuclear reaction shown above, what is the missing reactant?

   (A) ${}_4^9Be$
   (B) ${}_5^9B$
   (C) ${}_4^{10}Be$
   (D) ${}_5^{10}B$
   (E) ${}_5^{11}B$

36. **(D) is correct.** Adding up the atomic numbers in the products we get: $2 + 3 = 5$. So the reactant must be boron.

Adding up the atomic masses and keeping in mind that the neutron has a mass of 1, we get $y + 1 = 7 + 4$.

So the atomic mass must be 10.

37. A boiling water bath is sometimes used instead of a flame in heating objects. Which of the following could be an advantage of a boiling water bath over a flame?

   (A) The relatively low heat capacity of water will cause the object to become hot more quickly.
   (B) The relatively high density of water will cause the object to become hot more quickly.
   (C) The volume of boiling water remains constant over time.
   (D) The temperature of boiling water remains constant at $100\,°C$.
   (E) The vapor pressure of boiling water is equal to zero.

37. **(D) is correct.** The fact that boiling water maintains a constant temperature of $100°$ C is useful when a relatively low constant temperature is required. None of the other choices are true statements.

38. The addition of a catalyst to a chemical reaction will bring about a change in which of the following characteristics of the reaction?

    I. The activation energy
   II. The enthalpy change
 III. The value of the equilibrium constant

(A) I only
(B) II only
(C) I and II only
(D) I and III only
(E) II and III only

38. **(A) is correct.** The addition of a catalyst lowers the activation energy of a reaction, making it easier for the reaction to proceed, so (I) is correct.

Adding a catalyst has no effect on the enthalpy change or equilibrium conditions of a reaction, so (II) and (III) are wrong.

39.
$$2\,NO(g) + O_2(g) \rightarrow 2\,NO_2(g)$$

The reaction above occurs by the following two step process:

Step I: $NO(g) + O_2(g) \rightarrow NO_3(g)$

Step II: $NO_3(g) + NO(g) \rightarrow 2\,NO_2(g)$

Which of the following is true of Step II if it is the rate limiting step?

(A) Step II has a lower activation energy and occurs more slowly than Step I.
(B) Step II has a higher activation energy and occurs more slowly than Step I.
(C) Step II has a lower activation energy and occurs more quickly than Step I.
(D) Step II has a higher activation energy and occurs more quickly than Step I.
(E) Step II has the same activation energy and occurs at the same speed as Step I.

39. **(B) is correct.** The rate-limiting step in a reaction is the slowest step in the process.

When a reaction occurs slowly it is because very few collisions among reactant molecules have enough energy to overcome the high activation energy.

40.
$$...C_3H_7OH + ...O_2 \rightarrow ...CO_2 + ...H_2O$$

One mole of C_3H_7OH underwent combustion as shown in the reaction above. How many moles of oxygen were required for the reaction?

(A) 2 moles

(B) 3 moles

(C) $\dfrac{7}{2}$ moles

(D) $\dfrac{9}{2}$ moles

(E) 5 moles

40. **(D) is correct.** Backsolve. Start at (C).

Instead of using 1 as the coefficient for C_3H_7OH and $\dfrac{7}{2}$ for O_2, use 2 for C_3H_7OH and 7 for O_2. This won't change your result, and it will make the math easier.

If there are 2 moles of C_3H_7OH, then there must be 6 moles of CO_2 and 8 moles of H_2O.

That gives us 16 O's in the reactants and 20 O's in the products. So (C) is wrong and we should pick a larger number to put more O's on the reactant side. Try (D).

There are still 2 moles of C_3H_7OH, so there must still be 6 moles of CO_2 and 8 moles of H_2O. Now there are 9 moles of O_2. Now we have 20 O's in the reactants and 20 O's in the products, so (D) is the correct answer.

QUESTIONS	EXPLANATIONS

Questions 41–44 refer to the phase diagram below.

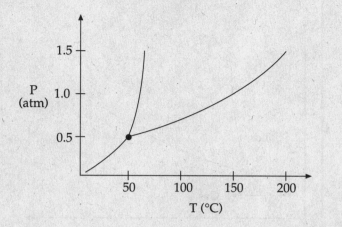

41. If the pressure of the substance shown in the diagram is decreased from 1.0 atmosphere to 0.5 atmosphere at a constant temperature of 100° C, which phase change will occur?

(A) Freezing
(B) Vaporization
(C) Condensation
(D) Sublimation
(E) Deposition

41. **(B) is correct.** The phase change will occur as shown in the diagram below.

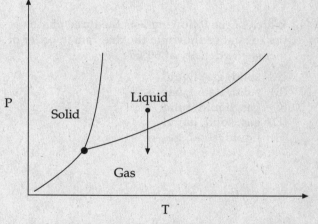

A phase change from liquid to gas is vaporization.

42. Under what conditions can all three phases of the substance shown in the diagram exist simultaneously in equilibrium?

(A) Pressure = 1.0 atm, Temperature = 150 °C
(B) Pressure = 1.0 atm, Temperature = 100 °C
(C) Pressure = 1.0 atm, Temperature = 50 °C
(D) Pressure = 0.5 atm, Temperature = 100 °C
(E) Pressure = 0.5 atm, Temperature = 50 °C

42. **(E) is correct.** At this point, called the triple point, all the phase change lines converge and all three phases are in equilibrium.

43. If the temperature of the substance shown in the diagram is increased from 10°C to 60°C at a constant pressure of 0.3 atmospheres, which phase change will occur?

   (A) Melting
   (B) Vaporization
   (C) Sublimation
   (D) Condensation
   (E) Deposition

43. **(C) is correct.** The phase change will occur as shown in the diagram below.

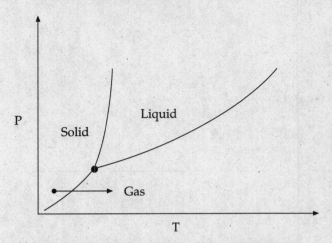

A phase change from solid to gas is sublimation.

44. Which of the following lists the three phases of the substance shown in the diagram in order of increasing density at 60°C?

   (A) solid, gas, liquid
   (B) solid, liquid, gas
   (C) gas, liquid, solid
   (D) gas, solid, liquid
   (E) liquid, solid, gas

44. **(C) is correct.** As pressure is increased, density will increase, so increasing density is shown by the arrow in the diagram below.

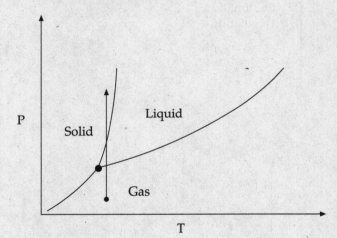

QUESTIONS	EXPLANATIONS

45. A solution to be used as a reagent for a reaction is to be removed from a bottle marked with its concentration. Which of the following is NOT part of the proper procedure for this process.

   (A) Pouring the solution down a stirring rod into a beaker.
   (B) Inserting a pipet directly into the bottle and drawing out the solution.
   (C) Placing the stopper of the bottle upside down on the table top.
   (D) Pouring the solution down the side of a tilted beaker.
   (E) Touching the stopper of the bottle only on the handle.

45. **(B) is correct.** The correct procedures listed here are designed to prevent spattering and spilling, (A) and (D), or contamination of the solution in the bottle, (C) and (E). Inserting a pipet directly into the bottle could contaminate the solution if the pipet wasn't perfectly clean.

46. $$N_2(g) + 3\,H_2(g) \leftrightarrows 2\,NH_3(g) + energy$$

   Which of the following changes to the equilibrium situation shown above will bring about an increase in the number of moles of NH_3 present at equilibrium?

   I. Adding N_2 gas to the reaction chamber
   II. Increasing the volume of the reaction chamber at constant temperature
   III. Increasing the temperature of the reaction chamber at constant volume

   (A) I only
   (B) II only
   (C) I and II only
   (D) I and III only
   (E) II and III only

46. **(A) is correct.** According to LeChatelier's law, the equilibrium will shift to counteract any stress that is placed on it.

   If N_2 is added, the equilibrium will shift to remove the excess N_2. This shift produces more products, and thus, more NH_3. So (I) is correct.

   Choice (II) is wrong because increasing the volume will cause the reaction to shift towards the side with more moles of gas. In this case the reactant side has more moles of gas (4 moles) than the product side (2 moles). So increasing the volume will decrease the number of moles of NH_3.

   Choice (III) is wrong because increasing the temperature will favor the endothermic direction, which in this case is the reverse reaction. So once again the number of moles of NH_3 is decreased.

47.
$$CH_4 + 2 O_2 \rightarrow CO_2 + 2 H_2O$$

If 16 grams of CH_4 reacts with 16 grams of O_2 in the reaction shown above, which of the following will be true?

(A) The mass of H_2O formed will be twice the mass of CO_2 formed.
(B) Equal masses of H_2O and CO_2 will be formed.
(C) Equal numbers of moles of H_2O and CO_2 will be formed.
(D) The limiting reagant will be CH_4.
(E) The limiting reagant will be O_2.

47. **(E) is correct.** Moles $= \dfrac{\text{grams}}{\text{MW}}$

Moles of $CH_4 = \dfrac{(16 \text{ g})}{(16 \text{ g/mol})} = 1$ mole

Moles of $O_2 = \dfrac{(16 \text{ g})}{(32 \text{ g/mol})} = 0.5$ moles

From the balanced equation, 2 moles of O_2 are used up for every mole of CH_4.

When all 0.5 moles of O_2 are used up, only 0.25 moles of CH_4 will be used up, so oxygen is the limiting reagant.

Choices (A), (B), and (C) are wrong because more moles of H_2O will be formed and a greater mass of CO_2 will be formed.

48. Which of the following sets of gases would be most difficult to separate if the method of gaseous effusion is used?

(A) O_2 and CO_2
(B) N_2 and C_2H_4
(C) H_2 and CH_4
(D) He and Ne
(E) O_2 and He

48. **(B) is correct.** From Graham's law, the rate of effusion of a gas depends on its molecular weight. The larger the molecular weight, the slower the rate of effusion.

In order for separation of gases by effusion to work, the gases must have different molecular weights, which will cause them to effuse at different rates. N_2 and C_2H_4 have the same molecular weight (28 g/mol), so they can't be separated by effusion.

49. Which of the following equilibrium expressions represents the hydrolysis of the CN^- ion?

(A) $K = \dfrac{[HCN][OH^-]}{[CN^-]}$

(B) $K = \dfrac{[CN^-][OH^-]}{[HCN]}$

(C) $K = \dfrac{[CN^-][H_3O^+]}{[HCN]}$

(D) $K = \dfrac{[HCN][H_3O^+]}{[CN^-]}$

(E) $K = \dfrac{[HCN]}{[CN^-][OH^-]}$

49. **(A) is correct.** The hydrolysis of the CN^- ion is shown by the reaction below.

$$CN^- + H_2O \leftrightarrow HCN + OH^-$$

Putting products over the reactants in the equilibrium expression and omitting water because it is a pure liquid, we get:

$$K = \dfrac{[HCN][OH^-]}{[CN^-]}$$

QUESTIONS	EXPLANATIONS

50. Which of the following is true under any conditions for a reaction that is spontaneous at any temperature?

  (A) ΔG, ΔS, and ΔH are all positive.
  (B) ΔG, ΔS, and ΔH are all negative.
  (C) ΔG and ΔS are negative, and ΔH is positive.
  (D) ΔG and ΔS are positive, and ΔH is negative.
  (E) ΔG and ΔH are negative, and ΔS is positive.

50. **(E) is correct.** For a spontaneous reaction, ΔG is always negative.

From the equation $\Delta G = \Delta H - T \Delta S$ we can see that the conditions that will make ΔG always negative are when ΔH is negative and ΔS is positive.

51. Which of the following pairs of compounds are isomers?

  (A) $HCOOH$ and CH_3COOH
  (B) CH_3CH_2CHO and C_3H_7OH
  (C) C_2H_5OH and CH_3OCH_3
  (D) C_2H_4 and C_2H_6
  (E) C_3H_8 and C_4H_{10}

51. **(C) is correct.** Isomers are different molecules that have the same collection of atoms arranged in different ways. Both of the molecules in choice (C) have 2 carbons, 6 hydrogens, and 1 oxygen.

52. A sample of an ideal gas confined in a rigid 5.00 liter container has a pressure of 363 mmHg at a temperature of 25° C. Which of the following expressions will be equal to the pressure of the gas if the temperature of the container is increased to 35° C?

  (A) $\dfrac{(363)(35)}{(25)}$ mmHg
  (B) $\dfrac{(363)(25)}{(35)}$ mmHg
  (C) $\dfrac{(363)(308)}{(298)}$ mmHg
  (D) $\dfrac{(363)(298)}{(308)}$ mmHg
  (E) $\dfrac{(363)(273)}{(308)}$ mmHg

52. **(C) is correct.** From the ideal gas laws, we know that with volume constant:

$$\frac{P_1}{T_1} = \frac{P_2}{T_2}$$

Solving for P_2, we get:

$$P_2 = \frac{P_1 T_2}{T_1} = \frac{(363)(308)}{(298)} \text{ mmHg}$$

53. If the temperature at which a reaction takes place is increased, the rate of the reaction will

  (A) increase if the reaction is endothermic and decrease if the reaction is exothermic
  (B) decrease if the reaction is endothermic and increase if the reaction is exothermic
  (C) increase if the reaction is endothermic and increase if the reaction is exothermic
  (D) decrease if the reaction is endothermic and decrease if the reaction is exothermic
  (E) remain the same for both an endothermic and an exothermic reaction

53. **(C) is correct.** An increase in temperature always increases the rate of a reaction, regardless of the change in enthalpy of the reaction.

Temperature change and enthalpy come into play in establishing whether reactants or products are favored at equilibrium according to LeChatelier's law, but increasing the temperature will bring the reaction to equilibrium more quickly, regardless of whether the equilibrium favors reactants or products.

QUESTIONS	EXPLANATIONS

54. Which of the following expressions is equal to the hydrogen ion concentration of a 1-molar solution of a very weak monoprotic acid, HA, with an ionization constant K_a?

(A) K_a
(B) K_a^2
(C) $2K_a$
(D) $2K_a^2$
(E) $\sqrt{K_a}$

54. **(E) is correct.** Use the equilibrium expression:

$$K_a = \frac{[H^+][A^-]}{[HA]} = \frac{y^2}{(1)}$$

For every HA that dissociates, we get one H^+ and one A^-, so $[H^+] = [A^-] = y$

The acid is weak, so we can assume that very little HA dissociates and that the concentration of HA remains 1-molar.

So, $[H^+] = y = \sqrt{K_a}$

---

55. $$2\,NO(g) + 2\,H_2(g) \rightarrow N_2(g) + 2\,H_2O(g)$$

Which of the following is true regarding the relative molar rates of disappearance of the reactants and appearance of the products?

   I. N_2 appears at the same rate that H_2 disappears.
  II. H_2O appears at the same rate that NO disappears.
 III. NO disappears at the same rate that H_2 disappears.

(A) I only
(B) I and II only
(C) I and III only
(D) II and III only
(E) I, II, and III

55. **(D) is correct.** For every mole of N_2 that appears, 2 moles of H_2 must disappear, so N_2 appears at half the rate that H_2 disappears, and (I) is wrong.

For every 2 moles of H_2O that appear, 2 moles of H_2 must disappear, so H_2O appears at the same rate that H_2 disappears, and (II) is correct.

For every 2 moles of NO that disappear, 2 moles of H_2 must disappear, so NO disappears at the same rate that H_2 disappears, and (III) is correct.

---

56. $$SO_4^{2-}, PO_4^{3-}, ClO_4^-$$

The geometries of the polyatomic ions listed above can all be described as

(A) square planar
(B) square pyramidal
(C) seesaw shaped
(D) tetrahedral
(E) trigonal bipyramidal

56. **(D) is correct.** All of these polyatomic ions have 32 valence electrons distributed in the Lewis structure shown below for ClO_4^-:

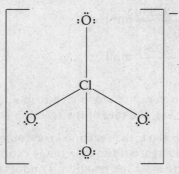

In these polyatomic ions, the central atom forms sp^3 hybrid orbitals, which have a tetrahedral structure. There are no unshared electron pairs on the central atom, so the geometry is tetrahedral.

QUESTIONS	EXPLANATIONS

57. $2 \, ZnS(s) + 3 \, O_2(g) \rightarrow 2 \, ZnO(s) + 2 \, SO_2(g)$

If the reaction above took place at standard temperature and pressure, what was the volume of $O_2(g)$ required to produce 40.0 grams of $ZnO(s)$?

(A) $\dfrac{(40.0)(2)}{(81.4)(3)(22.4)}$ L

(B) $\dfrac{(40.0)(3)}{(81.4)(2)(22.4)}$ L

(C) $\dfrac{(40.0)(2)(22.4)}{(81.4)(3)}$ L

(D) $\dfrac{(40.0)(3)(22.4)}{(81.4)(2)}$ L

(E) $\dfrac{(81.4)(2)(22.4)}{(40.0)(3)}$ L

57. **(D) is correct.** Moles $= \dfrac{\text{grams}}{\text{MW}}$

Moles of ZnO $= \dfrac{(40.0 \text{ g})}{(81.4 \text{ g/mol})}$

For every 2 moles of ZnO produced, 3 moles of O_2 are consumed.

So moles of $O_2 = \left(\dfrac{3}{2}\right)$(moles of ZnO)

$= \left(\dfrac{3}{2}\right) \dfrac{(40.0)}{(81.4)}$

At STP, volume of gas = (moles)(22.4 L)

So, volume of $O_2 = \left(\dfrac{3}{2}\right) \dfrac{(40.0)}{(81.4)} (22.4)$ L

58. Which of the following salts will produce a colorless solution when added to water?

(A) $Cu(NO_3)_2$
(B) $NiCl_2$
(C) $KMnO_4$
(D) $ZnSO_4$
(E) $FeCl_3$

58. **(D) is correct.** Zn^{2+} and SO_4^{2-} are both colorless in solution.

About the other answers:

(A) Cu^{2+} ions are blue in solution.
(B) Ni^{2+} ions are green in solution.
(C) MnO_4^- ions are purple in solution.
(E) Fe^{3+} ions are yellow in solution.

Most salts of transition metals produce colored solutions. That's because energy is released and absorbed when d subshell electrons change energy levels. This energy is manifested as visible light.

Zn^{2+} does not produce a colored solution because it has a full $3d$ subshell. The full subshell means that there are no empty orbitals for the d electrons to jump to. If there are no transitions, there is no light.

59. Copper (I) chloride will be LEAST soluble in a 0.02-molar solution of which of the following compounds?

    (A) NaCl
    (B) $CuNO_3$
    (C) $CaCl_2$
    (D) Na_2CO_3
    (E) KI

59. **(C) is correct.** According to the common ion effect, ions already present in a solution will affect the solubility of compounds that also produce those ions. So a solution containing Cu^+ ions or Cl^- ions will inhibit the solubility of CuCl.

A 0.02-molar solution of NaCl (A) will have a 0.02-molar concentration of Cl^- ions and a 0.02-molar solution of $CuNO_3$ (B) will have a 0.02-molar concentration of Cu^+ ions, so each of these choices will affect the solubility of CuCl.

The correct answer is $CaCl_2$ (C) because a 0.02 molar solution of $CaCl_2$ will have a *0.04-molar* concentration of Cl^- ions, so this solution will do the most to inhibit the solubility of CuCl.

Choices (D) and (E) have no effect on the solubility of CuCl.

60. Which of the following procedures will produce a buffered solution?

    I. Equal volumes of 1 M NH_3 and 1 M NH_4Cl solutions are mixed.
    II. Equal volumes of 1 M H_2CO_3 and 1 M $NaHCO_3$ solutions are mixed.
    III. Equal volumes of 1 M NH_3 and 1 M H_2CO_3 solutions are mixed.

    (A) I only
    (B) III only
    (C) I and II only
    (D) II and III only
    (E) I, II, and III

60. **(C) is correct.** A buffered solution can be prepared by mixing a weak acid or base with an equal amount of its conjugate.

In (I), equal amounts of NH_3 (a weak base) and NH_4^+ (its conjugate acid) are mixed, so (I) creates a buffer.

In (II), equal amounts of H_2CO_3 (a weak acid) and HCO_3^- (its conjugate base) are mixed, so (II) also creates a buffer.

In (III), equal amounts of a weak acid and base that are not conjugates are mixed. These two will neutralize each other and will not create a buffered solution.

QUESTIONS	EXPLANATIONS

61.

$$H_2(g) + I_2(g) \rightleftharpoons 2\,HI(g)$$

At 450 °C the equilibrium constant, K_c, for the reaction shown above has a value of 50. Which of the following sets of initial conditions at 450° C will cause the reaction above to produce more H_2?

   I. [HI] = 5-molar, [H_2] = 1-molar, [I_2] = 1-molar
   II. [HI] = 10-molar, [H_2] = 1-molar, [I_2] = 1-molar
   III. [HI] = 10-molar, [H_2] = 2-molar, [I_2] = 2-molar

(A) I only
(B) II only
(C) I and II only
(D) II and III only
(E) I, II, and III

61. (B) is correct. The reaction will proceed in the reverse direction and produce more H_2 when the reaction quotient Q is greater than K_c.

Q takes the form of the equilibrium constant.

$$Q = \frac{[HI]^2}{[H_2][I_2]}$$

For I: $Q = \frac{(5)^2}{(1)(1)} = 25.$ Q is less than K_c.

For II: $Q = \frac{(10)^2}{(1)(1)} = 100.$ Q is greater than K_c.

For III: $Q = \frac{(10)^2}{(2)(2)} = 25.$ Q is less than K_c.

So only (II) will produce more H_2.

62.

$$Cu^{2+}(aq) + Zn(s) \rightarrow Cu(s) + Zn^{2+}(aq)$$

A galvanic cell that uses the reaction shown above has a standard state electromotive force of 1.1 volts. Which of the following changes to the cell will increase the voltage?

   I. An increase in the mass of $Zn(s)$ in the cell.
   II. An increase in the concentration of $Cu^{2+}(aq)$ in the cell.
   III. An increase in the concentration of $Zn^{2+}(aq)$ in the cell.

(A) I only
(B) II only
(C) III only
(D) I and II only
(E) I and III only

62. (B) is correct. Let's look at the Nernst equation, which relates cell potential to concentration.

$$E = E° - \frac{0.059}{2}\log Q \text{ at } 25\text{ °C}$$

The smaller Q becomes, the larger E will become.

Remember, Q is the reaction quotient, which takes the form of K_{eq}, except with initial conditions instead of equilibrium conditions.

In this case $Q = \frac{[Zn^{2+}]}{[Cu^{2+}]}$, so increasing $[Cu^{2+}]$ decreases Q, which increases E.

So (II) is right and (III) is wrong.

The amount of solid has no effect, so (I) is wrong.

QUESTIONS	EXPLANATIONS

63. The nuclide $^{61}_{26}$Fe decays through the emission of a single beta (β^-) particle. What is the resulting nuclide?

    (A) $^{60}_{26}$Fe
    (B) $^{62}_{26}$Fe
    (C) $^{61}_{27}$Co
    (D) $^{62}_{27}$Co
    (E) $^{61}_{25}$Mn

63. **(C) is correct.** The number of nucleons doesn't change in beta decay, so the mass number must remain at 61.

In beta decay, a neutron is converted to a proton, so the atomic number increases by one.

The balanced nuclear reaction is as follows:

$$^{61}_{26}\text{Fe} \rightarrow\ _{-1}\beta + ^{61}_{27}\text{Co}$$

64. Which of the following statements is true regarding sodium and potassium?

    (A) Sodium has a larger first ionization energy and a larger atomic radius.
    (B) Sodium has a larger first ionization energy and a smaller atomic radius.
    (C) Sodium has a smaller first ionization energy and a larger atomic radius.
    (D) Sodium has a smaller first ionization energy and a smaller atomic radius.
    (E) Sodium and potassium will have identical first ionization energies and atomic radii.

64. **(B) is correct.** Sodium's valence electron is in the third energy level and potassium's valence electron is in the fourth energy level, so sodium's valence electron is closer to the nucleus than potassium's, so sodium must have a smaller atomic radius.

Also, because sodium's valence electron is closer to the nucleus, it is more difficult to remove, so sodium will have a higher first ionization energy.

65.   HCl(aq) + AgNO$_3$(aq) → AgCl(s) + HNO$_3$(aq)

One-half liter of a 0.20-molar HCl solution is mixed with one-half liter of a 0.40-molar solution of AgNO$_3$. A reaction occurs forming a precipitate as shown above. If the reaction goes to completion, what is the mass of AgCl produced?

    (A) 14 grams
    (B) 28 grams
    (C) 42 grams
    (D) 70 grams
    (E) 84 grams

65. **(A) is correct.** First we have to find the limiting reagant.

Moles = (molarity)(liters)

Moles of HCl = (0.20 M)(0.50 L) = 0.10 moles

Moles of AgNO$_3$ = (0.40 M)(0.50 L) = 0.20 moles

From the balanced equation, the two reactants are used up at equal rates. There is twice as much AgNO$_3$, so when the 0.10 moles of HCl have been used up, there will still be 0.10 moles of AgNO$_3$. So HCl is the limiting reagant.

From the balanced equation, for every mole of HCl consumed, 1 mole of AgCl is produced. So 0.10 moles of AgCl will be produced.

Grams = (moles)(MW)

Grams of AgCl = (0.10 moles)(143 g/mol)
    = 14 grams

QUESTIONS	EXPLANATIONS

66. $$H_2(g) + Cl_2(g) \rightarrow 2\,HCl(g)$$

Based on the information given in the table below, what is ΔH° for the above reaction?

Bond	Average Bond Energy (kJ/mol)
H–H	440
Cl–Cl	240
H–Cl	430

(A) −860 kJ
(B) −620 kJ
(C) −440 kJ
(D) −180 kJ
(E) +240 kJ

66. **(D) is correct.** The bond energy is the energy that must be put into a bond in order to break it. First let's figure out how much energy must be put in to the reactants in order to break their bonds.

To break 1 mole of H–H bonds, it takes 440 kJ.

To break 1 mole of Cl–Cl bonds, it takes 240 kJ.

So to break up the reactants, it takes +680 kJ.

Energy is given off when a bond is formed; that's the negative of the bond energy.

Now let's see how much energy is given off when 2 moles of HCl are formed.

2 moles of HCl molecules contain 2 moles of HCl bonds, so (2)(−430) kJ = −860 kJ are given off.

So the value of ΔH for the reaction is

(−860, E given off) + (680, E put in) = −180 kJ.

67. The first ionization energy for magnesium is 730 kJ/mol. The third ionization energy for magnesium is 7700 kJ/mol. What is the most likely value for magnesium's second ionization energy?

(A) 490 kJ/mol
(B) 1400 kJ/mol
(C) 4200 kJ/mol
(D) 7100 kJ/mol
(E) 8400 kJ/mol

67. **(B) is correct.** Magnesium has two valence electrons in the third shell, so we would expect to see a small jump between the first and second ionization energies.

The third electron must be removed from the second shell, so we would expect to see a much larger jump between the second and third ionization energies.

Choice (B) is the only answer that shows this relationship.

QUESTIONS	EXPLANATIONS

68. Molten NaCl is electrolyzed with a constant current of 1.00 ampere. What is the shortest amount of time, in seconds, that it would take to produce 1.00 mole of solid sodium? (1 faraday = 96,500 coulombs)

(A) 19,300 seconds
(B) 32,200 seconds
(C) 48,300 seconds
(D) 64,300 seconds
(E) 96,500 seconds

68. **(E) is correct.** First let's find out how many moles of electrons we need.

The half-reaction that reduces Na^+ to $Na(s)$ is as follows:

$Na^+ + e^- \rightarrow Na(s)$

So it takes 1 mole of electrons to produce 1 mole of $Na(s)$

Now let's find out how many coulombs we need.

$$\text{Moles of electrons} = \frac{\text{coulombs}}{96,500}$$

So coulombs = (moles of electrons)(96,500)

$\quad = (1)(96,500) = 96,500$ coulombs

Now we can find how many seconds it takes.

$$\text{Amperes} = \frac{\text{coulombs}}{\text{second}}$$

So, seconds $= \dfrac{\text{coulombs}}{\text{amperes}} = \dfrac{(96,500)}{(1)}$

$\quad = 96,500$ seconds.

69. How many moles of KCl must be added to 200 milliliters of a 0.5-molar NaCl solution in order to create a solution where the concentration of Cl^- ion is 1.0-molar? (Assume the volume of the solution remains constant.)

(A) 0.1 moles
(B) 0.2 moles
(C) 0.3 moles
(D) 0.4 moles
(E) 0.5 moles

69. **(A) is correct.** For every NaCl in solution, there's one Cl^- ion; and for every KCl we add, we get one Cl^- ion.

Let's find out how many moles of Cl^- ions are already in the solution.

Moles = (molarity)(volume)

Moles of $Cl^- = (0.5\ M)(0.2\ L) = 0.1$ moles

We're not changing the volume, so to double the concentration of Cl^- ions from 0.5-molar to 1.0-molar, we just double the number of moles of Cl^- ions. We do that by adding 0.1 moles of KCl.

70.
$$HCrO_4^- + Ca^2 \rightleftharpoons H^+ + CaCrO_4$$

If the acid dissociation constant for $HCrO_4^-$ is K_a and the solubility product for $CaCrO_4$ is K_{sp}, which of the following gives the equilibrium expression for the reaction above?

(A) $K_a K_{sp}$

(B) $\dfrac{K_a}{K_{sp}}$

(C) $\dfrac{K_{sp}}{K_a}$

(D) $\dfrac{1}{K_{sp} K_a}$

(E) $\dfrac{K_a K_{sp}}{2}$

70. **(B) is correct.** We can think of the reaction given in the question as the sum of two other reactions:

$$HCrO_4^- \leftrightarrows H^+ + CrO_4^{2-} \qquad K_{eq} = K_a$$

$$Ca^{2+} + CrO_4^{2-} \leftrightarrows CaCrO_4 \qquad K_{eq} = \frac{1}{K_{sp}}$$

Notice that we are using the reverse reaction for the solvation of $CaCrO_4$, so the reactants and products are reversed and we must take the reciprocal of the solubility product.

When reactions can be added to get another reaction, their equilibrium constants can be multiplied to get the equilibrium constant of the resulting reaction.

So $K_{eq} = (K_a) \left(\dfrac{1}{K_{sp}} \right) = \dfrac{K_a}{K_{sp}}$

71. A 100 gram sample of pure $^{37}_{18}Ar$ decays by electron capture with a half-life of 35 days. How long will it take for 90 grams of $^{37}_{17}Cl$ to accumulate?

(A) 31 days
(B) 39 days
(C) 78 days
(D) 116 days
(E) 315 days

71. **(D) is correct.** Because they have the same mass number, the mass of $^{37}_{17}Cl$ will accumulate at the same rate that the mass of $^{37}_{18}Ar$ disappears.

We're looking for the moment when 10 grams of $^{37}_{18}Ar$ remains.

Make a chart. Start at time = 0.

Half-lives	Time	Stuff
0	0 days	100 g
1	35 days	50 g
2	70 days	25 g
3	105 days	12.5 g
4	140 days	6.25 g

It takes between 3 and 4 half-lives for the amount of $^{37}_{18}Ar$ to decrease to 10 grams.

116 days is the only answer choice between 105 days and 140 days.

72. If the solubility of BaF_2 is equal to x, which of the following expressions is equal to the solubility product, K_{sp}, for BaF_2?

   (A) x^2
   (B) $2x^2$
   (C) x^3
   (D) $2x^3$
   (E) $4x^3$

72. **(E) is correct.** For BaF_2, $K_{sp} = [Ba^{2+}][F^-]^2$.

   For every BaF_2 that dissolves, we get one Ba^{2+} and two F^-.

   So if the solubility of BaF_2 is x, then $[Ba^{2+}] = x$, and $[F^-] = 2x$.

   So, $K_{sp} = (x)(2x)^2 = (x)(4x^2) = 4x^3$

73. When excess hydroxide ions were added to 1.0 liter of $CaCl_2$ solution, $Ca(OH)_2$ precipitate was formed. If all of the calcium ions in the solution were precipitated in 7.4 grams of $Ca(OH)_2$, what was the initial concentration of the $CaCl_2$ solution?

   (A) 0.05-molar
   (B) 0.10-molar
   (C) 0.15-molar
   (D) 0.20-molar
   (E) 0.30-molar

73. **(B) is correct.** Moles $= \dfrac{\text{grams}}{\text{MW}}$

   Moles of $Ca(OH)_2 = \dfrac{(7.4\text{ g})}{(74\text{ g/mol})} = 0.10$ moles

   One mole of $CaCl_2$ must have been consumed for every mole of $Ca(OH)_2$ produced, so there must have been 0.10 moles of $CaCl_2$ in the original solution.

   Molarity $= \dfrac{\text{moles}}{\text{liters}}$

   Molarity of $CaCl_2 = \dfrac{(0.10\text{ mol})}{(1.0\text{ L})} = 0.10$-molar

74. When a solution of $KMnO_4$ was mixed with a solution of HCl, Cl_2 gas bubbles formed and Mn^{2+} ions appeared in the solution. Which of the following has occurred?

   (A) K^+ has been oxidized by Cl^-.
   (B) K^+ has been oxidized by H^+.
   (C) Cl^- has been oxidized by K^+.
   (D) Cl^- has been oxidized by MnO_4^-.
   (E) MnO_4^- has been oxidized by Cl^-.

74. **(D) is correct.** The oxidation and reduction half-reactions are as follows:

   Cl^- is oxidized: $\quad 2\,Cl^- \rightarrow Cl_2 + 2e^-$

   MnO_4^- is reduced: $\ Mn^{7+} + 5e^- \rightarrow Mn^{2+}$

   So Cl^- is oxidized and MnO_4^- is the oxidizing agent.

QUESTIONS	EXPLANATIONS

75. $Ag^+ + e^- \rightarrow Ag \qquad E° = +0.8\ V$

$Cd^{2+} + 2e^- \rightarrow Cd \qquad E° = -0.4\ V$

Based on the reduction potentials given above, what is the reaction potential for the following reaction?

$$2\ Ag^+ + Cd \rightarrow 2\ Ag + Cd^{2+}$$

(A) −0.8 V
(B) −0.4 V
(C) +0.4 V
(D) +1.2 V
(E) +2.0 V

75. **(D) is correct.** We add the reduction potential for Ag^+ (+0.8 V) to the oxidation potential for Cd (+0.4 V, the reverse of the reduction potential) to get 1.2 V.

Remember, you ignore the coefficients in the reaction when you're calculating reaction potentials.

QUESTIONS	EXPLANATIONS

SECTION II-FREE RESPONSE

1.(a) Sulfur dioxide gas is bubbled through cold water.

(a) $SO_2 + H_2O \rightarrow H_2SO_3$

Oxide of a nonmetal + water → acid

(b) A solution of copper(II) chloride is mixed with a concentrated solution of ammonia.

(b) $Cu^{2+} + NH_3 \rightarrow Cu(NH_3)_4^{2+}$

Ammonia forms complex ions with transition metal ions.

(c) A solution of silver nitrate is added to a solution of potassium bromide.

(c) $Ag^+ + Br^- \rightarrow AgBr$

Silver bromide is insoluble; potassium nitrate is soluble (all nitrates are soluble).

(d) Ethane is burned in air.

(d) $C_2H_6 + O_2 \rightarrow CO_2 + H_2O$

Organic stuff + oxygen → carbon dioxide + water

(e) A piece of solid zinc is placed in a solution of copper(II) nitrate.

(e) $Zn + Cu^{2+} \rightarrow Zn^{2+} + Cu$

Zn is oxidized and Cu^{2+} is reduced.

(f) A piece of solid calcium is placed in distilled water.

(f) $Ca + H_2O \rightarrow Ca(OH)_2 + H_2$

Metal + water → base + hydrogen gas

(g) Chlorine gas is bubbled through a solution of sodium bromide.

(g) $Cl_2 + Br^- \rightarrow Cl^- + Br_2$

Cl_2 is reduced and Br^- is oxidized.

(h) A solution of sodium iodide and an acidified solution of sodium permanganate are mixed.

(h) $I^- + MnO_4^- + H^+ \rightarrow I_2 + Mn^{2+} + H_2O$

I^- is oxidized and MnO_4^- is reduced.

When a redox reaction takes place in acidified solution, there is always an H^+ on the reactant side and an H_2O on the product side.

QUESTIONS	EXPLANATIONS
2. A 0.20-molar solution of acetic acid, $HC_2H_3O_2$, at a temperature of 25 °C, has a pH of 2.73.	

(a) Calculate the hydroxide ion concentration, $[OH^-]$.

(a) Knowing the pH, we can calculate the pOH.

$pH + pOH = 14$

$2.73 + pOH = 14$

$pOH = 11.27$

Knowing the pOH, we can calculate $[OH^-]$

$[OH^-] = 10^{-pOH} = 10^{-11.27} = 5.4 \times 10^{-12}$

(b) What is the value of the acid ionization constant, K_a, for acetic acid at 25 °C?

(b) $K_a = \dfrac{[H^+][C_2H_3O_2^-]}{[HC_2H_3O_2]} = \dfrac{x^2}{0.200 - x}$

Knowing the pH, we can find $[H^+]$. We also know that every $HC_2H_3O_2$ molecule that dissociates will put 1 H^+ ion and 1 $C_2H_3O_2$ ion in solution.

$x = [H^+] = [C_2H_3O_2^-] = 10^{-pH} = 10^{-2.73} = 1.86 \times 10^{-3}$

$[HC_2H_3O_2] = 0.200 - x$

x is very small, so $[HC_2H_3O_2] = 0.200$

Now we can solve for K_a

$K_a = \dfrac{[H^+][C_2H_3O_2^-]}{[HC_2H_3O_2]} = \dfrac{x^2}{0.200} = \dfrac{(1.86 \times 10^{-3})^2}{(0.200)}$

$= 1.73 \times 10^{-5}$

(c) How many moles of sodium acetate must be added to 500. ml of a 0.200-molar solution of acetic acid in order to create a buffer with a pH of 4.00? Assume that the volume of the solution is not changed by the addition of sodium acetate.

(c) We can use the Henderson-Hasselbach expression to find out what value of $[C_2H_3O_2]$ will create a buffer with a pH of 4.

$pH = pK_a + \log \dfrac{[A^-]}{[HA]}$

$pH = pK_a + \log \dfrac{[C_2H_3O_2^-]}{[HC_2H_3O_2]}$

$pH = 4.00$

$pK_a = -\log(1.73 \times 10^{-5}) = 4.76$

$\log \dfrac{[C_2H_3O_2^-]}{[HC_2H_3O_2]} = pH - pK_a = 4.00 - 4.76 = -0.76$

$\dfrac{[C_2H_3O_2^-]}{[HC_2H_3O_2]} = 10^{-0.76} = 0.174$

$[HC_2H_3O_2] = 0.200\ M$

$[C_2H_3O_2^-] = (0.174)(0.200) = 0.035\ M$

Moles = (molarity)(volume) = (0.035)(0.500)
   = 0.018 moles

QUESTIONS	EXPLANATIONS

(d) In a titration experiment, 100. ml of sodium hydroxide solution was added to 200. ml of a 0.400-molar solution of acetic acid until the equivalence point was reached. What was the pH at the equivalence point?

(d) Because $HC_2H_3O_2$ dissociates to such a small extent, we can assume that all of the $C_2H_3O_2^-$ in the solution came from the NaC_2H_3O.

Use the base ionization constant for $C_2H_3O_2^-$.

$$K_b = \frac{[HC_2H_3O_2][OH^-]}{[C_2H_3O_2^-]}$$

$$K_b = \frac{10^{-14}}{K_a} = \frac{10^{-14}}{1.73 \times 10^{-5}} = 5.78 \times 10^{-10}$$

At the equivalence point, all of the acetic acid initially present has been converted to acetate ion. So the initial $[HC_2H_3O_2]$ is equal to $[C_2H_3O_2]$ at the equivalence point.

Moles = (molarity)(volume)

Moles of $C_2H_3O_2^-$ = (0.400 M)(0.200 L)
  = 0.080 moles

$$Molarity = \frac{moles}{volume}$$

$$[C_2H_3O_2^-] = \frac{(0.080\ mol)}{(0.200\ L + 0.100\ L)} =$$

$$\frac{(0.080\ mol)}{(0.300\ L)} = 0.267\ M$$

$[HC_2H_3O_2] = [OH^-] = x$

Now we can use the K_b equation to find x, the OH^- concentration.

We'll assume that x is much smaller than 0.267 M.

$$K_b = \frac{[HC_2H_3O_2][OH^-]}{[C_2H_3O_2^-]} = \frac{x^2}{0.267 - x} = \frac{x^2}{0.267}$$

$$K_b = 5.78 \times 10^{-10} = \frac{x^2}{0.267}$$

$x = [OH^-] = 1.24 \times 10^{-5}\ M$

Knowing $[OH^-]$, we can calculate pOH, and then pH.

pOH = $-\log[OH^-]$ = $-\log(1.24 \times 10^{-5})$ = 4.91

pH = 14 − pOH

pH = 14 − 4.91 = 9.09

QUESTIONS	EXPLANATIONS

3.
$$2 NO(g) + Cl_2(g) \rightarrow 2 NOCl(g)$$

The following data were collected for the reaction above. All of the measurements were taken at a temperature of 263 K.

Experiment	Initial [NO] (M)	Initial [Cl_2] (M)	Initial rate of disappearance of Cl_2 (M/min)
1	0.15	0.15	0.60
2	0.15	0.30	1.2
3	0.30	0.15	2.4
4	0.25	0.25	?

(a) Write the expression for the rate law for the reaction above.

(a) From experiments 1 and 2, we can see that when [Cl_2] doubles, the rate doubles, so the rate law is first order with respect to Cl_2. That is, $[Cl_2]^1$.

From experiments 1 and 3, we can see that when [NO] doubles, the rate quadruples, so the rate law is second order with respect to NO. That is, $[NO]^2$.

Rate = $k[NO]^2[Cl_2]$

(b) Calculate the value of the rate constant for the above reaction and specify the units.

(b) We'll use experiment 1 for our calculation.

$$k = \frac{\text{Rate}}{[NO]^2[Cl_2]} = \frac{(0.60\,M/\text{min})}{(0.15\,M)^2(0.15\,M)} = 180\ M^{-2}\ \text{min}^{-1}$$

(c) What is the initial rate of appearance of NOCl in experiment 2?

(c) From the balanced equation we can see that for every molecule of Cl_2 that disappears, 2 molecules of NOCl appear, so the rate of appearance of NOCl will be twice the rate of disappearance of Cl_2.

In experiment 2, the initial rate of disappearance of Cl_2 is 1.2 M/min, so the initial rate of appearance of NOCl will be 2.4 M/min.

(d) What is the initial rate of disappearance of Cl_2 in experiment 4?

(d) Use the rate law.

Rate = $k[NO]^2[Cl_2]$

Rate = $(180\ M^{-2}\ \text{min}^{-1})(0.25\ M)^2(0.25\ M)$
     = 2.8 M/min

QUESTIONS	EXPLANATIONS

4. $CH_4(g) + 2 O_2(g) \rightarrow CO_2(g) + 2 H_2O(l)$

The above reaction for the combustion of methane gas has a standard entropy change, $\Delta S°$, with a value of –242.7 J/mol-K. The following data are also available.

Compound	$\Delta H°_f$ (kJ/mol)
CH_4 (g)	-74.8
H_2O (l)	-285.9
CO_2 (g)	-393.5

(a)   What are the values of $\Delta H°_f$ and $\Delta G°_f$ for $O_2(g)$.

(a) $\Delta H°_f$ and $\Delta G°_f$ for $O_2(g)$ are both equal to zero. The enthalpy and free energy of formation of any element in its standard state are equal to zero.

(b)   Calculate the standard change in enthalpy, $\Delta H°$, for the combustion of methane.

(b) $\Delta H = \sum \Delta H°_f \text{(products)} - \sum \Delta H°_f \text{(reactants)}$

$\Delta H = [(-393.5) + (2)(-285.9)] \text{ kJ} - [-74.8] \text{ kJ}$

$\Delta H = [-965.3] \text{ kJ} - [-74.8] \text{ kJ}$

$\Delta H = -890.5 \text{ kJ}$

(c)   Calculate the standard free energy change, $\Delta G°$, for the combustion of methane.

(c) $\Delta G° = \Delta H° - T \Delta S°$

$\Delta G° = (-890,500 \text{ J}) - (298 \text{ K})(-242.7 \text{ J/K})$

$\Delta G° = -818,200 \text{ J} = -818.2 \text{ kJ}$

(d)   How would the value of $\Delta S°$ for the reaction be affected if the water produced in the combustion remained in the gas phase?

(d) $\Delta S°$ would become less negative. $H_2O(g)$ has more entropy than $H_2O(l)$, so the entropy of the products would be increased and the entropy change of the reaction would become more positive (less negative, that is).

QUESTIONS	EXPLANATIONS

5. Oxygen is found in the atmosphere as a diatomic gas, O_2, and as ozone, O_3.

(a) Draw the Lewis structures for both molecules.

(a)

Lewis structure for O_2

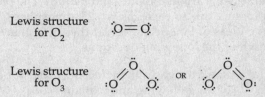

Lewis structure for O_3

(b) Use the principles of bonding and molecular structure to account for the fact that ozone has a higher boiling point than diatomic oxygen.

(b) O_3 is a polar molecule, while O_2 is nonpolar, so the dipole-dipole attractions between O_3 molecules are stronger than the van der Waals forces between O_2 molecules.

If you didn't recognize the polarity of O_3, you might have gotten some partial credit for noting that O_3 has more electrons than O_2, so O_3 will have stronger van der Waals forces between its molecules.

(c) Use the principles of bonding and molecular structure to account for the fact that ozone is more soluble than diatomic oxygen in water.

(c) Water molecules are polar. O_3 is a polar molecule, while O_2 is non-polar. So water molecules will be more strongly attracted to O_3 molecules than they are to the nonpolar O_2 molecules.

(d) Explain why the two bonds in O_3 are the same length and are longer than the bond length of the bond in diatomic oxygen.

(d) The bond in O_2 is a double bond. Ozone, however, has two resonance forms, each with a single and a double bond, so the two bonds in O_3 are each somewhere between a single and a double bond on average. The double bond in O_2 is stronger and shorter than the single/double resonance bonds in O_3.

QUESTIONS	EXPLANATIONS

6. At 25 °C and 1.0 atmosphere pressure, a balloon contains a mixture of four ideal gases: oxygen, nitrogen, carbon dioxide, and helium. The partial pressure due to each gas is 0.25 atmosphere. Use the ideas of kinetic molecular theory to answer each of the following questions.

(a) Rank the gases in increasing order for each of the following and explain.

    (i)   Density

    (ii)   Average kinetic energy

    (iii)   Average molecular velocity

(a)   (i)   He, N_2, O_2, CO_2.

$$Density = \frac{(mass)}{(volume)} \text{ and}$$

(mass in grams) = (moles)(MW).

The gases have equal partial pressures, so there are equal numbers of moles of each gas present in the balloon.

Helium has the smallest molecular weight (4), so there will be the smallest number of grams of helium in the given volume of the balloon. Carbon dioxide has the largest molecular weight (44), so the balloon will contain the largest number of grams of CO_2 per unit volume.

(ii) All of the gases will have the same average kinetic energy because average kinetic energy depends only on temperature.

$$KE_{avg} = \frac{3}{2}RT.$$

(iii) CO_2, O_2, N_2, He

All of the gases have the same average kinetic energy, and $KE = \frac{1}{2}mv^2$, so the larger the molecular weight, the smaller the average velocity. This relationship is given directly by the expression, $u_{rms} = \sqrt{\dfrac{3RT}{(MW)}}$.

QUESTIONS	EXPLANATIONS

(b) How would the volume of the balloon be affected by each of the following changes to the system?
 	
  (i) The temperature of the gases in the balloon were increased at constant pressure.
 	
  (ii) The gas mixture were replaced with an equal number of moles of pure oxygen.
	(b) (i) Volume increases.
	
	  $PV = nRT$. From the ideal gas law we can see that when T increases and P and n are held constant, V must increase to maintain equality.
	  (ii) Volume remains constant.
	
	  $PV = nRT$. For ideal gases, the identity of the gas is not important, only the number of moles, which we haven't changed.

(c) What changes to the temperature and pressure of the gases would cause deviation from ideal behavior and which gas would be most affected?	(c) Decreased temperature and increased pressure would eventually cause deviation from ideal behavior. Carbon dioxide would be most affected.
	
	  Deviation from ideal behavior occurs when gas molecules are brought very close together. When gas molecules are packed close together, the weak attractive forces between them become important. Also, in this situation, the volumes occupied by the individual gas molecules can no longer be ignored. Gas molecules are brought close together by low temperatures and high pressures.
	
	  Carbon dioxide would be the most affected of the four gases because it is the largest molecule and it has the most electrons. Because of this, the van der Waals forces among CO_2 molecules will be stronger than for the other gases.

QUESTIONS	EXPLANATIONS

7. Molten sodium chloride can be electrolyzed to form pure sodium and chlorine.

(a) Write the balanced equations for the half reactions that take place at the electrodes during the electrolysis. Indicate which half-reaction takes place at which electrode.

(a) $Na^+ + e^- \rightarrow Na$

Na$^+$ gains an electron, so it is reduced (GER).

Reduction takes place at the cathode (RED CAT)

$2 Cl^- \rightarrow Cl_2 + 2e^-$

Cl$^-$ loses an electron, so it is oxidized (LEO).

Oxidation takes place at the anode (AN OX).

(b) Describe how the pure sodium and chlorine are separated.

(b) Chlorine gas (Cl_2) bubbles out of the molten mixture, leaving pure molten sodium.

(c) For the electrolyzation of molten sodium chloride, will the value of each of the following be positive or negative?

(i) $E_{reaction}$

(ii) ΔG

(iii) ΔS

(c) (i) $E_{reaction}$ will be negative because E for both half-reactions is negative. The voltage source that drives the reaction must be strong enough to overcome the negative voltage for the reaction.

(ii) ΔG will be positive because the reaction is not spontaneous. Also, from the relationship $\Delta G = -nFE$ we know that ΔG and E always have opposite signs.

(iii) ΔS will be positive because the reactant is a liquid and the products are a liquid and a gas.

(d) Explain why, when the molten sodium chloride is replaced with an aqueous solution of sodium chloride, pure sodium is not produced.

(d) Water molecules are more easily reduced than sodium ions, so H_2O will be reduced at the cathode instead of Na$^+$.

QUESTIONS	EXPLANATIONS

8. $NaC_2H_3O_2$, $Ba(NO_3)_2$, KCl

Aqueous solutions of equal concentration of the three compounds listed above are prepared. What would an experimenter expect to observe when each of the following procedures is performed on each of the solutions?

(a) The pH of each solution is measured.

    (a) The $NaC_2H_3O_2$ solution will be slightly basic. The other two solutions will be neutral.

$NaC_2H_3O_2$ is a salt composed of the conjugate of a strong base and the conjugate of a weak acid, so it will create a basic solution.

$Ba(NO_3)_2$ and KCl are salts composed of conjugates of strong acids and bases, so they will create neutral solutions.

(b) Pb^{2+} ions are introduced into each solution.

    (b) A precipitate will form in the KCl solution. The other two solutions will show no change.

$PbCl_2$ is insoluble. $Pb(NO_3)_2$ and $Pb(C_2H_3O_2)_2$ are two of the very few soluble compounds of lead.

(c) SO_4^{2-} ions are introduced into each solution.

    (c) A precipitate will form in the $Ba(NO_3)_2$ solution. The other two solutions will show no change.

$BaSO_4$ is insoluble. Na_2SO_4 and K_2SO_4 are both soluble.

(d) The freezing point of each solution is measured and the three temperatures are compared.

    (d) The freezing points of the $NaC_2H_3O_2$ and KCl solutions will be less than $0°$ C and about the same. The freezing point of the $Ba(NO_3)_2$ solution will be lower than the other two.

Freezing point depression is a colligative property, so it will depend only on the number of particles in solution, not on their identity.

$NaC_2H_3O_2$ and KCl each dissociate into two ions per molecule, while $Ba(NO_3)_2$ dissociates into three ions per unit.

Since the concentrations of all three solutions are the same, the $Ba(NO_3)_2$ solution will have the greatest freezing point depression because it dissociates into the greatest number of particles. By the same reasoning, the freezing points of the $NaC_2H_3O_2$ and KCl solutions will be about the same.

QUESTIONS	EXPLANATIONS
9. Use chemical principles to explain each of the following.	
(a) A pressure cooker is used to cook food at higher temperatures than can be achieved using a regular pot.	(a) $PV = nRT$. With a constant volume, higher pressure makes for higher temperature. In a pressure cooker, much higher pressures are maintained than in normal pots, thus allowing for higher temperatures.
(b) Iron nails that are to be used outdoors are coated with zinc.	(b) Zinc is more easily oxidized than iron, so zinc will react with air and water before iron does. This helps to keep iron from rusting.
(c) Food kept in a refrigerator takes longer to spoil than food left out on a kitchen table.	(c) The spoiling of food is a chemical reaction, and like all chemical reactions, its rate depends on temperature. The higher the temperature, the faster the rate of reaction, and the lower the temperature, the slower the rate of reaction.
(d) When water is left standing in plumbing during extremely cold weather, there is a danger that the pipes will burst.	(d) Water expands when it freezes, so if a pipe is full of liquid water, there may not be enough space in the pipe for ice to form and the ice will break the pipe.

ABOUT THE AUTHOR

Paul Foglino has taught for The Princeton Review for more than a decade. He has written and edited course materials for the SAT, GRE, GMAT, and MCAT courses. He is coauthor of *Cracking the CLEP*. Foglino studied English and Electrical Engineering at Columbia University, but he remains convinced that he learned everything he ever needed to know in junior high school.

NOTES

NOTES

NOTES

NOTES

NOTES

NOTES

NOTES

NOTES

Free!

Did you know that The Microsoft Network gives you one free month?

Call us at 1-800-FREE MSN. We'll send you a free CD to get you going.

Then, you can explore the World Wide Web for one month, free. Exchange e-mail with your family and friends. Play games, book airline tickets, handle finances, go car shopping, explore old hobbies and discover new ones. There's one big, useful online world out there. And for one month, it's a free world.

Call **1-800-FREE MSN**, Dept. 3197, for offer details or visit us at **www.msn.com**. Some restrictions apply.

Microsoft Where do you want to go today?®

MSn.
The Microsoft Network

FIND US...

International

Hong Kong
4/F Sun Hung Kai Centre
30 Harbour Road, Wan Chai,
Hong Kong
Tel: (011)85-2-517-3016

Japan
Fuji Buibing 40, 15-14
Sakuragaokacho, Shibuya Ku,
Tokyo150, Japan
Tel: (011)81-3-3463-1343

Korea
Tae Young Bldg, 944-24,
Daechi- Dong, Kangnam-Ku
The Princeton Review- ANC
Seoul, Korea 135-280,
South Korea
Tel: (011)82-2-554-7763

Mexico City
PR Mex S De RL De Cv
Guanajuato 228 Col. Roma
06700 Mexico D.F., Mexico
Tel: 525-564-9468

Montreal
666 Sherbrooke St.
West, Suite 202
Montreal, QC H3A 1E7 Canada
Tel: (514) 499-0870

Pakistan
1 Bawa Park - 90 Upper Mall
Lahore, Pakistan
Tel: (011)92-42-571-2315

Spain
Pza. Castilla, 3 - 5º A, 28046
Madrid, Spain
Tel: (011)341-323-4212

Taiwan
155 Chung Hsiao East Road
Section 4 - 4th Floor,
Taipei R.O.C., Taiwan
Tel: (02)751-1243

Thailand
Building One, 99 Wireless Road
Bangkok, Thailand 10330
Tel: (662) 256-7080

Toronto
1240 Bay Street, Suite 300
Toronto M5R 2A7 Canada
Tel: (800) 495-7737
Tel: (716) 839-4391

Vancouver
4212 University Way NE,
Suite 204
Seattle, WA 98105
Tel: (206) 548-1100

National (U.S.)

We have over 60 offices around the U.S. and
run courses in over 400 sites. For the courses and
locations nearest you call **1 (800) 2/Review**
and you will be routed to the nearest office.

MORE EXPERT ADVICE

from

THE PRINCETON REVIEW

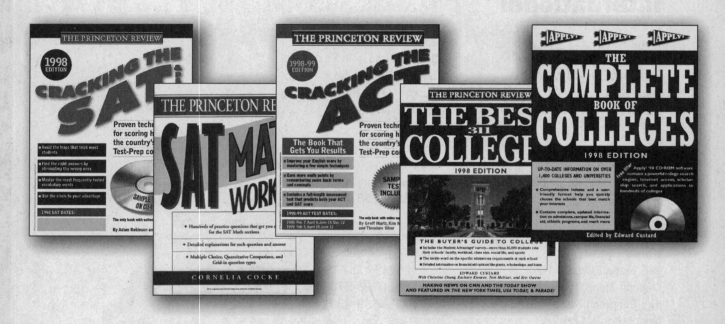

We help hundreds of thousands of students improve their test scores and get into college each year. If you want to give yourself the best chances for getting into the college of your choice, we can help you get the highest test scores, the best financial aid package, and make the most informed choices with our comprehensive line of books for the college-bound student. Here's to your success and good luck!

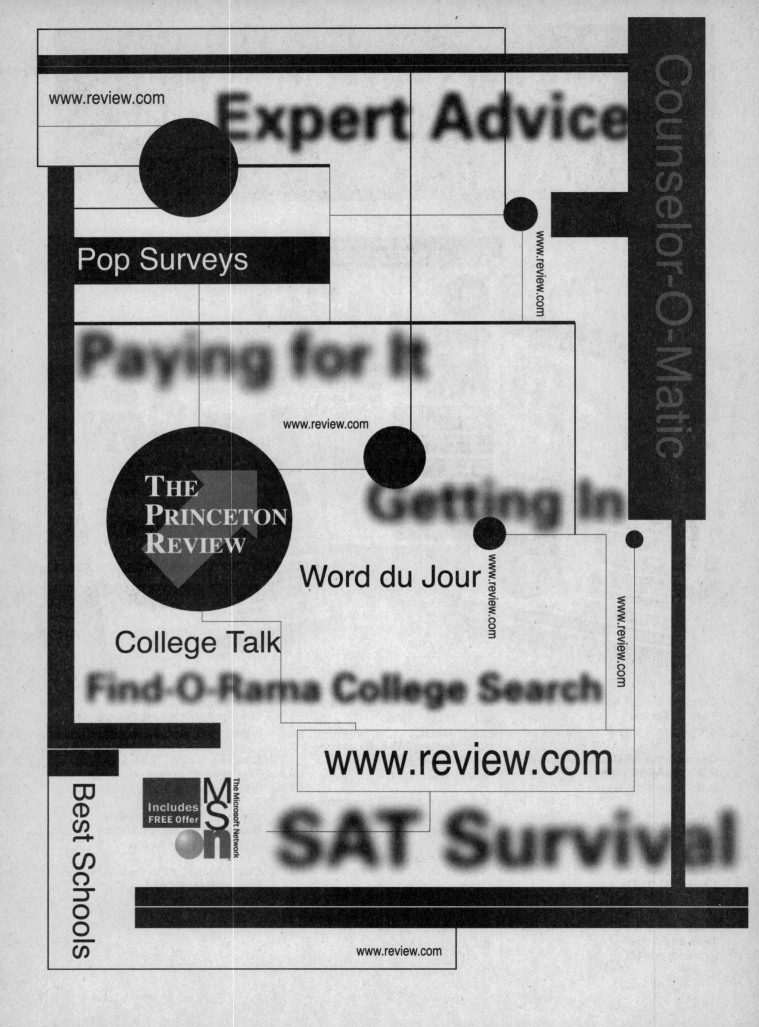